DATA BANK ON GEOGRAPHY

DATA BANK
ON
GEOGRAPHY

Compiled and Edited by
Arvind M. Dwivedi

ANMOL PUBLICATIONS PVT. LTD.
NEW DELHI - 110 002 (INDIA)

ANMOL PUBLICATIONS PVT. LTD.
4374/4B, Ansari Road, Daryaganj
New Delhi-110 002
www.anmolbooks.com

Data Bank on Geography

First Edition 2001
ISBN 81-261-1003-1

[Responsibility for the facts stated, opinions expressed, conclusions reached and plagiarism, if any, in this volume is entirely that of the Editor. The Publishers bear no responsibility for them, whatsoever.]

PRINTED IN INDIA

Published by J. L. Kumar for Anmol Publications Pvt. Ltd., New Delhi-110 002 and Printed at Tarun Offset Press, Delhi.

CONTENTS

PREFACE

In the present age of acute competitions in every walk of life the old adage 'survival of fittest' has apparently become a reality. Gone are the days when the degrees were enough to get a job. Now the thorough study of any subject is required to get through in any competitive examination. The objective multiple choice type questions are asked almost in all the competitions. In order to meet the increasing demand of the aspirants, we have prepared the Data Bank on Geography. It is concise, comprehensive and dependable which has a wide coverage of the syllabus.

The proportion of questions from Geography in General study has get tremendous increase in the recent past. Near about 15% questions are asked from this portion. In the present data bank we have touched all the corners of syllabus as well as the latest pattern of questions asked in UPSC, SSC, LIC, GIC, CDS, NDA and other central/state level examinations. We have taken utmost care in preparing the questions with particular gradation and level of the various examination.

Constructive criticism and valuable comments from actual users are welcome for further improvements in the subsequent editions of the book.

—**Arvind M. Dwivedi**

1
WORLD PHYSICAL GEOGRAPHY

1. The International Date Line is where the date changes exactly by how many days when it is crossed?
   (a) Four (b) Six
   (c) Eight (d) One.

2. The interior layer is the core or
   (a) Parysphere (b) Marysphere
   (c) Barysphere (d) Hydrophosphere.

3. The earth is not a perfect sphere it is little flattened at both ends like an orange and it could be called
   (a) Spherical (b) Circum
   (c) Geoid (d) Circumspherical.

4. Igneous rocks are formed due to cooling and solidification of
   (a) Sagma (b) Sediments
   (c) Magma (d) Breccia.

5. The earth spins on an elliptical orbit while revolving round the sun at a speed of
   (a) 20.5 miles/sec (b) 18.5 miles/sec
   (c) 20.2 miles/sec (d) 20.0 miles/sec.

6. Igneous rocks which contain a proportion of Silica they are said to be
   (a) Laves (b) Crystals
   (c) Acid (d) Diorite.

7. The earth's make up is of several concentric layers and the outer layer of the earth's crust is

(a) Biosphere (b) Stratosphere
(c) Lithosphere (d) Lithosphere.

8. Igneous rocks cooled and solidified at some depth are known as

(a) Conglomerate (b) Plutonic rocks
(c) Cynian rocks (d) None.

9. The upper part of the earth which forms the continents are made up of

(a) Metamorphic rocks (b) Sedimentary rocks
(c) Metasedimentary rocks (d) Granitic rocks.

10. The Granite rocks poured out of volcanoes as lavas and soliditfy quickly on the earth's surface are called

(a) Plutonic rocks (b) Cynian rocks
(c) Hermanian rocks (d) Volcanic rocks.

11. The lower ozone of the earth which farms the ocean floor are made up of mainly continuous zones of denser

(a) Igneous rock (b) Strato igneous rocks
(c) Metamorphic rocks (d) Basaltic rocks.

12. Longitude shown as a series of semi circles on the globe that run from pole to pole cutting the equator is known as

(a) Angular distance
(b) Parallels
(c) Meridians
(d) Convergence of the poles.

13. In how many Standard Time Zones the whole world has been divided and by what degree they differ from the next?

(a) 26 & 12° in longitude (b) 32 & 12° in longitude
(c) 24 & 15° in longitude (d) 24 & 12° in longitude.

14. ---------is the point from which all other meridians radiate eastwards and westwards up to 180°.

(a) Advanced meridian (b) Prime meridian

(c) Restarted meridian (d) Actual meridian.

15. CIS which extends through almost 165° of longitude is divided into how many line zones

(a) 12 (b) 11
(c) 24 (d) 14.

16. The Royal Astronomical Observatory is located at

(a) Greenwich (b) Rhine Valley
(c) Las Vegas (d) Arkansas.

17. Both Canada and USA have five time zones

(a) Atlantic, Pacific, Northern, Southern, Western
(b) Atlantic, Eastern, Central, Mountain and Pacific Time zones
(c) Atlantic, Eastern, Western, Polar and Pacific Time zones
(d) Atlantic, Eastern, Tundras, Polar and Pacific Time zones.

18. As the earth rotates from west to east every 15° we go eastwards the local time is . . . by 1 hour. And conversely when we go westwards the local time is . . . by 1 hour.

(a) retarded and advanced (b) advanced and tarded
(c) advanced and fixed (d) none.

19. The difference between the local time of the Atlantic and Pacific coasts is nearly of how many hours ?

(a) Six (b) Three
(c) Four (d) Five.

20. A system of standard time is observed by all countries and adopt their standard time from the central meridian of their countries. The Government of India has accepted the meridian of . . . for the standard time.

(a) 82.5° east (b) 81.2° east
(c) 83.4° east (d) 89.2° east.

21. The brief period between sunset and complete darkness is termed as

(a) Dawn (b) Faint rays
(c) Oblique rays (d) Twilight.

22. For aprecise location on a map each degree is sub-divided into 60 minutes and each minute into how many seconds?
(a) 90 sec. (b) 180 sec.
(c) 160 sec. (d) 60 sec.

23. As the earth is slightly flattered at the poles the linear distance of a degree of latitude at the pole is little ------than at the equator.
(a) Shorter (b) Wider
(c) Longer (d) None.

24. Which two days are termed equinoxes meaning equal nights
(a) 21 March and 23 Sept. (b) 21 March and 20 Sept.
(c) 21 March and 21 Sept. (d) 20 March and 21 Sept.

25. Which two days are the summer solstice and winter solstice?
(a) 21 June and 20 Dec. (b) 21 June and 21 Dec.
(c) 21 June and 23 Dec. (d) 21 June and 22 Dec.

26. Which orogenic movement is the latest of all ?
(a) Alphine (b) Caledonian
(c) Hercynian (d) Scandinavian.

27. Name of the highest peak in Western Malaysia is
(a) Kilimanjaro (b) Doda Bhatta
(c) Gunong Tahan (d) Gunog Parah.

28. The Upfolded waves caused by the expansion or contraction of some part of the earth are called
(a) Synclines (b) Par Synclines
(c) Anticlines (d) Mega anticlines.

29. The orogenic or mountain building movement that occurred in the per Cambrain times dates back to
(a) 660-3800 million years ago

(b) 550-4280 million years ago
(c) 600-3000 million years ago
(d) 600-3500 million years ago.

30. The down fold or the troughs are due to expansion or contraction of some part of the earth are called
(a) Synclines (b) Anticlines
(c) Mega anticlines (d) Low synclines.

31. The mare recent three organic movements are
(a) Caledonian, Phyledonian and Hermedonian
(b) Caledonian, Hermedonian and Syberdonian
(c) Caledonian, Hercynian and Alpine
(d) None.

32. The Himalayas Rockies, Andes and Alps comes under the category of
(a) Black mountains
(b) Fold mountains
(c) Residual mountains
(d) Compressional mountains.

33. The important ranges that were formed during the Hercynian earth movements are
(a) Rhine and Mt. Blanc (b) Rhine and Vegas
(c) Rhine and Fuji (d) Ural and Appalachians.

34. The Alps and Himalayas were formed during the
(a) Cameroonian movement
(b) Hercynian movement
(c) Syberdonian movement
(d) Alpine movement.

35. What leads to the formation of metamorphic rocks?
(a) Heat and sun rays (b) Heat and steam
(c) Heat and pressure (d) None.

36. Solution of rocks is dominant in-------
(a) Sandstone region (b) Limestone region

(c) Volcanic region (d) None of these.

37. The highest peak in western Malaysia is composed of
(a) Marble stones (b) Resistant graphite
(c) Hard slate (d) Resistant quartzite.

38. Carbonaceous rocks are also organically formed but they formed by
(a) Animal residue (b) Human waste
(c) Finer clay (d) Swamps and Forests.

39. The word "Dykes" and "Sills" are associated with
(a) Metamorphism (b) Hercynian
(c) Volcanism (d) Hydroism.

40. When larger pebbles are firmly cemented to form a rock, it is called as
(a) grit (b) conglomerate
(c) clay (d) pebble chips.

41. Sedimentary rocks are greatly distinguished from other rocks by virtue of
(a) extensive saturation (b) extensive hollowness
(c) extensive layers (d) compositions.

42. Sedimentary rocks are made up of materials brought by different agents of erosion or even animals and they are . . . and often contain . . . of animals, plants and different micro-organisms
(a) Crystalline and leftover
(b) Crystalline and fossils
(c) Crystalline and signs
(d) Non-crystalline and fossils.

43. Sedimentary rocks are classified under three major categories in respect to its origin and composition. They are
(a) Mechanically, Chemically, Canonically formed, Sedimentary rocks
(b) Chemically, Organically, Canonically formed, Sedimentary rocks

(c) Chemically, Biologically, Astronomically formed, Sedimentary rocks

(d) Mechanically, Organically and Chemically formed, Sedimentary rocks.

44. --------is the most familiar kind of Sedimentary rocks.

(a) Carbon stone (b) Hard stone

(c) Meta stone (d) Sand stone.

45. The most common example of organically formed Sedimentary rocks are

(a) Chalk and clay stone (b) Quartz and granite

(c) Chalk and quartz (d) Limestone and chalk.

46. Fold mountains are also called the mountains of

(a) Depression (b) Elevation

(c) Fracture plane (d) Denudation.

47. Volcanoes which are accumulated and built up from material ejected from fissures in the earth's crust is known as

(a) Table lands (b) Cinder

(c) Volcanic mountains (d) Lava stretch.

48. Fold mountains contain many volcanic activity and have many active valcanoes specially in the

(a) Circum-Atlantic fold mountain system

(b) Circum-Indian fold mountain system

(c) Circum-Pacific fold mountain system

(d) None.

49. Mt. Fuji (Japan) and Mt. Mayon are example of

(a) Black mountains (b) Volcanic mountains

(c) Fold mountains (d) Table lands.

50. The fold mountains have very rich mineral resource of

(a) Tin, tungstan, copper

(b) Silver, bronze, iron

(c) Tin, iron, aluminium

(d) Tin, copper, gold and petroleum.

51. Mt. Catopaxi is located in
    (a) France (b) Brazil
    (c) Canada (d) Ecuador.

52. A mountain mass formed by the uplift of land between 'faults' or by the subsidence of land outside the faults is known as
    (a) Residual mountain (b) Fold mountain
    (c) Elevated mountain (d) Black mountain.

53. Mt. Agung is located in
    (a) Thailand (b) Malaysia
    (c) Bali (d) Bhutan.

54. Unique feature of Black mountains are
    (a) Alps, Andes, Rockies
    (b) Appalachians, Kilimanjro, Fuji
    (c) Ural, Vesivuous, Aravali
    (d) Hunsruck, Vosgos, Black forest of the Rhineland.

55. A mass of solidified lava filling the centralovent of a Volcano is known as
    (a) Volcanic rubbles (b) Volcamass
    (c) Volcanic neck or plug (d) Verano.

56. By and large Black mountains are due to
    (a) Compression (b) Tension
    (c) Breakage (d) Venting.

57. Fine particles of lava ejected from a Volcano after eruption is known as
    (a) Volcanic dust (b) Shield Volcano
    (c) Vernal (d) None.

58. A lump of lava which are rounded in shape and are thrown out of a valcano in the liquid state, but solidifies as it fall outside is known as
    (a) Virazone (b) Veplean
    (c) Veranillo (d) Volcanic bomb.

59. Mt. Manodnock, an example of Residual mountain is located in

(a) North Korea (b) USA
(c) South Korea (d) Yugoslavia.

60. With some Volcanoes the overflow of lava takes place quietly and generally covers a large and wide area, which is termed as

(a) Venting Volcano (b) Shield Volcano
(c) Blocked Volcano (d) Saturated Sheets.

61. Residual mountains also evolve from plateoux which have been------by rivers into hills and valleys

(a) Met (b) Overlapped
(c) Dissected (d) Lifted.

62. Mauna Lao is an example of shield Volcano located in

(a) Italy (b) Haiti
(c) Addis Ababa (d) Hawaii.

63. Examples of dissected plateaux where the down cutting streams have eroded the uplands into mountains of denudation is

(a) Highlands of Australia (b) Highlands of Chile
(c) Highlands of Burma (d) Highlands of Scotland.

64. Mt. Pelee is on the island of

(a) Madagascar (b) Sri Lanka
(c) Martinique (d) None.

65. Mt. Meropi an example of Volcanic mountain is in

(a) Java (b) Bangladesh
(c) Sumatra (d) Singapore.

66. Small rock fragments ejected from a Volcano but are smaller in size to Volcanic bombs but larger than Volcanic ash is called

(a) Largely (b) Lapics
(c) Landes (d) Lappilli.

67. Plateaus those are formed by earth-movements and causes uplift and one of considerable size and uniform altitude are said to be

(a) Tectonic Plateau (b) Tetra Plateau
(c) Timvana Plateau (d) None.

68. When the normal level of the land is lowered by the agents of denudation, some very resistant areas are left which forms

(a) Reprisal (b) Bergschrund
(c) Ria (d) Residual mountains.

69. A plateau bounded by steep cliff like faces which lead abruptly down to the sea or the adjoining lowlands are known as

(a) Talus (b) Talus creep
(c) Table land (d) None.

70. Plateaus, which have been formed in association with mountains and are partly or completely enclosed by them are known

(a) Inversion Plateau (b) Interzonal Plateau
(c) Intermontane Plateau (d) Internched Plateau.

71. Some of the best known Volcanic plateaus are Antrlim plateau of

(a) Northern Ireland (b) Southern Scotland
(c) Northern London (d) Norther Sussex.

72. Deccan Plateau in India is an example of

(a) Interzonal Plateau (b) Intermontane Plateau
(c) Tectonic Plateau (d) None.

73. The most remarkable plateau built by lava is the . . . which is twice as big as Malaysia.

(a) Bulgaria-snake plateau
(b) African-Rhino plateau
(c) Columbia-Snake plateau
(d) Yugoslavia-Snake plateau.

74. South Africa provides the best known example of a
   (a) Low land (b) Elevated
   (c) Scrap land (d) Table land.

75. Which of the following is an important Pacific atoll
   (a) Great Barrier Reef (b) Wake Island
   (c) Fanafuti Atoll (d) Sudbury Cay.

76. Example of intermontane plateau is . . . . between the Himalayas and the Kunlun
   (a) Travi plateau (b) Tiga plateau
   (c) Tibet plateau (d) None.

77. When erosion of plateaus are made by rivers in vertical corrasion from and abrasion by winds it dissects the plateaus into steep sided tabular masses termed as
   (a) Mesas and Buffers (b) Mesas and Buttes
   (c) Mesas and Bummers (d) Mesas and Butick.

78. Molten lava may come out of the earth's crust and spread over its surface to form successive sheets of basaltic lava and solidify to form a
   (a) Volcanic plateau (b) Lesser plateau
   (c) Loose plateau (d) Lyining plateau.

79. An example of the dissected plateau is
   (a) Burmese highland (b) Indonesian highland
   (c) Scottish highland (d) Southern highland.

80. Messa and Buttes are common feature of
   (a) Arid and Tundra areas
   (b) Arid and evergreen areas
   (c) Arid and semi-arid areas
   (d) Desert and plain areas.

81. The following figure shows
   (a) Thrust fault (b) Normal fault
   (c) Slip fault (d) Step fault.

82. Most obvious examples of the structural plains are

(a) Russian platform, Bulgarian platform and Great plains of U.S.A.

(b) Russian platform, Polish platform and Bulgarian platform

(c) Russian platform, Czech platform and Danish platform

(d) Russian platform, Central lowlands of Australia, Great plains of U.S.A.

83. Minas Gerais mines area is in

(a) Brazil (b) Kenya

(c) Uganda (d) Sudan.

84. The lying down of materials brought by various agents transportation and rise gently towards adjacent highlands are laid to be

(a) Structural plains (b) Accumulated plains

(c) Drift plains (d) Depositional plains.

85. A--------is an area of low-land, either level or undulated seldom rises more than a few hundred feet above from sea-level and from the base land of a country

(a) Plane (b) Plain

(c) Clean plane (d) None.

86. Active erosion in the upper course results in large quantities of alluvium being brought down to the lower course and deposited to from extensive

(a) alluvial plains, flood plains, forest plains

(b) flood plains, deltaic plains, forest plains

(c) flood plains, deltaic plains, glaciated plains

(d) None.

87. When the plains are traversed by rivers they have immense economic importance like that of

(a) Thames, Rhine, Gobi plains

(b) Indo Gangetic, Mississippi, Yang-tze plains

(c) Nigara, Victoria, Kiev-plain

(d) Periyar, Sene, Ghaghra.

88. The alluvials plains, flood plain and deltaic plains from the most-------agricultural plain of the world.

(a) Unproductive (b) Semi-productive
(c) Productive (d) Semi-unproductive.

89. The horizontally bedded rocks, relatively undisturbed by the crustal movement and are structurally depressed areas are

(a) Outwash plains (b) Structural plains
(c) Stratified plains (d) Stepped plains.

90. The Nile Delta of Egypt is noted for . . . cultivation

(a) Jute and wheat (b) Wheat and grapes
(c) Wheat and tabacco (d) Rice and cotton.

91. The Ganges Delta is noted for

(a) Wheat and Rice (b) Wheat and Maize
(c) Jute and Rice (d) Wheat and Barley.

92. Example of Loess plain is found in

(a) South West China (b) North West China
(c) Eastern China (d) Central China.

93. The Hwang Ho deltaic plains supports

(a) only rice (b) a wide range of crops
(c) only wheat (d) exclusively maize.

94. Many of the Loess covered plains in the world are

(a) Industrial regions
(b) Fertile agriculture regions
(c) Fishing regions
(d) None.

95. The mass of rocks and finely ground rock flour dragged along in the lower part of the ice of a glacier and left behind when ice melts are known as

(a) Till plain (b) Tierra plain
(c) Timber plain (d) Loess plain.

96. The load of a river rabs against the sides and the bottom of the river's channel and these are slowly worn away. The Process is called

(a) erosion (b) abrasion
(c) corrosion (d) spilting.

97. A plain which borders the sea coast and extends from the sea to the nearest elevated land, it may be formed by the deposition of solid matters is termed as

(a) crest plain (b) coastal plain
(c) cluse plain (d) cold plain.

98. In the Sahara the extensive areas of flat desert plain from which the fine sand has been blown away leaving the surface converted with small stones and gravel are termed as

(a) Ray (b) Rege
(c) Relict (d) Reef.

99. Deposition of fine silt or dust which is generally held to have been transported its present position by the wind is known as

(a) Lode (b) Lock
(c) Loess (d) Loxodrome.

100. When winds blow aeolian deposits from interior deserts or barren surfaces and deposit them upon hills, valleys or plains forms

(a) Till plain (b) Drift plain
(c) Loess plateau (d) Intersected plateau.

101. Which country is estimated to have 35000 lakes occupying 10% of the total land surface of the country

(a) Australia (b) Denmark
(c) Surinam (d) Finland.

102. An isolated hill in an arid or semi-arid region usually has a rounded Summit and steep sides of bare rocks termed as

(a) instability (b) inselberg
(c) insular (d) incised.

103. When a mass of magma cuts across the bedding planes and forms a wall like feature it is called a

(a) Dyke (b) Diastrophism
(c) Diathermancy (d) Detritus.

104. Magma while thrusting its way to the surface may cool and solidify with in the crust as -----rocks resulting in -----land forms

(a) Sedimentary, invent (b) Hard, soft
(c) Very hard, massive (d) Plutanic, intrusive.

105. An example of Dyke is Cleveland Dyke of

(a) Hampshire (b) Birmingham
(c) Neveda (d) Yarkshire.

106. Rocks formed by either plutonic or volcanic activity are called --------rocks

(a) Sedimentary (b) Metamorphic
(c) Granite (d) Igneous.

107. A large and very resistant Dyke of quartzite forms along ridge to the north of

(a) Bangkok (b) Kuala Lampur
(c) Djakarta (d) Rangoon.

108. When an intrusion of magma is made horizontally along the bedding planes of sedimentary rocks the resultant intrusion is called

(a) Sill (b) Simon
(c) Sinkhale (d) None.

109. A large blistor of igneous maund with a dome shaped upper surface and a level base fed by a pipe-like conduit from below is termed as

(a) laccolith (b) phacolith
(c) racolith (d) none.

110. Best example of Sill is great when Sill in

(a) Northern America (b) Latin America
(c) Central America (d) Northern England.

111. An example of laccolith is the laccoliths of the Henry Mountains in

(a) Utah U.S.A. (b) Dallas U.S.A.
(c) Denver U.S.A. (d) Harvard U.S.A.

112. Another form of igneous intrusion with a sauser shape is formed and results into a shallow basin is known as

(a) High fluidity (b) Dome
(c) Cone (d) Lopolith.

113. The Bushveld lopoliths of Transvaal in . . . are good examples

(a) South Africa (b) North Africa
(c) Eastern Africa (d) Central Venezuela.

114. Some times the active lava vent pours red hot lava forming the

(a) Whole (b) Lava pit
(c) Ash pit (d) Dust pit.

115. A lens-shaped mass of igneaus rocks occupying the Crest of an Anticlinear the bottom of a syncline are being fed by a conduit from beneath is known as

(a) Pharalith (b) Phamalith
(c) Phacalith (d) Phakhalith.

116. The best example of the lava-pit is------where thousands of lava fountain rise and fall in the dazzling-pit.

(a) Hampshire (b) Hamburg
(c) Helemaumau (d) Hanoi.

117. An example of a phacolith is cardan hill Shrapshire in

(a) U.S.A. (b) France
(c) Canada (d) England.

118. The less fluid lava that explodes more Vicelently from ----- with large central oraters and steep slopes.

(a) ash and cinder cones (b) ash and dust cones
(c) ash and lava cones (d) ash and magma.

119. The two volcanic mountains were once through by people to be extinct and yet both erupted most violently which they are?

(a) Mt. Vesurins and Mt. Karkatau
(b) Mt. Anthens and Mt. Hamphis
(c) Mt. Thames and Mt. Blanc
(d) None.

120. Small volcanic mountain Mt. Paricutin not exceeding 1000 feet is in

(a) Los Angeles (b) Mexico
(c) Japan (d) Spain.

121. Volcanic cones are most typical of the extrusive features. The highly fluid lava build up a feature known as

(a) Mud dome (b) Ash dome
(c) Lava dome (d) None.

122. The Nuovo is in

(a) Italy (b) Mexico
(c) Azerbaijan (d) Naples.

123. The Valcanoes of------have the best developed lava domes.

(a) Sicily (b) Japan
(c) Phillipines (d) Hawaii.

124. Some times lava flows are so viscous that they solidify after a short distance when they are confined in river valleys and are known as

(a) lava tongues (b) lava mouth
(c) ash tongues (d) none.

125. The fine particles after hurled from the vent of a Volcano may be shot so high in the sky that it travels round the world several times before it eventually comes to rest is known as

(a) volcanic dust (b) mud dust
(c) sand dust (d) caldera dust.

126. Mt. Vesvikius standing 4000 feet above the Bay of Naples erupted violently on--------overwhelmed by a mud flow of ashes and cinders almost 50 feet thick

(a) 24 August BC 79 (b) 24 August AD 79
(c) 24 August AD 97 (d) 24 Sept. AD 97.

127. Mt. Etna is in
(a) Paris (b) Copenhegan
(c) Helsinki (d) Sicily.

128. Mt. Krakatau the greatest volcanic explosion known to men took place in . . . where vibrational set up enormous waves over two feet high and drowned 36000 people in the coastal districts of Indonesia
(a) Jan. 1883 (b) Jan. 1983
(c) Jan. 1842 (d) August 1883.

129. Mt. Sterombedi whose frequent eruptions that make the summit glow have earned for it the name
(a) Torch of the sea
(b) Lighthouse of the mediterranean
(c) Sun of the mediterranean
(d) Thunder of the mediterranean.

130. Mt. Pelle of the West Indies erupted in . . . where St. Pierre the capital of Martinique was completely destroyed
(a) May 1902 (b) May 1903
(c) May 1904 (d) June 1902.

131. Some volcanoes may have greatly enlarged depression called calderas caused by the subsidence of much of the volcano into the magma beneath and water may collect in the crater or the caldera forming
(a) Subsidence lake (b) Depressed lake
(c) Uplifted lake (d) Crater.

132. The greatest concentration of volcano is in the Circum-Pacific region popularly termed as the
(a) Pacific ring of lava (b) Pacific ring of light
(c) Pacific ring of fire (d) Pacific ring of thunder.

133. Best examples of crater or caldera lake is Lake Toba in

(a) Java (b) Bali
(c) Sumatra (d) Nepal.

134. Mt. Madeira and Mt. Ascension are on the
(a) Pacific coast (b) Atlantic coast
(c) Arabian coast (d) Mediterranean coast.

135. Mt. Etna and Mt. Stromboli are in the
(a) Mediterranean region (b) Tundra region
(c) Taiga region (d) Coniferous region.

136. The Himalayas have
(a) no active volcanoes (b) many active volcanoes
(c) five active volcanoes (d) one active valcano.

137. Thousands of hot springs are found in
(a) Germany (b) Canada
(c) U.S.A. (d) Iceland.

138. In Africa, Mt. Kilimanjaro and Mt. Kenya both probably extinct volcanoes are found along the
(a) East African Rift valley
(b) West African Rift valley
(c) North African Rift valley
(d) Central Africa.

139. Earthquakes are usually caused by movement along 'faults' and produce gigantic tidal waves called by the Japanese is
(a) Sunamen (b) Tsunamis
(c) Tremar (d) None.

140. The active Volcano of Mt. Cameroon is in
(a) North Africa (b) South Africa
(c) East-North Africa (d) West Africa.

141. One of the greatest earthquakes ever known was the Great Lisbon earthquake on
(a) 1 Nov. 1755 (b) 1 Nov. 1758
(c) 1 Nov. 1786 (d) 2 Nov. 1786.

142. A hot spring which at regular intervals throws a Jet of hot water and steam into the air the Jet rises to 100-200 ft. and occurs in the volcanic regions is known as

(a) Geothermal water (b) Geyserite
(c) Geyser (d) Geysive.

143. The great Tokyo-Yokohama earthquake was on

(a) 1 Sept. 1923 (b) 1 Sept. 1924
(c) 2 Sept. 1942 (d) 1 Sept. 1920.

144. The world's best known Geyser is cold, faithful in

(a) National Australian Park
(b) Rock Garden Sydney
(c) Hot Park Canberra
(d) Yellow Stone National Park U.S.A.

145. The great Morocco earthquake at Agadir sealed the fate of 10000 people in

(a) 1940 (b) 1941
(c) 1942 (d) 1960.

146. Springs found in any part of the earth where water sinks deep enough beneath the surface to be heated by the interior forces are known as

(a) Fountains (b) Hot springs
(c) Jet stream (d) Hot ejection.

147. The world's distribution of earthquakes concides closely with that of volcanoes, lie along the

(a) Atlantic line (b) Pacific Ring of fire
(c) Sea of Japan (d) Red Sea.

148. 20% of the earthquakes take place in the . . . including Asia Minor the Himalayas and parts of North-West China.

(a) Mediterranean Belt
(b) Red Sea
(c) Dead Sea
(d) Mediterranean Himalayan Belt.

149. -------is the most important single agent of denudation
(a) Glacier (b) Wind
(c) Human-being (d) Running water.

150. The initial stream that exists as a consequence of the slope is called the
(a) insequent stream (b) sufficient stream
(c) consequent stream (d) insufficient stream.

151. To find the precise depths of ocean floors and map of the relief of the oceans, the older echosounding technique have now been replaced by
(a) electronic gauge
(b) gauge metre
(c) radar sounding and electrical echo devices
(d) None.

152. The term Loess' actually comes from a village in Alsaca in
(a) France (b) China
(c) Italy (d) Malaysia.

153. The earth's rotation deflects freely moving objects including ocean currents to the right. In the northern hemisphere this is in . . . direction
(a) deflected (b) circular
(c) clockwise (d) anticlockwise.

154. 'Hills of sand' formed by accumulation of sand and shaped by the movement of winds reshaped and redeposited into a variety of feature is known as
(a) multiple sand features (b) sand dust
(c) dust devil (d) dunes.

155. The ocean currents those flow from equatorial regions polewards have a higher surface temperature and are
(a) cold currents (b) freezing currents
(c) normal currents (d) warm currents.

156. Inselbergs are typical of many desert and semi-arid landscapes and common in

(a) Northern Nigeria, Kalahari desert
(b) Northern Nigeria, Eastern Australia
(c) Northern Nigeria Western Australia, Kalahari desert
(d) None of these.

157. The highest water temperatures are found in enclosed seas in the tropics, that is the
(a) Black Sea (b) Red Sea
(c) Caspian Sea (d) None of these.

158. The cold water chills any wind that blows onshore so that the Chilean and Peruvian coasts are practically
(a) Rainfall (b) Normal rain
(c) Rainless (d) Heavy rain.

159. The island which are build up by coral animals of various species are found both near the shores of the mainland and in the midst of the ocean is said to be
(a) Coral islands (b) Mid island
(c) Emerging island (d) Animal island.

160. A Coral Reef in the shape of a ring or horse shoe enclosing a lagoon is known as
(a) Auriole (b) Aurora
(c) Aurora (d) Atoll.

161. A reef which lies at some distance from the share, its outer side rises from deep water where no reef building corals live and the lagoon is wide and deep is known as
(a) Barrow reef (b) Barricaded reef
(c) Barrier reef (d) None.

162. The best known Barrier reef is the Great Barrier heef of the coast is
(a) Brisbane (b) Sydney
(c) Merryland (d) Queensland.

163. A chain of rock lying at or near the surface of the sea and built up principally by immense number of corals polyps, both on and behind the reef, fragments of shells, Coral and

Coral Sand are piled up by wind and wave and a new land is thus formed is called

(a) Coral reef (b) Coral land

(c) Coral fragments (d) Coral wind.

164. The most famous international oceanographic research centre is the International Council for the Exploration of the Sea with its headquarters at

(a) Brussel (b) Helsinki

(c) Copenhagen (d) Sicily.

165. Regarding the origin of Coral Reefs, the glacial control theory of-------put forward in 1910 is of much importance.

(a) R.A. Daly (b) R.A. Dell

(c) R.A. David (d) R.A. Davidson.

166. The Suvadiva Atoll is in

(a) Indonesia (b) Manner

(c) Maldives (d) Australia.

167. The Grand bank of new found land is in the

(a) Dead sea (b) Caspian sea

(c) North sea (d) South sea.

168. The greatest known ocean deep is the

(a) Marika Trench (b) Marina Trench

(c) Mariana Trench (d) Marrica Trench.

169. The Tonga Trench and the Japanese Trench is in

(a) Atlantic ocean (b) Pacific ocean

(c) Indian ocean (d) None of these.

170. World's greatest sea parts are located on

(a) Coral shelves (b) Continental shelves

(c) Atoll shelves (d) Down warping shelves.

171. The line joining places having an equal degree of salinity is known as

(a) Isohytes (b) Isohalines

(c) Isomers (d) Isophytes.

172. The highest salinity recorded is of Lake Van in
(a) Egypt (b) Israel
(c) Asia Minar (d) Africa.

173. Albatrass plateau is in the
(a) Pacific ocean (b) Atlantic ocean
(c) Indian ocean (d) None.

174. Aleutian Rench is in the
(a) Indian ocean (b) Atlantic ocean
(c) Pacific ocean (d) Gulf of Mexico.

175. Hanging valley is very common in
(a) High mountain (b) Sub-arctic region
(c) Glaciared areas (d) Coastal belt.

176. When the earth is at the maximum distance from the sun it is called
(a) Aphelion (b) Perihelion
(c) Equinox (d) Sidereal

177. A land mass always obstructs and diverts a current. Like the shoulder of Brazil at cape sao Roque, divides the west flowing equatorial current into the
(a) Agulhas current (b) Florida current
(c) Sargasso current (d) Cayenne current.

178. The Irminger Current or east Greenland Current flows between Greenland and
(a) Canada (b) Iceland
(c) England (d) None.

179. The cold water chills any wind that blows on-shore so that the Chilean and Peruvian coasts are partically
(a) Rainless (b) Full of rain
(c) Heavy rain (d) Normal rain.

180. Net growth rate of population is determined by
(a) Gross reproduction rate
(b) The birth rate and the death rate

(c) The pressure of population
(d) The birth rate in a country.

181. The water movement in the ocean result from the combined action of density of water and
(a) weight (b) mass
(c) winds (d) weather.

182. The undulating plain lying two to three miles below sea level and covering two-thirds of the ocean floor, is known as
(a) Shallow plain (b) Wave plain
(c) Abyssal plain (d) Sedumented plain.

183. Magmas that reach the surface and solidify form
(a) extensive land forms (b) intensive land forms
(c) none of the above (d) extrusive land forms.

184. The temperature gradient in the earth's interior has been found to be
(a) 36°C/Km. (b) 28°C/Km
(c) 32°C/Km (d) 40°C/Km.

185. Gutenberg discontinuity is the Zone between
(a) crust and upper mantle
(b) lower mantle and outer care
(c) upper mantle and lower mantle
(d) outer care and inner care.

186. The pressure gradient in the earth's interior is
(a) 0.32 kb/km (b) 0.20 kb/km
(c) 0.45 kb/km (d) 0.28 kb/km.

187. 80% of the surface rocks are
(a) Metamorphic (b) Igneous
(c) Sedimentary (d) None of the above.

188. In the 16 km depth, from surface of the earth about what percentage rocks are igneous
(a) 75 (b) 85
(c) 95 (d) 90.

189. Basic lava is one of the liquid products of Volcanism. Its features are
(a) less viscous and less mobile
(b) more viscous and less mobile
(c) less viscous and more mobile
(d) None of the above.

190. Which of the following is not true about phyllite?
(a) It is in a more metamorphosed form than slate
(b) It has lustre due to mica particles
(c) It is in a less metamorphosed slate than schist
(d) They are more metamorphosed than schist.

191. The mean distance of the Earth from Sun is
(a) 150 million km (b) 300 million km
(c) 250 million km (d) 400 million km.

192. March 21, is also known as
(a) Summer Solstice (b) Autumn Equinox
(c) Spring Equinox (d) Winter Solstice.

193. Experiment have proved that 90% of the earth's crust is composed of . . . elements
(a) 8 (b) 6
(c) 15 (d) 12.

194. A huge mass of igneous rocks which after removal of the overlying rocks forms a massive and resistant upland region is called
(a) Laccolith (b) Lapolith
(c) Batholith (d) Phacolith.

95. At Idaho, the biggest . . . is found
(a) Laccolith (b) Lapolith
(c) Phacolith (d) Batholith.

196. Which of the following is not effect of the earth's revolution
(a) Parallels are equally spaced
(b) All parallels are circular except the poles which are point

(c) Parallels intersect merideans at an acute angle
(d) Parallels are the true east-west lines.

197. The direction of the drift of continents were towards the equator and
(a) towards the west (b) towards the east
(c) towards the south (d) towards the north.

198. Who holds the view that "Earth gave birth to moon"?
(a) Jeans (b) A. Holmes
(c) Melash (d) Ptolemy.

199. Which element is the major element of the earth crust
(a) Aluminium (b) Iron
(c) Oxygen (d) Silican.

200. Who formulated the concept of Tsotasy?
(a) Dutton (b) Bullen
(c) Jeffreys (d) Suess.

201. Which of the following are the examples of regional metamorphism
(a) Hot gases vapour and liquid
(b) Hot Magma
(c) Geothermal heat
(d) None of the above.

202. Which of the following is not the proponent of continental subsidence theory?
(a) Joly (b) Gregory
(c) Daly (d) Holmes.

203. Transportation action of rivers include
(a) By suspension
(b) By traction
(c) By solution and saltation
(d) All of the above.

204. Which of the following does not cause folding
(a) Intrusions

(b) Isostatic settling
(c) Stress
(d) Tangentential Compression.

205. Which of the following is not a landforms created due to faults
(a) Nappe
(b) Black or Horst mountain
(c) Drag
(d) Rift valley.

206. Which of the following is most important agent of erosion?
(a) Moving ice
(b) Winds
(c) Running water
(d) None of the above.

207. Graphite is a metamorphosed form of which of the following rocks?
(a) Peat
(b) Biturminous coal
(c) Shale
(d) None of the above.

208. Faults are not caused by
(a) Convectional current with in earth
(b) Different compaction
(c) Stress
(d) None of the above.

209. Which of the following is not related to glacial erosion?
(a) Attrition
(b) Abrasion
(c) Plucking
(d) Frost wedging.

210. Gobi desert is an example of
(a) Low latitude deserts
(b) Polar deserts
(c) Desert in the Lee of mountains
(d) Desert of continental interior.

211. Kimberley Plateau a lava plateau is in
(a) Asia
(b) Australia
(c) Africa
(d) S. America.

212. What is the term used to describe cultivation on hill slopes with small patches of land in descending order

(a) hill farming (b) slope cultivation
(c) contour farming (d) truck farming.

213. Seacles Dry lakes is situated in
(a) Scotland (b) Ireland
(c) California (d) Mexico.

214. The mean elevation of land is
(a) 840 m (b) 100 m
(c) 1220 m (d) 1160 m.

215. The Lot desert of N. Africa stretches right across the continent whereas the hot desert of Australia does not. This is because
(a) A cool current flows along the west coast of Australia
(b) Australia has great extent from west the east
(c) South-East Australia lies under trade winds
(d) Australia is in a higher latitude.

216. Bathyl is a
(a) Littarol deposit (b) Shallow sea deposit.
(c) Intermediate deposit (d) Deep sea deposit.

217. Bog-Boga is a mud volcano and situated in
(a) Baku (b) Pelee
(c) Naples (d) Mongolia.

218. The care of the Rockies is composed of
(a) Igneous rocks (b) Metamorphic rocks
(c) Sedimentary rocks (d) None of the above.

219. The ralative humidity of a region is low when
(a) the wet and dry bulb thermometers read differently
(b) the wet and dry bulb thermometers read the same
(c) the difference between the reading of the wet and dry bulb thrmometers is large
(d) The temperature are low.

220. Which of the following statement is not true about Coral Reefs

(a) Extensive coral formation develop between 15o N to 15o S
(b) Great Barrier Reef is situated on the cast coast of Australia
(c) Coral Reefs do not develop between 30o N and 30o S on the Western costs
(d) All of them are true.

221. Which of the following statement is wrong?
(a) Low salinity of equator is noticed
(b) There is high salinity is Tropics
(c) There is a tendency for salinity to increase from west to east
(d) Low salinity is found in closed seas.

222. The mean depth of sea is
(a) 3500 m (b) 3800 m
(c) 4200 m (d) 4500 m.

223. Which of the following is not one of the various stages of the evolution of fold of mountains
(a) Geosynclinal stage (b) Exogenetic stage
(c) Orogenetic stage (d) Epeirogenetic stage.

224. Which of the following lake was formed by diastrophic forces
(a) Reelfoot (b) Pepin
(c) Bhimtal (d) Wular.

225. Which river is known as sorrow of Bengal
(a) Damodar (b) Tapi
(c) Padma (d) Narmada.

226. The island which are build up by coral animals of various species are found both near the shores of the mainland and in the midst of the oceans is said to be
(a) Mud island (b) Emerging island
(c) Coral islands (d) Animal islands.

227. Desert occupy about . . . % of the surface of the earth.

(a) 20 (b) 30
(c) 35 (d) 25.

228. Malaspina glacier is situated in
(a) Alaska (b) Norway
(c) Greenland (d) Siberia.

229. The Iceward side of a mountain which does not receive rain is known as the
(a) desert area (b) dry zone
(c) adiabatically dry area (d) rain-shadow area.

230. Dew is caused when
(a) the sky is overcast at night
(b) the wind is too dry to cause rainfall
(c) humid air condenses on cool surface
(d) the air is colder than the earth's surface.

231. Hail consists of
(a) masses of ice in layers one above the other
(b) water droplers
(c) granular ice
(d) crystals of ice.

232. An upper air wind system wish very high velocities in certain parts of the atmosphere is called
(a) jet strem (b) a cyclone
(c) an anticyclone (d) monsoon.

233. Which one is an anticyclone
(a) high pressure system with clockwise winds in the northern hemisphere
(b) low pressure system with clockwise winds in the northern hemisphere
(c) low pressure system with clockwise winds in hemisphere
(d) None of the above.

234. The difference in the duration of day and night increases as one moves from the . . . to the . . . .

(a) Poles, equator
(b) Tropic of Cancer
(c) Tropic of Cancer, tropic of Capricorn
(d) Equator, poles.

235. What is the tidal bore?
(a) A high tidal wave moving upstream in the mouth of a river
(b) A tidal wave resulting from seismic activity
(c) A formation of polyps just above high tide level
(d) A deposit of sand in coastal areas.

236. Which of the following are wrongly matched?
(1) Tropic of Cancer - 23½ degree N Latitude
(II) Tropic of Capricorn 66½ degree N Latitude
(III) International Date Line - 0 degree longitude
(IV) Antarctic Circle - 66½ degree S latitude
(a) I (b) II & III
(c) I, II & IV (d) None of these.

237. Equinoxes occur on
(a) January 4 and July 23
(b) March 21 and December 22
(c) March 21 and Septmeber 23
(d) December 22 and June 21.

238. The longest day in Australia will be on
(a) December 22 (b) March 22
(c) June 11 (d) September 24.

239. Most of the weather phenomena take place in the
(a) stratosphere (b) ionosphere
(c) tropopanse (d) troposphere.

240. The South pole experiences continuous light at the time of
(a) summer solstice (b) vernal equniox
(c) autumnal equinox (d) winter solstice.

241. Which of the following will never get the vertical rays of the sun?
(a) Mumbai (b) Srinagen
(c) Trivandrum (d) Srinagar.

242. Which planet takes the longest time to go once around the sun
(a) Pluto (b) Uranus
(c) Neptune (d) Jupiter.

243. The most prominent gases in the atmosphere, in terms of volume, are
(a) hydrogen and nitrogen
(b) oxygen and carbon dioxide
(c) nitrogen and methane
(d) nitrogen and oxygen.

244. Which of the following is wrong?
(a) When the sun shines vertically over the equator, it is called an equinox
(b) The sun shines vertically over the Tropic of Cancer at the time of the winter solstice
(c) The sun never shines vertically beyond the tropics
(d) At the poles there is light for half the year.

245. The standard time of India is
(a) 4 1/2 hours behind Greenwich time
(b) 4 hours ahead of Greenwich time
(c) 5 1/2 hours ahead of Greenwich time
(d) 5 1/2 hours behind Greenwich time.

246. The water content in the atmosphere
(a) increases as temperature increases
(b) it not dependent on temperature
(c) cannot be measured
(d) remains unchanged as temperature changes.

247. What is the name given to winds blowing from sub-tropical high pressure region to the equator?

(a) Northerlies (b) Doldrums
(c) Westerlies (d) Trades.

248. Which layer of the atmosphere maintains an almost uniform temperature
(a) ionosphere (b) tropopanse
(c) stratosphere (d) troposphere.

249. Name the instrument used for measuring humidity ?
(a) Barometer (b) Hygrometer
(c) Thermometer (d) Hydrometer.

250. The moon's period of revolution with reference to the sun is
(a) equal to one sidereal month
(b) equal to one solar month
(c) equal to one synodie month
(d) none of these.

251. Light from the nearest star reaches the earth in
(a) 43 minutes (b) 4.3 years
(c) 4.3 minutes (d) 4.3 seconds.

252. Which comet appears every 76 years ?
(a) Donati's (b) Holme's
(c) Halley's (d) Alpha Centauri.

253. What is the unit of measurement of distances of stars from the earth
(a) Nautical miles (b) Kilometres
(c) Fathoms (d) Light years.

254. When the tide-producing forces of the earth around the sun and moon act in a straight line complementing each other, it produces
(a) tidal bornes (b) neap tides
(c) normal tides (d) spring tides.

255. When the tide-producing forces of the sun and moon act in a straight line complementing each other it produces
(a) normal tides (b) tidal bones

(c) spring tides (d) neap tides.

256. The rate of rotation of the earth on its axis is highest on
(a) March 3 (b) July 4
(c) December 22 (d) It never changes.

257. What is the International Date Line?
(a) It is the 0 degree longitude
(b) It is the 90 degree east longitude
(c) It is the equator
(d) It is the 180 degree longitude.

258. Which planet is closest to the sun
(a) Earth (b) Pluto
(c) Mercury (d) Jupiter.

259. The mass of the earth is about ------times of that of the moon.
(a) 81 (b) 82
(c) 83 (d) 84.

260. The earth is at its maximum distance from the sun on
(a) January 3 (b) July 4
(c) September 22 (d) December 22.

261. How much of the surface of the moon is visible from the earth?
(a) only about 40% (b) more about 40%
(c) about 59% (d) None of these.

262. Which of the statement does not prove the sphericity of the earth?
(a) The shadow of the earth at the time of the solar eclipse is circular
(b) If the earth were flat one would come across some sharp edges
(c) The sunrise is not visible from all places at the same time
(d) The altitude of the stars from various points on the earth's surface varies.

263. What is the relationship between solar day sidereal day ?
   (a) Solar day is shorter than sidereal day
   (b) Both are equal
   (c) Solar day is longer than sidereal day
   (d) None of these.

264. We always see the same face of the moon because
   (a) It takes equal time for both revolution around the earth and rotation on its own axis
   (b) It is smaller than the earth
   (c) It revolves on its axis in a direction opposite that of the earth
   (d) It rotates at the same speed as the earth around the sun.

265. What is incoming solar radiation known as?
   (a) insolation (b) reflection
   (c) refraction (d) radiation.

266. The velocity of winds is governed by
   (a) Farrel's Law (b) Rotation of the earth
   (c) Pressure gradient (d) Temperature.

267. Identify the Sedimentary rocks
   (1) Basalt (2) Limestone
   (3) Shale (4) Granite.
   (5) Quartzite
   (a) 1 & 2 (b) 2 & 3
   (c) 3 & 4 (d) 2 & 5.

268. Which of the following one not a planetary wind?
   (a) trades (b) drainage winds
   (c) easterlies (d) westerlies.

269. How much pressure is exerted by the atmosphere at sea level
   (a) five kg. per sq. cm. (b) one pound per sq. cm.
   (c) two kg. per sq. cm. (d) one kg per sq. cm.

270. Where is the doldrums belt located?

(a) on the tropic of Cancer
(b) on the tropic of Capricorn
(c) near the equator
(d) near the polar areas.

271. Which gas in the atmosphere absorbs ultraviolet rays
(a) methane (b) nitrogen
(c) helium (d) ozone.

272. The fall in air temperature with increasing elevation is known as
(a) thermal anomaly (b) temperature fall
(c) thermal volocity (d) lapse rare.

273. The stratosphere is said to be ideal for flying jet aircraft. This is because
(a) this layer is out of the firing range of anti-aircraft guns
(b) of the absence of clouds and other weather phenomena
(c) this layer is rich in ozone which reduces fuel consumption
(d) the temperature is constant and ideal for aircraft engine efficiency.

274. Identify the factors responsible for change in seasons of the earth's surface
(I) Rotation of the earth
(II) Revolution of the earth
(III) Inclination of the axis of the earth
(IV) Rotation of the sun
(a) I and III (b) I, II and IV
(c) I and IV (d) I and II.

275. Arrange the planets correctly in descending order in terms of number of their satellites
1. Uranus 2. Jupiter
3. Saturn 4. Mars
(a) 4, 2, 3, 1 (b) 3, 2, 1, 4
(c) 2, 3, 4, 1 (d) 2, 3, 1, 4.

276. 'Horse latitudes' is the term applied to the
(a) O° - S N and S latitudes
(b) 40° - 60° N and S latitudes
(c) 30° - 40° N and S latitudes
(d) Polar circles.

277. Which one of the following is a great circle
(a) Tropic of Capricorn (b) Tropic of Cancer
(c) Equator (d) Polar Circle.

278. What is meant by the term 'Midnight Sun'
(a) Sun shining in the polar circles for long time
(b) Twilight
(c) Very bright moon
(d) Rising sun.

279. Where is famous Tuscarora Deep located
(a) Off Japan
(b) Near USA
(c) Off Lakshadweep
(d) Near the Australian coast.

280. Which is the shortest route from Moscow to San Francisco?
(a) over land (b) over the North Pole
(c) via Canada (d) over the South Pole.

281. What is the vapour pressure ?
(a) barometric pressure
(b) the pressure of vapour in air
(c) pressure only due to vapour in the air
(d) pressure in the clouds.

282. What is fog?
(a) A cirro straters cloud (b) a low straters cloud
(c) an alrocumulus cloud (d) a cumulonimbus cloud.

283. The temperature at which the air is fully saturated is called
(a) dew point (b) saturation point
(c) condensation point (d) critical temperature.

284. What is tornado?
(a) a very high ocean wave
(b) a planetary wind
(c) a very low pressure centre
(d) a very high pressure centre.

285. The coastal part of the sea-bed which is structurally a part of the landmars is called the
(a) oceanic plateau (b) continental shelf
(c) deep sea plain (d) continental slope.

286. Which ones are wrongly matched?
(I) Typhoons - China Sea
(II) Hurricanes - Indian Ocean
(III) Cyclone - West Indies
(IV) Tornadoes - Australia.
(a) I, III and IV (b) I, II and IV
(c) I, II and III (d) II, III and IV.

287. What is stated in terms of grams of water vapour per kilogram at moist air?
(a) relative humidity (b) vapour pressure
(c) absolute humidity (d) specific humidity.

288. What is the importance of ozone in the atmosphere
(a) It provides condensation nuclei
(b) It creates the greenhouse effect on earth
(c) It helps scatter blue light
(d) It provides protection against ultraviolet radiation.

289. Rainfall caused due to the presence of the mountains in the way of winds is called
(a) cyclone rain (b) orographic rain
(c) advectional rain (d) convectional rain.

290. When humidity is expressed as a percentage, it is called
(a) relative humidity (b) percentage humidity
(c) absolute humidity (d) specific humidity.

291. Assertion (A) : Eclipses do not occur on all full moon and new moon days

Reason (R) : The moon revolves round the earth in an elliptical orbit

(a) A and R are true but R does not explain A
(b) A is true but R is false
(c) A and R are true and R correctly explains A
(d) Both A and R false.

292. What will happen if the temperature of water is lowered from 8° C to 3° C?

(a) Water will freeze
(b) The volume will first increase then decrease
(c) The volume will first decrease then increase
(d) No change would take place.

293. Farrel's Law is concerned with the

(a) Velocity of winds (b) Direction of winds
(c) Intensity of waves (d) None of these.

294. What is the most common salt in sea water

(a) Sodium chloride (b) Calcium carbonate
(c) Potassium chloride (d) Magnesium sulphare.

295. The crystal layer of the earth is also called

(a) Sima (b) Sial
(c) Nife (d) Moho.

296. Which group does the black cotton soil of India belong

(a) Chernozem (b) Laterite
(c) Alluvial (d) Podzol.

297. Which is an organic rock

(a) Slare (b) Marble
(c) Coal (d) Granite.

298. Metamorphic rocks originate from

(a) Sedimentary rocks
(b) Igneous rocks

(c) Both igneous and sedimentary rocks
(d) None of these.

299. Isochrones are lines joining places with equal
(a) forest
(b) rainfall
(c) longitude
(d) travelling time from a point.

300. Plains formed due to the filling up of lakes are called
(a) kanst plains (b) floods plains
(c) alluvial plains (d) peneplains.

301. The term 'nife' refers to
(a) crust of the earth (b) core of the earth
(c) earthquakes (d) ocean beds.

302. What does the term 'lithosphere' refer to
(a) Interior of the earth (b) Crust of the earth
(c) Plants and animals (d) None of these.

303. What is Gulf Stream?
(a) a cold current in the Atlantic Ocean
(b) a cold current in the Pacific Ocean
(c) a warm current in the Pacific Ocean
(d) a warm current in the Atlantic Ocean.

304. The term 'epicenter' is associated with
(a) earthquakes (b) folding
(c) earth's interior (d) haulting.

305. With what type of climate is the pedogenic regime of podzolisation associated
(a) hot and dry (b) equatorial
(c) humid temperature (d) cool and dry.

306. The Red Sea is an example of a
(a) faulted structure (b) folded structure
(c) residual structure (d) lava structure.

307. Plateaus situated in between plains and mountains are called
(a) peninsular plateaus (b) piedmont plateaus
(c) intermontane plateaus (d) continental plateaus.

308. Lines joining places experiencing a thunders form at the same time are known as
(a) isohytes (b) isobronts
(c) isophenes (d) isochrones.

309. Richer Scale is used for
(a) Measuring humidity of emperature
(b) Measuring the intensity of earthquakes
(c) For measuring the purity of milk
(d) Measuring the alcohol in various drugs.

310. The latest theory suggesting the movement of the continents relative to one another is the
(a) Plate tectonics theory (b) Kant theory
(c) Tetrahederal theory (d) Continental drift.

311. Which soil is most common in the Indo Gangetic plains
(a) regur (b) laterite
(c) podzol (d) alluvial.

312. The theory suggesting that the continents of South America and Africa were once joined together was the
(a) Kant theory
(b) Tetrahederal theory
(c) Continental drift theory
(d) None of these.

313. Plains formed in limestone regions are called
(a) peneplains (b) kanst plains
(c) alluvial plains (d) floods plains.

314. The pedogenic regime of calcification is commonly associated with
(a) mid-latitude steppelands
(b) hot humid areas

(c) coastal areas
(d) cool temperature areas.

315. One of the warm currents in the Indian Ocean is the
(a) Curoshio current (b) Humbdt current
(c) Agulhas current (d) Labrador current.

316. In which of the following areas is salininy likely to be highest
(a) North Pacific (b) Indian Ocean
(c) North Atlantic (d) Red Sea.

317. Most of the people of the middle-east belong to the----- group of people
(a) Mediterranean (b) Negro
(c) Alpine (d) Nodric.

318. Isobaths are used to show
(a) time (b) rainfall
(c) pressure (d) depth.

319. As one moves from the equator to the poles along a meridian
(a) the variety of plants and animals decrease
(b) the variety of animals increases and plants decreases
(c) the variety of plants and animals increase
(d) the variety of plants increases and animals decreases.

320. Isonif lines are the isopleths
(a) frost (b) sunshine
(c) rainfall (d) snowfall.

321. Bindibu are natives of
(a) Alpine (b) Mestizoes
(c) Amerinds (d) Bushman.

322. The aborigines of North America are called
(a) Hamites (b) Red Indians
(c) Semites (d) Mestizoes.

323. The rate of erosion in a stream is highest where
(a) depth is greater (b) the river joins the sea
(c) breadth is greater (d) flow is fast.

324. Isoholines are the isopleths of
(a) salinity (b) height
(c) transport cost (d) hail.

325. What is measured on the Richter Scale
(a) depth (b) wind velocity
(c) earthquakes (d) heat.

326. Laterisation occurs in
(a) cool temperature areas (b) poorly drained areas
(c) warm humid areas (d) viterine tracts.

327. Which continent has the highest density of population
(a) Europe (b) Asia
(c) Africa (d) North America.

328. Lapps in habit
(a) East Africa
(b) South American grasslands
(c) European tundra
(d) European steppes.

ANSWERS

1.	(d)	2.	(c)	3.	(c)	4.	(c)
5.	(b)	6.	(c)	7.	(d)	8.	(b)
9.	(d)	10.	(d)	11.	(d)	12.	(c)
13.	(c)	14.	(b)	15.	(b)	16.	(a)
17.	(b)	18.	(b)	19.	(d)	20.	(a)
21.	(d)	22.	(d)	23.	(c)	24.	(c)
25.	(d)	26.	(a)	27.	(c)	28.	(c)
29.	(d)	30.	(a)	31.	(c)	32.	(b)
33.	(d)	34.	(d)	35.	(c)	36.	(b)
37.	(d)	38.	(d)	39.	(c)	40.	(b)
41.	(c)	42.	(d)	43.	(d)	44.	(d)

45. (d)	46. (b)	47. (c)	48. (c)
49. (b)	50. (d)	51. (d)	52. (d)
53. (c)	54. (d)	55. (c)	56. (b)
57. (a)	58. (d)	59. (b)	60. (b)
61. (c)	62. (d)	63. (d)	64. (c)
65. (c)	66. (d)	67. (a)	68. (d)
69. (c)	70. (c)	71. (a)	72. (c)
73. (c)	74. (d)	75. (b)	76. (c)
77. (c)	78. (a)	79. (b)	80. (c)
81. (a)	82. (d)	83. (a)	84. (d)
85. (b)	86. (a)	87. (b)	88. (c)
89. (b)	90. (d)	91. (c)	92. (b)
93. (b)	94. (b)	95. (a)	96. (c)
97. (b)	98. (a)	99. (c)	100. (c)
101. (d)	102. (b)	103. (a)	104. (d)
105. (d)	106. (d)	107. (b)	108. (a)
109. (a)	110. (d)	111. (a)	112. (d)
113. (a)	114. (b)	115. (c)	116. (c)
117. (d)	118. (a)	119. (a)	120. (b)
121. (c)	122. (d)	123. (d)	124. (a)
125. (a)	126. (b)	127. (d)	128. (d)
129. (b)	130. (a)	131. (d)	132. (c)
133. (c)	134. (b)	135. (a)	136. (a)
137. (d)	138. (a)	139. (b)	140. (d)
141. (a)	142. (c)	143. (a)	144. (d)
145. (d)	146. (b)	147. (b)	148. (d)
149. (d)	150. (c)	151. (c)	152. (a)
153. (c)	154. (d)	155. (a)	156. (c)
157. (b)	158. (c)	159. (a)	160. (d)
161. (c)	162. (d)	163. (a)	164. (c)
165. (a)	166. (c)	167. (d)	168. (c)
169. (a)	170. (b)	171. (b)	172. (c)
173. (a)	174. (c)	175. (b)	176. (a)
177. (b)	178. (b)	179. (a)	180. (c)
181. (c)	182. (c)	183. (d)	184. (c)
185. (b)	186. (d)	187. (c)	188. (c)
189. (c)	190. (d)	191. (a)	192. (d)
193. (a)	194. (c)	195. (b)	196. (c)
197. (a)	198. (a)	199. (d)	200. (a)
201. (d)	202. (b)	203. (d)	204. (c)
205. (a)	206. (d)	207. (b)	208. (b)

209. (a)	210. (d)	211. (b)	212. (d)
213. (c)	214. (a)	215. (b)	216. (c)
217. (a)	218. (a)	219. (c)	220. (c)
221. (c)	222. (b)	223. (b)	224. (a)
225. (a)	226. (c)	227. (b)	228. (a)
229. (d)	230. (c)	231. (a)	232. (a)
233. (a)	234. (d)	235. (a)	236. (b)
237. (c)	238. (a)	239. (d)	240. (d)
241. (d)	242. (a)	243. (d)	244. (b)
245. (c)	246. (a)	247. (d)	248. (c)
249. (b)	250. (c)	251. (b)	252. (c)
253. (d)	254. (c)	255. (c)	256. (d)
257. (d)	258. (c)	259. (a)	260. (b)
261. (c)	262. (a)	263. (c)	264. (a)
265. (a)	266. (c)	267. (b)	268. (b)
269. (d)	270. (c)	271. (d)	272. (d)
273. (b)	274. (a)	275. (b)	276. (c)
277. (c)	278. (a)	279. (a)	280. (b)
281. (c)	282. (b)	283. (a)	284. (a)
285. (b)	286. (a)	287. (d)	288. (d)
289. (b)	290. (a)	291. (a)	292. (c)
293. (b)	294. (a)	295. (b)	296. (a)
297. (c)	298. (c)	299. (d)	300. (a)
301. (b)	302. (b)	303. (d)	304. (a)
305. (c)	306. (a)	307. (b)	308. (b)
309. (b)	310. (a)	311. (d)	312. (c)
313. (b)	314. (a)	315. (c)	316. (d)
317. (a)	318. (d)	319. (a)	320. (d)
321. (c)	322. (b)	323. (d)	324. (a)
325. (c)	326. (c)	327. (a)	328. (c)

2
CLIMATE, SOIL, VEGETATION & NATURAL REGIONS

1. On maps places of equal temperature are joined by lines called
   (a) isohyte (b) isohaline
   (c) isotherm (d) isomar.

2. The places having the same mean annual rainfall are joined by a line called
   (a) isoheyet (b) isobar
   (c) isohel (d) isotherm.

3. The ratio between the actual amount of water vapour and the total amount the air can hold at a given temperature expressed as a percentage is called the
   (a) absolute humidity (b) normal humidity
   (c) saturated humidity (d) relative humidity.

4. Air exerts a pressure on the earth's surface which varies from place to place and from time to time can be fairly accurately measured by the instrument called
   (a) Barmometer (b) Preno meter
   (c) Air meter (d) Barometer.

5. On maps places of equal pressure are joined by lines called
   (a) isohyet (b) isobars
   (c) isoline (d) isotherm.

6. Humidity is a measure of the dampness of air atmosphere which varies from place to place. The actual amount of water vapour present in the air and expressed in grams per cubic metre is called the

   (a) absolute humidity (b) relative humidity
   (c) saturated humidity (d) normal humidity.

7. The condensation of water vapour in the air causes small droplets of water to float about forming clouds at ground level and occurs in wet air when the relative humidity is over 75% is called the formation of

   (a) fog (b) hill fog
   (c) mist (d) radiation.

8. The Clouds which appear as white globular masses forming ripples in a 'mackerel sky' is said to be

   (a) Cirrocummulus (b) Cirrus
   (c) Cirrostratus (d) Cumulus.

9. The term . . . is used in connection with the reduction of visibility in regions of low humidity caused by smoke and dust particles in an industrial area or might be due to unequal refraction of light in air of different densities in the lower atmosphere

   (a) Bad visibility (b) Haze
   (c) Haphazard visibility (d) Hallucination.

10. Light soils reflect more heat than darker soils which are better absorbers. Such soild differences may give------to variations in the temperature of the region.

    (a) lowering (b) rise
    (c) none (d) static.

11. Along the equator and within five degrees north and south is the equatorial low pressure belt where there is intense heating with expanding air and ascending connection currents. This equatorial belt is termed as

    (a) expanding air belt (b) convectional current
    (c) rain shadow area (d) doldrums.

12. The denser, greyish looking clouds with a 'watery look' and have a fibrous or striated structure through which the Sun's rays shine faintly is said to be

(a) Cumulonimbus clouds (b) Altocumulus clouds
(c) Altostratus clouds (d) Stratocumulus clouds.

13. On maps places with an equal degree of cloudiness are joined by lines known as

(a) isomars (b) isoclouds
(c) isorephs (d) isobath.

14. Much of the precipitation experienced on the windward slopes of the north-east of West Malaysia. Western New Zealand, Western Scotland, Assam hills of the Indian sub-continent is

(a) Convectional rain (b) Orographic or relief rain
(c) Frontal rain (d) Cyclonic rain.

15. In the hilly areas a hot day followed by a calm cloudless night during which the aircools more rapidly over that higher ground may induce cold, heavy air to flow down the slope and accumulate at the valley bottom pushing the warmer air

(a) upwards (b) horizontal
(c) vertical (d) downwards.

16. On maps places with equal sun-shine duration are joined by lines called

(a) isohec (b) isohels
(c) isotope (d) isobath.

17. Dry soils like sands are very sensitive to temperature changes, where as wet soils like clay retain much......and warm up or cool down mare.......

(a) moisture, slowly (b) moisture, effectively
(c) moisture, quickly (d) None.

18. A fibrous looking cloud appears like wisps in the blue sky its often called 'mares' tails which indicates a fair weather and often gives a brilliant sunset is known as

(a) Stratus clouds (b) Cirrus clouds
(c) Cumulus (d) Cirrostratus.

19. Quite often, the ice-pellets exist as frozen rain-drops, meeting and re-freezing on their way down and this forms
(a) Radiation fog (b) Hill fog
(c) Snow hail (d) Sleet.

20. A dark and dull looking cloud, clearly layered, brings continuous rain, snow or sleet is known as
(a) Cumulonimbus clouds (b) Nimbus clouds
(c) Altocumulms clouds (d) None.

21. If moist air ascends rapidly to the cooler lay of the atmosphere, the water droplets freeze into ice pellets and fall to the earth as
(a) smong (b) snow
(c) hailstone (d) none.

22. A thin white looking sheet which causes the sun and the moon to have 'halos' is said to be
(a) Cirrocumulus (b) Cirrostratus
(c) None (d) Cumulus.

23. Beyond the stratosphere is the--------which goes several hundred miles up and has electrically conducting layers which make short-wave radio transmission possible over long distances
(a) Stratosphere (b) Ionosphere
(c) Hydrosphere (d) Cumulossphere.

24. The instrument for measuring relative humidity is the ------ which has wet and dry bulb thermometer
(a) Anemometer (b) Hydrometer
(c) Hygrometer (d) Altimeter.

25. When the relative humidity reaches 100 per cent, the air is completely saturated and the air-temperature is said to be ----- further cooling will condense the water vapour into clouds or rain?

(a) dew point (b) humidity point
(c) none (d) saturation point.

26. A round-topped and flat based cloud which forms a whitish grey glabular mass, indicates a fair weather is known as
(a) cumulus clouds (b) cirrocumulus
(c) cirronimbus (d) cirrus clouds.

27. The lowest layer in which the weather is confined is known as
(a) Troposphere (b) Ionosphere
(c) Cumulosphere (d) Stratosphere.

28. The best regions for the production of---------is the Himalayan foot hills of India and Bangladesh, the central highlands of Sri Lanka Western Java.
(a) Tea (b) Teak
(c) Cocoa (d) Coffee.

29. About 30°N and South, the air comparatively dry and the winds are calm and light. It is a region of descending air currents or wind divergence and referred as
(a) Frontal (b) Cyclonic area
(c) Horse latitudes (d) Leeward area.

30. Burma alone accounts for as much as three-quarters of the world's -------production
(a) Sal (b) Deodar
(c) Teak (d) Mahogany.

31. As one goes further north and south of the equator particularly in the coastal districts open to the influences of the trades, the tendency is towards a monsoonal pattern with the heaviest rainfall coming in the summer months in the northern hemisphere and--------, -------, -------- in the southern hemisphere
(a) Dec., Jan. April (b) Dec., Jan., March
(c) Dec., Jan., Feb. (d) Jan., Feb., March.

32. The Tropical marine climate is experienced along the eastern coasts of tropical lands, receiving steady rainfall from the.........all the time............

(a) Easterlies (b) Trade winds
(c) Westerlies (d) Planetary winds.

33. At the North and South Poles 90° N and South, where the temperatures are permanently low, are the Polar--------
(a) high pressure belts (b) none
(c) low presssure belts (d) Semi-low pressure belts.

34. The equatorial regions are generally
(a) Heavily populated (b) None
(c) Sparsely populated (d) Normally populated.

35. In Africa, the domesticated animals are attacked by a disease called 'ngana' caused by
(a) Tsetse flies (b) Jungle flies
(c) Wild flies (d) Animal flies.

36. From the sub-tropical high pressure belts, winds blow towards the temperate low pressure belts as the variable westerlies. But under the effect of the------they become the south westerlies in the northern hemisphere and the north-westerlies in the southern hemisphere.
(a) coriolis force (b) gravitational force
(c) convectional force (d) gravitational pull.

37. Coffee originated in Ethiopia and Arabia where it is still grown, but-------now accounts for almost half the world's production of coffee
(a) Sri Lanka (b) Brazil
(c) China (d) India.

38. One of the tropical crop that has achieved an amazing success is
(a) Cocoa (b) Pulse
(c) Maize (d) Mustard.

39. The Fohn is experienced in the valleys of the northern Alps particularly in Switzerland in ------- Chinook winds are experienced on the eastern slopes of the Rokies in U.S.A. and Canada in--------

(a) Winter, summer (b) Spring, winter
(c) Winter, spring (d) Spring, autumn.

40. For Burma------is the second greatest money-earner after rice
(a) coffee (b) teak
(c) spices (d) cocoa.

41. The hard wood, mahogany and ebony are types of
(a) Seasonal tropical trees (b) Equatorial trees
(c) Tropical marine trees (d) Tropical monsoon trees.

42. Cocoa is most extensively cultivated in------bordering the Gulf of Guinea
(a) East Africa (b) South Africa
(c) West Africa (d) South-east Africa.

43. The Savanna or Sudan climate is transitional type of climate found between the equational forests and the trade wind -
(a) Cold desert (b) Rocky desert
(c) Hot desert (d) Sandy desert.

44. Gazelle is ------------animal.
(a) Herbivorous (b) None
(c) Carnivorous (d) Omnivorous.

45. Khartoum is in the interior of
(a) Sudan (b) Kenya
(c) Somalia (d) Uganda.

46. Both the Fohn and Chinook winds are dry winds .experienced on the side of mountains when descending air becomes compressed with-------pressure
(a) Steep, increased (b) Iceward, increased
(c) Vertical, static (d) Leeward, decreased.

47. Many remote parts of the Amazon basin, the Congo basin and Borned are without modern communication lines, the--------form the only natural highways.
(a) Old railway tracks (b) Kucha roadways
(c) Rivers (d) Half metalled roads.

48. Match the following

(a)	Typhoon	1.	China Sea
(b)	Tropical	2.	Guinea lands of West Africa
(c)	Hurricanes	3.	West Indian Islands in Caribbean
(d)	Tornadoes	4.	The Indian Ocean

	(A)	(B)	(C)	(D)
(a)	1	4	3	2
(b)	1	3	4	2
(c)	1	3	2	4
(d)	1	2	4	3.

49. The most outstanding feature of the equational climate is its great uniformity of

(a) rainfall (b) temperature
(c) pressure (d) humidity.

50. The natural vegetation tropical monsoon lands are------- types

(a) Coniferous (b) Savanna
(c) Deciduous (d) Tundra.

51. In West Africa, the North-East Trades, in fact blow off-shore from the Sahara Desert and reach the Guinea Coast as a dry, dust-laden wind called locally the

(a) Hermes (b) Harmattan
(c) Harmatch (d) None.

52. In the Amazon basin the Indian tribes collect wild rubber, where as in the Congo basin, the Pygmies gather--------

(a) Nuts (b) Wheat
(c) Maize (d) Barley.

53. ----------is the most important staple crop and is grown in tropical lowlands wherever the rain exceeds 70 inches.

(a) Wheat (b) Barley
(c) Rice (d) Sugarcane.

54. Sirocco is a hot dry, dusty wind which originates in the ---------desert, and it is most frequent in springs and normally lasts for only a few days

(a) Atacama (b) Sahara
(c) Gobi (d) Kalahari.

55. The Chindwin river is in the northern
(a) Indonesia (b) Burma
(c) Korea (d) Thailand.

56. In true Savanna lands, the grass is tall and the 'elephant grass' may attain a height of even
(a) 60 ft. (b) 65 ft.
(c) 15 ft. (d) 50 ft.

57. The Sahara single largest stretch desert has an area of ------- square miles which is larger than all the States of U.S.A. put together
(a) 3.5 million (b) 7.3 million
(c) 9.5 million (d) 5.3 million.

58. Shifting cultivation is called by different names in different countries
(A) Ladang (1) Java
(B) Taungya (2) Burma
(C) Tamraj (3) Malaysia
(D) Humah (4) Thailand

	A	B	C	D
(a)	2	4	1	3
(b)	2	4	3	1
(c)	4	3	2	1
(d)	3	2	4	1.

59. The Savanna landscape is typified by tall grass and
(a) Tall trees (b) Medium trees
(c) Skeletal (d) Short trees.

60. Rain in Mediterranean reaches its peak in the month of
(a) August (b) July
(c) October (d) November.

61. In the Savanna region, trees grow best towards the equatorical humid latitudes or along the bank but ----- in height and density away from the equator.

(a) decrease (b) increase
(c) have mild change (d) remains same.

62. Within the Savanna lands of the tropics live many different tribes, Maria is one of them and is confined to the Maria reserves in

(a) Syria (b) Uganda
(c) Kenya and Tanzania (d) Kenya and Somalia.

63. The Australian Savanna is located south of the monsoon strip running from west to east-north of the

(a) Tropic of Cancer (b) Tropic of Capricorn
(c) Equator (d) Pole.

64. In the month of July, Rome has as much as------hours of sunlight and with the Mediterranean palm trees around tourists feel very much as if they are in the tropics.

(a) 10 (b) 09
(c) 11 (d) 08.

65. Hakodate and Kushiro and large fishing parts of

(a) Korea (b) Japan
(c) China (d) Vietnam.

66. In Cold wet regions, leaching helps to produce a grey soil which is known as a

(a) Podzol (b) Chernozem
(c) Laterite (d) None.

67. All soils contain mineral particles (inorganic material) humus (organic material), water and

(a) snow (b) air
(c) none (d) ice.

68. The Polar type of climate is found mainly north the Arctic circle in the northern hemisphere and includes the coastal strip of Greenland, the barren grounds of northern Canada and also the barren ground of

(a) California (b) Mexico
(c) Alaska (d) St. Luis.

69. Laterite soils are mainly composed if iron and ------- compounds

(a) Copper (b) Bronze

(c) Tin (d) Aluminium.

70. The term 'igloos' is associated with the

(a) Tribes of Africa

(b) Local population of Gobi desert

(c) Tribes of Central Asia

(d) Eskimos.

71. Which type of soils are generally red because of the presence of iron oxides

(a) desert soils (b) podzol

(c) chernozem (d) laterite soils.

72. Most of the World's wheat is grown on the

(a) Peat soils (b) Chernozems

(c) Wind deposited soils (d) Terra Rossa soils.

73. The laterite soils are unsuitable for agricultural activities because of lack of humus and high content of

(a) toxic (b) acidity

(c) rates (d) gravels.

74. The soil which contain large quantities of chlorides, sulphates, calcium and patassium is known as

(a) Saline soils (b) Bog soils

(c) Meadow soils (d) Arogean soils.

75. With the declining reserve of iron-ore around Lake Superior, the Great Lakes industrial concerns are using more and more iron from large iron ore deposits in

(a) Alaska (b) Yarmouth

(c) Labradar (d) Halifax.

76. ----------are probably the richest soils in the world, formed under a natural vegetation of grass in the temperate latitudes and are rich in humus

(a) Chirnozems (b) Red soils
(c) Temperate Brown soils (d) Peat soils.

77. The type of soils which are found in humid tropical regions where volcanic activity occurred in the past geological ages is called
(a) Brown soils (b) Dark soils
(c) Grey soils (d) Black soils.

78. When rainfall is greater than evapration water moves downwards in the soil and mineral matter is removed from the top layer and deposited in the layer beneath. These deposits give rise to a hard layers, which is called a
(a) Partuberance (b) Hard pan
(c) Solid pan (d) Hard shape.

79. The black soils are found in north-west Deccan trap of India, northern Argentina, Kenya and
(a) Syria (b) Somalia
(c) Morocco (d) Sudan.

80. The method by which the fields are ploughed, horrowed and sown along the contours instead of up and down the slopes, and makes the rain water stand in level furrows and soak into the ground is called
(a) Terrace farming (b) Sheet ploughing
(c) Harrowed ploughing (d) Contour ploughing.

81. The Desert soils are grey to brown in colour and they occur chiefly in parts of West U.S.A. and in between the Caspian Sea and Lake
(a) Aral (b) Ajerbaizan
(c) Ural (d) Kirgisthan.

82. The most important factor in thunderstorm development is
(a) temperature inversion
(b) atmospheric stability
(c) abundance of moisture in lower layers
(d) atmospheric instability.

83. In the Deccan trap as the black soil is very useful for the cultivation of cotton, they are called as the black cotton soils or the

(a) relvant soils (b) regur soils
(c) asset soils (d) regular soils.

84. The height of thunderstorms may vary from

(a) 20 to 40 kms (b) 4 to 20 kms
(c) 10 to 50 metres (d) 100 to 500 metres.

85. Due to the lack of vegetation cover, the rain instead of sinking into the ground washes the soil down slope, and each succeeding rain-storm washes away a thin layer of top soil is called the

(a) Share erosion (b) Slip erosion
(c) Sheet erosion (d) Top erosion.

86. The largest number of temperate cyclones originate mostly over the

(a) Arctic Ocean (b) Indian Ocean
(c) North Atlantic Ocean (d) North Pacific Ocean.

87. A kind of soil associated with the area where the land is poorly drained, such as swamps, marshes or bogs is

(a) Alkaline soils (b) Hydrographic soils
(c) Metamorphic soil (d) Hydrated soil.

88. Sclerophyllus natural vegetation is found in

(a) Mediterranean regions (b) Tundra regions
(c) Equatorial regions (d) Monsoon regions.

89. The Terra-Rossa soils are red in colour formed in limestone regions under

(a) Tundra conditions (b) Polar conditions
(c) Semi-arid conditions (d) Taiga conditions.

90. When rainfalls more heavily, the run off scours out deep grooves which grow wider and deeper, giving rise to bad lands or ravines this type of erosion is known as

(a) Rill erosion (b) Slip erosion
(c) Groove erosion (d) Gully erosion.

91. Zones separating different air masses are called
(a) Cols (b) Fronts
(c) Cyclones (d) None of the above.

92. In parts of India, Srilanka, Sumatra, Java the soil erosion is chiefly caused by
(a) over grazing by cattle (b) over grazing by goat
(c) shifting cultivation (d) centralized cultivation.

93. Caillison-coalescence theory was propounded to explain
(a) Cyclones (b) Tornado
(c) Precipitation (d) Anticyclones.

94. The--------are found in the East of the Caspian Sea and West U.S.A typical for the growth of steppe grasslands which are suitable for live stock raising
(a) Wind deposited soils (Laess)
(b) Brown or grey soils
(c) Hydrographic soils
(d) Chestnut soil.

95. Due to a series of drier years, crop fails and the land is abandoned, at this stage when the land is bare wind erosion sets in one of the worst cases of such erosion occurred in the 1930s in mid-western states of the U.S.A. and the area devastated here is called that
(a) erosion belt (b) dust stretch
(c) erosion extension (d) dust bowl.

96. Erosion caused by hydraulic pressure exerted by moisture penetrating into the soil during heavy rains, when unable to percolate further down to impermeable soil or rock strata, a great mass of over-lying soil on sheep land comes down and is called
(a) slip erosion (b) slide erosion
(c) share erosion (d) none.

97. Ground Banks of New foundland is one of the largest fishing grounds, the reason being abundant availability of ----- a fish feeding

(a) Plankton (b) Plantova
(c) Germs (d) Salty Germs.

98. The uniformity of precipitation of the Laurentian climate of North America is due to the influence of Atlantic and that of the

(a) Great deserts (b) Great mountains
(c) Great rivers (d) Great lakes.

99. In Canada, due to the greater reserves of coniferous softwoods and their overriding importance in Industrial uses, the annual production of ------hardwood is much less significant

(a) Coniferous (b) Deciduous
(c) Pallinated (d) Monsoonal.

100. It is said that New foundland experiences more-------than any other part of the world.

(a) Tarrential rain (b) Orographic rain
(c) Rain (d) Drizzle.

101. In the Kalahari Desert the discovery of--------has brought many whitemen to the 'land of thirst' as is often called

(a) Iron, Mica (b) Tin, Aluminium
(c) Diamond, Copper (d) Copper, Gold.

102. In South America, there are two distinct regions of Savanna north and south of the equator, namely the lanes of the Orinoco basin and the Campos of the

(a) Columbian highlands (b) Brazilian highlands
(c) Mexican highlands (d) None.

103. In South America, the Atacama or Peruvisan Desert is the driest of the deserts with less than------inches of annual rainfall.

(a) 10.2 (b) 12.0
(c) 12.5 (d) 00.5.

104. The rainiest part of Europe is the steep hills of the eastern Adriatic with 182 inches recorded at------about 3,600 ft. above the sea level.

(a) Crkven (b) Crkvem
(c) Crkvial (d) Crkvike.

105. The Hansa are a tribe settled cultivators who inhabit the Savahha lands of the Bauchi Plateau of northern

(a) Kenya (b) Nigeria
(c) Yuganda (d) Tanzania.

106. In the deserts of North America, ---------is mind in Nevada.

(a) Gold (b) Copper
(c) Diamond (d) Mica.

107. The Mediterranean lands are also known as the

(a) World's industries lands
(b) World's teak lands
(c) World's archard lands
(d) World's grasslands.

108. In the northern hemisphere tine grasslands are far more extensive and are entirely continental, in Eurasia they are called the

(a) Prairies (b) Pustoz
(c) Steppes (d) None.

109. The Mistral is a cold wind in the Mediterranean land rushing down the ------valley in violent gusts between 40 and 80 miles per hour.

(a) Rhone (b) None
(c) Rhine (d) Rhokdec.

110. ----------is the next most popular cereal.

(a) Barley (b) Rice
(c) Wheat (d) Maize.

111. In the Mediterranean lands, most of the precipitation comes in winter when the westerlies shift---------

(a) Towards tropic of Capricorn

(b) Towards tropic of Cancer
(c) Equator wards
(d) Pole wards.

112. In winter when the Mistral is most frequent the temperature of the wind may be

(a) below freezing point (b) above 40°F
(c) above 50°F (d) above 70°F.

113. The Sirocco blows outwards in a southerly direction from the desert interiors into the cooler Mediterranean

(a) Seas (b) Highlands
(c) Plateax (d) Plains.

114. In North America, the grasslands are quite extensive, lie between the foothills of the Rockies and the Great Lakes astride the American-Canadian border is known by the name

(a) Prairies (b) Pustoz
(c) Prarires (d) Hameries.

115. The Sirocco is very prominent wind and it is called by other local names in different native countries. In Egypt it is called by the name

(a) Khermonge (b) Khamti
(c) Khamteke (d) Khamsin.

116. Generally farms are small in size but there are also large holdings called 'haciendas' in

(a) Portugal (b) California
(c) Spain (d) Italy.

117. The Pines, Fires, Cedars which have needleshaped leaves and tall straight trunks, appear more on the cooler highlands and where droughts are less severe is

(a) Tropical Monsoon trees
(b) Temperate Evergreen trees
(c) Tropical trees
(d) Evergreeen Coniferous trees.

118. Mediterranean lands accounts for three-quarters of the World production of wine and the average wine consumption of the Mediterranean countries is about-------- gallons per head per annum.

(a) 100 (b) 90
(c) 80 (d) 15.

119. Conditions in the Mediterranean do not suit grass, because most of the rain comes in the----------season when growth is slow.

(a) Spring (b) Hot
(c) Autumn (d) Cold.

120. The Mediterranean lands account for per cent of the World's exports of citrus fruits

(a) 40 (b) 20
(c) 50 (d) 70.

121. When Sirocco crosses over Mediterranean Sea, the Water vapour is observed and is slightly cooled, but even then it is still hot and dry with a temperature of over

(a) 135°F (b) 120°F
(c) 105°F (d) 125°F.

122. Other important fruits of the Mediterranean lands are

(a) Pea-nuts, Chest-nuts
(b) Peaches, Apricots, Cherries, Figs
(c) Mango, Guava
(d) Jackfruit, Banana, Lichis.

123. The Nager Desert is in---------where elaborate system of irrigation canals enables both fruits and cereals to be successfully raised.

(a) Sudan (b) Egypt
(c) Israel (d) Portugal.

124. Mediterranean climate also supports many field crops and -----is the leading food crop.

(a) Rice (b) Maize
(c) Wheat (d) Barley.

125. A type of cold north-easterly wind experienced along the Adriatic Coast is called the------which usually occurs in winter when the atmospheric pressure over continental Europe is higher than that of the Mediterranean Sea.

(a) Boma (b) Bara
(c) Hara (d) Kora.

126. In few localities of the Mediterranean like the Ebro basin in Spain, the Po Valley in Italy and in California-------has been successfully cultivated and their yields are some of the highest in the world.

(a) Rice (b) Spices
(c) Maize (d) Pulses.

127. The trees are normally low, even stunted, with massive trunks, deeply fissioned barks small leathery leaves and a wide-spreading root system in search of water are of

(a) The hot west equatorial types
(b) The Warm Temperate Western Margin or Mediterranean types
(c) The hot desert types
(d) The Savanna or Sudan types.

128. The various Mediterranean oranges are of distinctive types, like the Seville oranges of---------are small but very sweet and suitable for making marmalade

(a) California (b) Portugal
(c) Italy (d) Spain.

129. In case of Argentina and Uruguay, the grasslands extend right to the Sea and enjoy much martime influenced and is known by the name

(a) Pampas (b) Pampov
(c) Pustaz (d) Pamkos.

130. Three-quarters of the world's what is-------what, sown in winter or late autumn is hard wheat with a low moisture content and best for bread making

(a) Winter (b) Rainy
(c) Spring (d) Summer.

131. One of the climatic feature associated with the China type of climate in Southern China is the occurrence of

(a) Severe cold winds (b) Typhoons
(c) Hurricane (d) Tornado.

132. In the Southern Australia alongwith Murray Darling basin, the grasslands are better known as

(a) Don (b) Downs
(c) Downev (d) Dover.

133. The Gulf states of U.S.A. have lowland-------where trees grow close together with thick undergrowth and leafy branches.

(a) evergreen coniferous forests
(b) monsoonal forests
(c) coniferous forests
(d) deciduous forests.

134. In South Africa, the grasslands are sandwiched between the Drakensberg and the Kalahari desert and are further sub-divided into the mare tropical---------in the north and temperate-----in the south

(a) None (b) Bush veld, narrow veld
(c) Bush veld, high veld (d) Bush veld, low veld.

135. In the Monsoon China, apart from rice and tea, one of the most extensively grown is

(a) Mulberries (b) Cocoa
(c) Barley (d) Wheat.

136. On the eastern slopes of the Rokies in Canada and U.S.A. a local wind similar to the Fohn in Switzerland called the ----- comes in a South Westerly direction. It is hot wind and may rain the temperature by 40° within 30 minutes.

(a) None (b) Chinook
(c) Harmattan (d) Manhattan.

137. The Monsoon China is the world's greatest---------growing area, which accounts for a third of the world's rice.

(a) Rice (b) Coffee
(c) Cocoa (d) Mulberries.

138. The Scientific plant breeding has now devised cold resistant varieties that can mature within---------days, which has resulted in the northward extension of the wheat cultivation into the Peace River region is Canada.

(a) 75 (b) 110
(c) 70 (d) 60.

139. The warm temperate Eastern Margin are the homes of a number of valuable timber species. In eastern Australia the most important are

(a) None (b) Eucalyptus trees
(c) Serum trees (d) Sal trees.

140. The Bedouin is a tribe found in the

(a) Arabian desert (b) Gobi deserts
(c) Thar deserts (d) Great Australian deserts.

141. The warm temperate Eastern Margin (China type) climate is typified by a warm, moist summer and a cool, dry winter, with mean monthly temperature varies between--------and is strongly modified by maritime influence.

(a) 15°F and 20°F (b) 10°F and 25°F
(c) 60°F and 95 F (d) 40°F and 78°F.

142. The Temperate grasslands even as recently, as the last century were dominated by nomadic and semi-nomadic peoples like the --------of the Asiatic Steppes.

(a) Kirghiz (b) Kirgns
(c) Remen (d) Kirghiven.

143. In the Natal, the warm--------current encourages heavy precipitation along the coast and many species of palm trees thrive

(a) Mozambique (b) Gulf
(c) Mexican (d) Labradar.

144. The temperate grasslands have now been ploughed up for extensive, mechanized wheat cultivation and the tufted

grasses have been replaced by the more nutritious grass for cattle and sheep rearing

(a) Anfalingo (b) Lucerne or alfalfa
(c) Levy (d) Long.

145. Besides the widespread cultivation of maize, fruits and cotton in the corn and cotton belts of U.S.A.---------is also grown.

(a) Tabacco (b) Rubber
(c) Mustard (d) Sugarcane.

146. The climate of most parts of China a modified form of monsoonal climate is called the Temperate monsoon or------ type of climate.

(a) None (b) Continental
(c) China (d) Mexico.

147. Most intensively formed areas are the basin of the Si-kiang, Yang-tze and -------they are also the most densely populated areas.

(a) Hang-Tse (b) Hocho-min
(c) Hwang-Ho (d) Chung-min.

148. In the Southern hemisphere the China type of climate is experienced along the warm temperate eastern coastlands of all the three continents—the Natal where cane sugar thrives, the maize belt of Parana - Paraguay-Uruguay basin and in the-------with its eucalyptus forests.

(a) New South Wales (b) Alberta
(c) British Columbia (d) New Columbia.

149. The coal temperate western margins are under the permanent influence of the Westerlies all round the year, they are the regions of much cyclonic activity typical of------ and said to experience--------type of climate.

(a) Australia, New South Wales
(b) France, French
(c) Britain, British
(d) Germany, Rhine.

150. In the southern hemisphere, sheep rearing is the chief occupation of

(a) New Zealand (b) Sudan
(c) Egypt (d) Australia.

151. The above mentioned regions of question no. 115 accounts for more than half the world's production of corn, but only ------- percent of the world's export, far most of the corn is used for fattening of animals, mostly cattle and pigs.

(a) 25 (b) 3
(c) 20 (d) 15.

152. Britain is the home of some of the best known sheep breeds like Leicesters, Lincoln which are dual purpose, mutton and

(a) Wool (b) Eyes
(c) Skin (d) Bone.

153. The British type of climate has adequate rainfall throughout the year with a tendency towards a slight winter or autumn maximum from

(a) Orographic sources (b) Cyclonic sources
(c) Conventional sources (d) Moist wind sources.

154. The produce such as lettuces, cabbages, cauliflowers, tomatoes, onions, peas and fruits are seldom shipped, but conveyed by high speed conveyances such as truks or vans. A particular term is used in the United States for these kind of form products. It is

(a) Van farming (b) Conveyance farming
(c) Road farming (d) Truck farming.

155. Corn or Maize is grown right from the Gulf coast to the Mid-West South of the Great Lakes, with the greatest concentration in the corn belt of Nebraska, Iowa and------

(a) Neveda (b) Dallas
(c) Ohio (d) Columbia.

156. Relief can make great differences in the annual amount of rainfall. For instance, the Western slopes of the Southern Alps of South-Island, New Zealand have as much as 200

inches of rainfall, while the conterbury plain in the-------area has as little as 25 inches.

(a) Rainfed (b) Rainless
(c) Rain deficit (d) Rain shadow.

157. In Britain the Scottish Highlands is a major --------area.

(a) Holiday resort (b) Leather-tanning
(c) Sheep-rearing (d) Industrial.

158. The Gulf type of climate with its long, hot growing season with 200 days frost free and a moderately high temperature of about 75°F, permits one of the best climate for

(a) Cotton growing (b) Mustard growing
(c) Coffee growing (d) Mulberry growing.

159. In the higher up Scandinavian mountains the Rockies, the Southern Andes, Southern Alps of New Zealand, the deciduous trees are generally replaced by the-------which can survive a higher altitude lower temperature and poor soils.

(a) None (b) Conifers
(c) Bamboo thickets (d) Grasslands.

160. Though New Zealand has only 4 per cent of the world's sheep population, it accounts for two-thirds of the world's mutton exports and------ of world wool exports

(a) one-tenth (b) two-third
(c) three-fourth (d) one-sixth.

161. The chief food crop raised in the Gulf states are

(a) Corn or maize (b) Rice
(c) Millets (d) Wheat.

162. There is much oceanic influence on both the temperature and the precipitation on the British type climate, and thus it is also referred as

(a) North-East European Maritime climate
(b) North-West European Maritime climate
(c) North-East Cool climate
(d) North-West Cool climate.

163. In Australia, high speed boats ply across the Bass Strait daily from Tasmania to rush vegetables, apples, beans etc. to major cities in mainland Australia and the Australians have nicknamed Tasmania

(a) 'Garden State' (b) 'Natural State'
(c) 'Heaven State' (d) 'Apple State'.

164. The Sea Island Cotton grown in the islands off the coast of Georgia and---------is long stapled and is one of the best known quality in the world.

(a) East Dakata (b) South Carolina
(c) North Dakata (d) South Dakata.

165. In British Columbia, mixed farming is restricted only to the most favoured parts of the Western

(a) Grasslands (b) Coasts
(c) Lowlands (d) Highlands.

166. Unlike the equatorial forests, the deciduous trees occur in pure stands and have greater---------value from the commercial point of view.

(a) Sericulture (b) Lumbering
(c) Farming (d) Hunting.

167. The natural vegetation of the British Type of Climate is

(a) Temperate grasslands (b) Deciduous forests
(c) Evergreen forests (d) Conferous forests.

168. In the production of wood pulp (by both chemical and mechanical methods) the---------is the leader.

(a) Sweden (b) Norway
(c) U.S.A. (d) Japan.

169. The climate of Siberian type of characterized by a bitterly cold winter of long duration and a--------

(a) no summer (b) cool brief summer
(c) very hot brief summer (d) hot summer.

170. The Laurentian type of climate has cold dry winters and warm--------summers

(a) Wet (b) Excess dry
(c) Dry (d) Cool.

171. Liquid resins and wood alcohols are important chemically processed by products of
(a) Fossils (b) Natural oil
(c) Pipal (d) Timbers.

172. In Canada, the most important fur bearing animals sought offer is muskrat, ermine mink and
(a) Golden fox (b) Silver fox
(c) Polar Beer (d) Beer.

173. The Siberian or "Sub-Arctic" type of climate has a great continuous belt across North America, Europe and
(a) Asia (b) South America
(c) Australia (d) Africa.

174. In the field of newsprint paper---------is the leading one, accounting for almost half of the world's total annual production.
(a) Norway (b) Canada
(c) CIS (d) Finland.

175. The Laurentian type of climate is found only in two regions. They are - north-eastern, north-American including eastern Canada, north-east U.S.A. and the other region is eastern Coastlands of Asia which includes
(a) Eastern Siberia, North-China, Manchuria, Korea and Northern Japan
(b) Eastern Siberia, West China, West Korea
(c) Eastern Siberia, East China, West Korea
(d) Eastern Siberia, East China, East Manchuria.

176. The world's greatest softwood producers are CIS, U.S.A. Canada and
(a) Poland
(b) Brazil
(c) Mexico

(d) Fenoscandian countries (Finland, Norway, Sweeden).

177. For driving the saw-mills and lumbering industry of North America and Europe which of the following cheap energy is used?

(a) Hydro-electricity (b) Thermal energy
(c) Wind energy (d) Solar energy.

178. In North America, the Sub-Arctic (Siberian) belt stretches from Alaska across Canada into Labradar and is found on the high

(a) Rocky Mountains (b) Mt. Blano
(c) Andes Mountains (d) Appalachian Mountains.

179. An immediate type of climate between the British and the Siberian type of climate is

(a) The Temperate Polar climate
(b) The Cool Temperate Eastern Margin (Laurentian) climate
(c) The Semi-Arctic Polar climate
(d) The Arctic climate.

180. The coniferous forest belts of Eurasia and North America are the richest sources of---------for use in building construction, furniture, matches, paper and pulp.

(a) None (b) Semi hardwood
(c) Hardwood (d) Softwood.

181. The conifer has a two-year fructification cycle. The seeds are pollinated in one year and dispessed in the following year, and there is no annual replacement of new leaves as in deciduous trees, the same leaf remains on the tree for as long as

(a) 3 years (b) 2 years
(c) 5 years (d) 1 year.

182. The predominant vegetation of Siberian type of climate is evergreen coniferous, and the greatest single bond of the coniferous forest is the -------- in Siberia

(a) Patchy Coniferous (b) Deep Coniferous
(c) Tundra (d) Taiga.

183. Probably the most important occupation of the Siberian type of climate is promoted by the
(a) None (b) Sheep rearing industry
(c) Lumbering industry (d) Fur industry.

184. These are four major species in the coniferous forest. They are
(a) Pine, Spruch, Larch, Fir
(b) Pine, Spur, Larkech
(c) Pine, Spur, Larv
(d) Pine, Spur, Lark.

185. In the 'Sub-Arctic' (Siberian) region, occasionally cold northerly polar winds such as the Blizzard of--------and Buran of------ below violently at 50 m.p.h.
(a) Canada, Eurasia (b) Germany, Europe
(c) Poland, Europe (d) Switzerland, Asia.

186. Some of the lowest temperatures in the world are recorded in Verkhoyansk, as low as ------- was once recorded.
(a) - 75°F (b) - 70°F
(c) - 90°F (d) -60 °F.

187. In Tasmania and Southern Chile, Sheep rearing has always been a predominant occupation with surplus sheep products for the
(a) Local market use (b) International trade
(c) Domestic use (d) Home consumption.

188. The equatorial rainforests are luxuriant and contain trees of various heights, the coniferous forest are more uniform and grows------
(a) straight and tall (b) very thick and short
(c) wide and tall (d) wide and short.

189. The most remarkable characteristic of the Laurentian climate of north America is its uniformity of
(a) None (b) Chilliness
(c) Precipitation (d) Dryness.

190. The fertile valley of Annapolis is the world's most renowned region for apples and is in

(a) Nova Scatia (b) St. John's
(c) Halifax (d) Darmouth.

191. The meeting of the warm Gulf stream and the cold Labradar current on the coastal waters off---------- produces dense mist and fog.

(a) New York (b) New Foundland
(c) Costarica (d) Canada.

192. The Pilagic fish live near the surface and . . . . fish live near the bottom of shallow seas.

(a) Dalecin (b) Demersal
(c) Daniel (d) Duncan.

193. Of the annual precipitation of 30 to 60 inches in the Laurentian type, two-thirds of its precipitation comes in the

(a) Autumn (b) Spring
(c) Winters (d) Summers.

194. The warm Kuroshio has played an important part in making the climate of Japan less extreme, with the meeting of cold Oyashio from the north it produces fog and mist, making the -------- Japan a 'Second New Foundland'.

(a) West (b) North
(c) East (d) South.

195. The "Pearl culture" is associated with the

(a) Japanese fishing
(b) Fishing grounds of Boston
(c) Fishing parts of Halifax
(d) Fishing parts of Yarmouth.

196. The soil which is found in the flood area where water drainage is better than marshes

(a) Desert soils (b) Saline soils
(c) Meadow soils (d) Bog soils.

197. Which soil area is known as the Bread Basket of the World?
(a) Prairie soil
(b) Meadow soil
(c) Chernozem
(d) Chestnut and Brown soils.

198. Where there is a bag salt lake
(a) Texas (b) Sasketchwan
(c) Utah (d) Alberta.

199. Prairie soils lack the excess of
(a) None (b) Calcium Carbonate
(c) Phosphorus (d) Nitrogen.

200. In the direct absorption of insalation the most significant part is played by
(a) Water vapour (b) Clouds
(c) Gases (d) Dust particles.

201. Rill erosion creates
(a) Ravines (b) V-shaped valley
(c) Ugly topography (d) Erosion of soil.

202. The average annual temperature in tundra climate is
(a) 0°C (b) 5°C
(c) -12°C (d) 15°C.

203. Who make initial studies in the field of Biogeography
(a) Simon
(b) Alexander Van Humboldf
(c) E.W. Russell
(d) None of these.

204. Zerophytes represent the class of vegetation found in
(a) Humid microthermal climate
(b) Tropical rain forest
(c) Semi-arid steppes
(d) Taiga.

205. Biotic succession is a--------
   (a) dynamic process
   (b) limited self-renewing process
   (c) static process
   (d) both (a) and (b).

206. The maximum frequency of hurricanes is found in between latitudes
   (a) 10° to 15° (b) 15° to 20°
   (c) 20° to 25° (d) 25° to 30°.

207. Soil is biochemically withered part of
   (a) Bedrock (b) Inorganic
   (c) Parent material (d) Regolith.

208. Tornadoes may be called
   (a) Local winds (b) The most violent storms
   (c) Whirl winds (d) V-shapped depressions.

209. Cyclones cause floods in the —
   (a) North plains (b) South plains
   (c) Hilly areas (d) Deccan plateau.

210. The immediate cause of wind is
   (a) Pressure differences (b) Temperature differences
   (c) Rotation of the earth (d) Humidity differences.

211. Illite montmorillinite and kaolinite are —
   (a) kinds of soils in U.S.A.
   (b) kinds of protozoa present in the soil
   (c) clay minerals
   (d) kinds of soil microbes.

212. Rozov and Eranova scheme of soil classification is most recent and comprehensive. It is not based on
   (a) profile evolution and interrelationship
   (b) soil forming processes
   (c) soil properties
   (d) environmental factors.

213. Petterssen has classified fog dissipation process into the categories
   (a) Heating
   (b) Vertical mixing
   (c) Condensation and sublimation
   (d) All of the above.

214. The hierarchial system of soil classification is based on
   (a) Soil temperature/atmosphere regimes
   (b) Soil moisture regimes
   (c) Diagnostic horizons
   (d) All of the above.

215. The diameter of the hurricane eye varies from—
   (a) 20 to 40 Km. (b) 40 to 60 Km.
   (c) 60 to 100 Km. (d) 100 to 500 Km.

216. Which of the following has given the most scientific soil classification
   (a) Dokuchaiev (b) Fallou
   (c) Richthofen (d) Kellogg.

217. Hurricane derive their energy from
   (a) Atmospheric stability
   (b) Latent heat of condensation
   (c) Temperature inversion
   (d) None of these.

218. 'Frost-smoke' is known by the name '______' in the mountain regions of North America.
   (a) Samze (b) Pogonip
   (c) Smog (d) None of these.

219. Which of the following is not found in saline soils?
   (a) Boron (b) Sulphate
   (c) Sodium (d) Carbonate.

220. Close to the equator the tropical cyclone do not occur because of

(a) convective activity (b) Light and variable winds
(c) Weak coriolis forces (d) All of these.

221. Thunderstorm originate from
(a) Stratus clouds (b) Cumulonibus clouds
(c) Altocumulus clouds (d) Cirrus clouds.

222. In a tropical cyclone, the pattern of isobars is
(a) circular (b) semi-circular
(c) rectangular (d) elliptical.

223. Dokuchaiev has studied soils into an equilibrium in relationship with the vegetational climax and basic types. How many basic types are there?
(a) 2 (b) 3
(c) 4 (d) 6.

224. Ice-crystal theory of presipitation has been put forward by
(a) Petterssen (b) Bergeron
(c) Tor Bergeron (d) Evans.

225. About half of the atmosphere lies below an attitude of
(a) 5.6 Km. (b) 8.2 Km.
(c) 10 Km. (d) 12 Km.

226. The process involved in adiabatic change of temperature is
(a) Chemical (b) Physical
(c) Advectional (d) None of these.

227. 'Torrential rain' is a characterstic feature of
(a) Orographic precipitation
(b) Convectional precipitation
(c) Cyclonic precipitation
(d) None of these.

228. Which of the statement is not true
(a) The troposphere is the lowest layer of earth
(b) It extends upto 10 kms. near the poles
(c) Climate and weather condition take place in stratosphere

(d) Temperature decrease with height.

229. Soil contain

(a) Nitrogen (b) Oxygen
(c) Carbondioxide (d) All of the above.

230. All the weather changes are closely related to .

(a) humidity variations (b) temperature changes
(c) pressure variations (d) cyclonic activity.

231. The last great ice-age existed in

(a) Pliocene period (b) Pleistocene period
(c) Triassic period (d) Miocene period.

232. Fogs produced in the coastal areas of Japan are

(a) radiation fogs (b) upslope fogs
(c) advection fogs (d) frontel fogs.

233. Marine foods mostly come from

(a) Continental rise (b) Continental slope
(c) Continental sheif (d) Abyssal plains.

234. Soil have delicately interwoven and interacting balanced systems. These subsystems are

1. inorganic minerals and resulting texture
2. organic matter
3. soil organism
4. soil atmosphere

(a) Only 1 and 2 (b) Only 2 and 3
(c) Only 3 and 4 (d) All of the above.

235. The drifting ice-fields are called

(a) Ice-flows (b) Icebergs
(c) Glaciers (d) None of these.

236. One of the forms of precipitation is

(a) frost (b) sleet
(c) dew (d) sublimation.

237. Sunspots are

(a) undulations on the solar surface
(b) huge magnetic storms on the solar suface
(c) places with adequate sunshine
(d) None of the above.

238. The rain shadow effect is related with
(a) drizziling
(b) orographic precipitation
(c) convectional precipitation
(d) none of the above.

239. To reach the earth's suface the rays of the sun take about
(a) 18 minutes (b) 12 minutes
(c) 8 minutes (d) 15 minutes.

240. The thermal equator is found
(a) at the equator
(b) south of geographical equator
(c) north of geographical equator
(d) at the tropic of Cancer.

241. Extra-trophical cyclones have
(a) eye (b) fronts
(c) diverging winds (d) none of the above.

242. The intensity of insolation depends on
(a) altitude (b) latitude
(c) longitude (d) winds.

243. The insolation reaching the earth's surface is equal to
(a) 28 billion horse power (b) 18 billion horse power
(c) 35 billion horse power (d) 23 billion horse power.

244. Which of the following is not a low cloud
(a) cirrocumulus (b) cumulus
(c) nimbostratus (d) stratocumulus.

245. The origin of the simplest life is attributed to
(a) Achaezoic Era (b) Cambrain Era
(c) Proterzoic Era (d) Carboniferous Era.

246. Air mass concept was developed by
   (a) Abercomby (b) Petterssen
   (c) Picardly (d) Vilhelm Bjerknes.

247. An adiabatic change of temperature is caused by
   (a) an increase in the moisture content of an air parcel
   (b) expansion or compression of an air parcel
   (c) increasing amount of dust particles in an air parcel
   (d) horizontal movement of an air parcel.

248. 'Smaze' is a type of
   (a) precipitation
   (b) fog which is an admixture of haze and smoke
   (c) atmospheric disturbance
   (d) frost.

249. In taiga region the average temperature of the coldest month is
   (a) continental steep climate
   (b) mid latitude desert climate
   (c) savanna climate
   (d) none of these.

250. Chernozem is also known as
   (a) Loam (b) Red soil
   (c) Leterite soil (d) Black soil.

251. Soil formation is influenced by
   (a) climate
   (b) topography
   (c) plant and animal organism
   (d) all of the above.

252. Which of the following has the diameter 1-0.05 mm.
   (a) Clay (b) Gravel
   (c) Silt (d) None of these.

253. Which of the following is not a cold current
   (a) Gulf stream (b) Guinea current
   (c) Canarise current (d) Curoshio current.

254. Summer time Continental Polar air masses have their source regions
   (a) in the central parts of high latitude continents
   (b) in central Canada and Siberia
   (c) over the oceans in higher latitudes
   (d) none of these.

255. The carbon dioxide theory of climatic change was advanced by
   (a) Arthur Holmes (b) T.C. Chamberlin
   (c) Kennely (d) Solberg.

256. The 'albedo' of the earth as a whole is
   (a) 35% (b) 40%
   (c) 42% (d) 46%.

257. Inversion of temperature represents
   (a) increases of temperature with latitude
   (b) decreases of temperature with latitude
   (c) uniform temperature
   (d) increase of temperature.

258. The dry adiabatic lapse rate is GEO
   (a) 5°C (b) 10°C
   (c) 15°C (d) 20°C.

259. The normal lapse rate of temperature per kilometre is
   (a) 5.6°C (b) 6.4°C
   (c) 7.9°C (d) 8.2°C.

ANSWERS

1.	(c)	2.	(a)	3.	(d)	4.	(d)
5.	(b)	6.	(a)	7.	(c)	8.	(a)
9.	(b)	10.	(b)	11.	(b)	12.	(c)
13.	(c)	14.	(b)	15.	(a)	16.	(b)
17.	(a)	18.	(b)	19.	(d)	20.	(b)
21.	(c)	22.	(b)	23.	(b)	24.	(c)
25.	(c)	26.	(a)	27.	(a)	28.	(a)

29.	(c)	30.	(c)	31.	(c)	32.	(b)
33.	(a)	34.	(c)	35.	(a)	36.	(a)
37.	(b)	38.	(a)	39.	(b)	40.	(b)
41.	(b)	42.	(c)	43.	(c)	44.	(a)
45.	(a)	46.	(b)	47.	(c)	48.	(a)
49.	(b)	50.	(c)	51.	(b)	52.	(c)
53.	(c)	54.	(b)	55.	(b)	56.	(c)
57.	(a)	58.	(d)	59.	(d)	60.	(c)
61.	(a)	62.	(c)	63.	(b)	64.	(c)
65.	(b)	66.	(a)	67.	(b)	68.	(c)
69.	(d)	70.	(d)	71.	(d)	72.	(b)
73.	(b)	74.	(a)	75.	(c)	76.	(a)
77.	(d)	78.	(b)	79.	(c)	80.	(d)
81.	(a)	82.	(c)	83.	(b)	84.	(b)
85.	(c)	86.	(c)	87.	(b)	88.	(a)
89.	(c)	90.	(d)	91.	(b)	92.	(c)
93.	(c)	94.	(d)	95.	(d)	96.	(a)
97.	(a)	98.	(d)	99.	(b)	100.	(d)
101.	(c)	102.	(b)	103.	(d)	104.	(c)
105.	(b)	106.	(b)	107.	(c)	108.	(c)
109.	(a)	110.	(a)	111.	(c)	112.	(a)
113.	(a)	114.	(a)	115.	(d)	116.	(c)
117.	(d)	118.	(d)	119.	(d)	120.	(d)
121.	(c)	122.	(b)	123.	(c)	124.	(c)
125.	(b)	126.	(a)	127.	(b)	128.	(d)
129.	(a)	130.	(a)	131.	(b)	132.	(b)
133.	(d)	134.	(c)	135.	(a)	136.	(b)
137.	(a)	138.	(b)	139.	(b)	140.	(a)
141.	(d)	142.	(a)	143.	(a)	144.	(b)
145.	(a)	146.	(c)	147.	(c)	148.	(a)
149.	(c)	150.	(a)	151.	(b)	152.	(a)
153.	(b)	154.	(d)	155.	(c)	156.	(d)
157.	(c)	158.	(a)	159.	(b)	160.	(d)
161.	(a)	162.	(b)	163.	(a)	164.	(b)
165.	(c)	166.	(b)	167.	(b)	168.	(c)
169.	(b)	170.	(a)	171.	(d)	172.	(b)
173.	(a)	174.	(b)	175.	(a)	176.	(d)
177.	(a)	178.	(a)	179.	(b)	180.	(d)
181.	(c)	182.	(d)	183.	(c)	184.	(a)
185.	(a)	186.	(d)	187.	(b)	188.	(a)

189.	(c)	190.	(b)	191.	(b)	192.	(d)
193.	(b)	194.	(a)	195.	(c)	196.	(c)
197.	(c)	198.	(c)	199.	(b)	200.	(b)
201.	(a)	202.	(c)	203.	(b)	204.	(c)
205.	(d)	206.	(a)	207.	(d)	208.	(b)
209.	(d)	210.	(a)	211.	(c)	212.	(b)
213.	(d)	214.	(d)	215.	(a)	216.	(d)
217.	(b)	218.	(b)	219.	(a)	220.	(c)
221.	(b)	222.	(a)	223.	(b)	224.	(c)
225.	(a)	226.	(b)	227.	(b)	228.	(c)
229.	(d)	230.	(c)	231.	(b)	232.	(c)
233.	(c)	234.	(d)	235.	(a)	236.	(b)
237.	(b)	238.	(b)	239.	(c)	240.	(c)
241.	(b)	242.	(b)	243.	(d)	244.	(a)
245.	(a)	246.	(d)	247.	(b)	248.	(b)
249.	(a)	250.	(d)	251.	(d)	252.	(c)
253.	(c)	254.	(a)	255.	(b)	256.	(a)
257.	(a)	258.	(b)	259.	(b)		

3
HUMAN GEOGRAPHY

1. Rostow has put forward the best Knowhow-spatial model for economic development it identifies five stages of development. In which stage of economic development in India still lying.
   (a) The preconditions for take off stage
   (b) Take of stage
   (c) The drive to maturity stage
   (d) None of these.

2. Large cities of the world have been experiencing growth
   (a) Horizontal only (b) Vertical only
   (c) Both (a) and (b) (d) None of these.

3. Which theory tries to explain the hierarchical pattern of Indian cities?
   (a) Central place theory (b) Primate city concept
   (c) Rank-size rule (d) All of the above.

4. The urban population of India is next only to
   (a) U.S.A. (b) U.S.S.R
   (c) both (a) and (b) (d) None of these.

5. According to concentric zone theory, a typical city would take the form of---------concentric zones of the land use
   (a) 4 (b) 5
   (c) 6 (d) 7.

6. The multiple nuclei theory has been put forward by
   (a) E.W. Burgess (b) H. Hyot
   (c) Harris & Ullman (d) Moser and Scott.

7. The concentric zone theory has been advanced by
   (a) E.W. Burgess (b) H. Hyot
   (c) Harris and Ullman (d) None of these.

8. According to the Rank-size rule propounded by Zipf, the population size from largest to lowest follow
   (a) Geometric progression
   (b) Harmonic progression
   (c) Arithmetic progression
   (d) None of the above.

9. The area which follows a continuum of the typical urban area as well as rural area is known as
   (a) Urban sphere of Inference
   (b) Rural-Urban fringe
   (c) Rural fringe
   (d) None of these.

10. A technique of principal component analysis was adopted for classification of cities for establishing similarity rather than dissimilarity by which of the following geographer
    (a) Nelson and Jefferson (b) Taylor and Smith
    (c) Moser and Scott (d) None of the above.

11. Nelson has put forward his theory of classification of cities. His theory is based on
    (a) Occupation groups of the urban population
    (b) Population density of the urban area
    (c) Employment data
    (d) None of these.

12. Which is the next stage development of a metropoolis?
    (a) greater city (b) concubation
    (c) megapolis (d) None of these.

13. Who has given one of the best known and earliest of the functional classification of cities?
    (a) Christaller (b) Mark Jefferson
    (c) Harris (d) Taylor.
14. Who has put forward the law of primate city?
    (a) Mark Jefferson (b) Christaller
    (c) Lewis Mumford (d) None of these.
15. Who pioneered the theory of rank-size rule
    (a) Lewis Mumford (b) Zipf
    (c) Christaller (d) Weber.
16. "A city is in fact the physical form of the highest and the most types of associative life" who has defined thus
    (a) Lewis Mumford (b) C.K. Zipf
    (c) Hoover (d) D.M. Smith.
17. Rural nucleated settlements can be classified in many categories which of the following does not belong to that
    (a) Rectangular (b) Linear
    (c) Colinear (d) Starlike.
18. The size of the village is determined by the factors
    (a) The size of the population
    (b) Stage of development of the village
    (c) Land fertility
    (d) All of the above.
19. In Isolated settlement the farmer wishes to live on his own land. This type of settlement is found in
    (a) Western U.S.A. (b) Canadian Ranches
    (c) Australian Ranches (d) All of the above.
20. Dispersion indicates a
    (a) Close relationship between the dwelling and place of work
    (b) An inverse relationship between the dwelling and the place of work

(c) A remote relationship between the dwelling and place of work

(d) none of these.

21. Nucleated form of settlements develop in

(a) lowland areas with rich soils

(b) highlands with forests

(c) sandy area

(d) None of these.

22. Which of the following statement is true?

(a) GNP is a better measure than GDP

(b) GDP is a better measure than GNP

(c) GNP would be larger than GDP if the country has a trade surplus

(d) None of these.

23. Which is known as "the land of rising sun"?

(a) Norway (b) Japan

(c) South Korea (d) Sweden.

24. Which of European races have the features -----broad heads, thick set bodies, light skin and straight to wavy brown hair?

(a) Nardic Race (b) Alpine Race

(c) Mediterranean Race (d) None of the above.

25. Narrow faced, hirsute and of slight build these are features of

(a) Chinese (b) Mongoloid

(c) Japanese (d) None of these.

26. Long noses are prevalent among

(a) Eskimos (b) Negroes

(c) Mongoloid (d) None of these.

27. Which of the following does not rise in the Alps

(a) Rhine (b) Dainube

(c) Rhone (d) Po.

28. The major characteristics of the Europeans are

(a) Aggressive (b) Acquisitive
(c) Progressive (d) All of the above.

29. Anglo-American realm is known for its
(a) Rawness (b) Hawness
(c) Spaciousness (d) All of the above.

30. Which of the following realms is known of Iberian tongues?
(a) European realm (b) Latin-American realm,
(c) Anglo-American realm (d) None of these.

31. Which of the following is not a sub - region of Pacific realm?
(a) Melanesia (b) Polynesia
(c) Andulasia (d) Micronesia.

32. Which Realm is known as "Vegetable Civilization"?
(a) The Oriental Realm (b) Polar Realm
(c) Pacific Realm (d) European Realm.

33. Capitalism, Industrialism and Urbanism has reached its peak in
(a) Latin-American Realm
(b) European Realm
(c) Anglo-American Realm
(d) Pacific Realm.

34. Which one of the following is not an example of forced migration?
(a) Expulsion of Indians from Uganda
(b) Expulsion of Chinese from Vietnam
(c) Movement of Kampuchean tours people to country side
(d) Movement of Jews to Israel.

35. Which type of migration is very popular these days?
(a) daily (b) seasonal
(c) semiopermanent (d) permanent.

36. Northern hemisphere has the population concentration of more than---------per cent of world population.

(a) 80 (b) 85
(c) 75 (d) 90.

37. Four out of five people in the world live within the height of ---------from sea-level
(a) 300 m (b) 400 m
(c) 500 m (d) 700 m.

38. Which of the following is not the population problem of the developed countries?
(a) Housing and health (b) Small work force
(c) Rural population (d) Aging population.

39. Human occupy the------trophic level in ecosystem
(a) lowest (b) medium
(c) highest (d) none of these.

40. Humans are
(a) Herbivores (b) Carnivores
(c) Omnivores (d) None of these.

41. Which points are taken into consideration while judging the races?
(a) Skin and hair colour
(b) Eye colour
(c) Form and shape of the face of Jaw
(d) All of these.

42. Baltic race is famous for its
(a) Blonde hair (b) Wavy hair
(c) Long and straight hair (d) None of these.

43. Eye or ocpicanthic fold is also known as
(a) Nordic fold (b) Negro fold
(c) Mongoloid fold (d) None of these.

44. Which of the following forests are most sparsely populated?
(a) Forest of Congo (b) Ahazonian forest
(c) Coniferous forests (d) None of these.

45. Which is the most effective for the opening of a country for dense inhabitation?
    (a) Opening of the railways
    (b) Clearing of the forests
    (c) Establishment of Industrial complexes
    (d) Both (a) and (c).

46. What is the approximate world population density per wquare kilometre?
    (a) 30-35 (b) 40-45
    (c) 50-55 (d) 20-25.

47. Which of the geographical conditions determine the density and distribution of population?
    (a) Climate and relief
    (b) Rock structure and mineral sources
    (c) Availability of water
    (d) All of the above.

48. The people—Malaya, and the Polynesians and Melanesian vary in colour from
    (a) Brown to black (b) Black to grey
    (c) Grey to fair (d) None of these.

49. He is possibly no more inventive than Chinese, put he is unrivalled in common sense and insight of practical application. This is said about the
    (a) Americans (b) Europeans
    (c) Mongolians (d) Negroes.

50. Which of the following is an artistic craftsman and a great organizer?
    (a) Negro (b) Red Indian
    (c) Australian (d) Mongolian.

51. Short, slender, dark - haired, dark complex and very long heads are the attributes of
    (a) Nordic Race (b) Alpine Race
    (c) Mediterranean Race (d) None of these.

52. The aborigines of Australia, a primitive race how few in no. are dark skinned and have
    (a) Curly hair (b) Shaggy hair
    (c) Long and straight hair (d) Woolly hair.

53. Which of the following is not an attribute of the Nordic Race?
    (a) Tall (b) Fair hair
    (c) Blue or grey eyes (d) Round head.

54. The Bushmen and Hottentots of Kalahari are
    (a) Dark skinned (b) Brown skinned
    (c) Yellow skinned (d) Fair skinned.

55. Most of the people who live in North Europe belong to
    (a) Nordic race (b) Alpine race
    (c) Mediterranean race (d) None of these.

56. Which of the following is not a feature of Negroes
    (a) Thick lips (b) Broad flat nose
    (c) Grey eyes (d) Woolly hair.

57. The hair of the Caucasian is oval in cross section and is
    (a) Straight (b) Wavy
    (c) Woolly (d) None of these.

58. A unit of organized group of men, women and children making a living out of their surrounding environment, which vary in size, complexity and stage of development is said to be a
    (a) Concentration (b) Location
    (c) Settlement (d) None of these.

59. The type of settlement which are one family, few family residences scattered about in isolated places, separated from one another by open country or by geographical barriers and life for the settlers is simple, quite and much the same all the year round is said to be
    (a) Nucleated settlements
    (b) Dispersed settlements

(c) Fragmented settlements
(d) None of these.

60. The type of settlements which are groupings of several family residences have collective amenities to survey the community like shop-houses, markets, schools, places of worship etc. is said to be
(a) Dispersed settlement (b) Congested settlements
(c) Broken settlement (d) Nucleated settlements.

61. -----------settlement is most typical of rural areas, highlands of Malaysia, the Scrublands of Central Australia and the Wheat-farms in the Canadian Prairies.
(a) Dispersed (b) Fragmented
(c) Nucleated (d) Unilinear.

62. 'Sungei Sumum' is the ---------type of nucleated settlements
(a) Indonesian (b) Japanese
(c) Burmese (d) Malaysian.

63. Paris basin is drained by river
(a) Seine (b) Sinomg
(c) Nanking (d) Sungeiklang.

64. An indented coastline has calm waters and is sheltered from the waves of the open sea, particularly well suited for-------- where off shore islands offer an added protection.
(a) Seaport (b) Fishing
(c) Floating city (d) None of these.

65. ----------- is ideally sited on Port Phillip Bay and protected by protruding headlands on both sides of the entrance so for one of the best sheltered natural harbours of the southern hemisphere
(a) Adelaide (b) Melbourne
(c) Brisbane (d) Perth.

66. The river Shannon is in
(a) Canada (b) Australia
(c) South Korea (d) Ireland.

67. The Salt Lake city situated near the Great Salt Lake of Utah, is one of the largest-----------settlements in the Rocky mountains.
(a) Fragmented (b) Dispersed
(c) Nucleated (d) None of these.

68. Rome is located on the river
(a) Tubec (b) Euphrates
(c) Rosem (d) Tiber.

69. --------- towns are historical and religious centres frequented by pilgrims from all parts of the globe.
(a) Commercial (b) Mining
(c) Administrative (d) Ecclesiastical.

70. The ports that specialize in receiving and redistributing goods to the neighbouring countries and to different corners of the world is said to be
(a) Entrè ports (b) Packet ports
(c) Royal ports (d) Linear ports.

71. The smaller ports closer to deep ocean waters and serve a larger port further inland which can no longer be reached by the larger ships is said to be
(a) Outlet ports (b) Linear ports
(c) Outports (d) Inports.

72. Who pioneered the "Theory of demographic transition"?
(a) R. Nurkse (b) C.P. Blacker
(c) D.M. Smith (d) None of these.

73. India is still in the-------- stage of theory of demographic transition.
(a) 1st stage (b) IIIrd stage
(c) IInd stage (d) IVth stage.

74. Match the following Demo transition
A. 1st Stage 1. Depopulation stage
B. IInd Stage 2. Population explosion stage

C. IIIrd Stage 3. Primitive stage
D. IVth Stage 4. Equilibrating stage.

75. Asia accounts for the how much population of the world population.

(a) 48 (b) 53
(c) 58 (d) 62.

76. Which of the following accounts for the highest population percentage of the world population.

(a) South America (b) Europe
(c) North America (d) Australia.

77. Population density is maximum in which of the following countries.

(a) Indonesia (b) India
(c) China (d) Japan.

78. Which one of the following is not related to population in direct ways?

(a) Fertility (b) Morality
(c) Migration (d) Occupational structure.

79. Over the past decade the increase in world population has been at a rate of approximately

(a) 72 million persons per year
(b) 77 million persons per year
(c) 82 million persons per year
(d) 87 million persons per year.

80. UN has projected a world population of --------- by the end of this century.

(a) 6.0 billion (b) 7.5 billion
(c) 7 billion (d) 8.0 billion.

81. The Polar Eskimos use dogs popularly known as--------to carry their loads.

(a) Husk (b) Harrier
(c) Huskies (d) Handerton.

82. It is estimated that lands South of the Tropic of Capricorn contains less than------- percent of the world's population.
(a) 5 (b) 10
(c) 12 (d) 16.

83. Some important ways of relieving the world population problems are
(a) Cut down the rate of population increase
(b) Increase food yields
(c) Migration
(d) All of the above.

84. The problem of food shortages is greatest in
(a) Japan and Bangladesh
(b) Bangladesh, Indonesia, India, China
(c) Burma and Bangladesh
(d) East Europe and Bangladesh.

85. The greatest assets of North-West Europe are
(a) Coal and Iron deposits (b) Copper and aluminium
(c) Teak wood (d) None of these.

86. What is the most important factors that enable the small countries of North-West Europe to support its large population.
(a) Industrialization (b) Huge oil wells
(c) Fishing (d) Foreign aid.

87. Though the Amazon River floods extensively and is navigable for thousands of miles up-stream, absence of------ and lack of commercial enterprises results to few towns and fewer posts.
(a) Metropolis (b) Sophisticated Bonds
(c) Productive hinterland (d) None of these.

88. Due to the geographical conditions, the Amazon will have ------- population for many years to come.
(a) High (b) Very high
(c) High explosion of (d) Sparse.

89. Migration can be defined as a
   (a) A permanent move to a new country or a region which is geographically well defined
   (b) Move from a country to a state
   (c) Intra move with in a state
   (d) None of these.

90. Australia was lonely settled by
   (a) Involuntary migration of convicts who were departed from England
   (b) Voluntary migration of Agricultural search of land, food and habitation
   (c) Both (a) and (b)
   (d) None of these.

91. Economic density is defined as
   (a) A ratio between the requirements of a population and the resources not able to match the requirements
   (b) A ratio between the requirements of a population and the resources made available to it by production in the areas it occupies
   (c) Both (a) and (b)
   (d) None of these.

92. Japan, though a small country has become an industrial giant because of
   (a) Work motivation and urge to known the best skills by the people
   (b) Very advanced agro industry
   (c) Very advanced in oil and natural gas industries
   (d) None of these.

93. If a country is at a relatively advanced stage of development, it is termed as
   (a) Under developed country
   (b) Developing country
   (c) Developed country
   (d) All of these.

94. In South-East Asia, the predominant form of economy is
(a) Leather exports (b) Handicraft
(c) Subsistence agriculture (d) Silk exports.

95. The form of ritual or established process for public worship is termed of
(a) Ghetto (b) Granaie
(c) Liturgy (d) None of these.

96. The majority of the countries at the present time are under
(a) Stage 1st of demographic transition
(b) Either stage 2nd or stage 3rd of demographic transition
(c) Stage 4th of demographic transition
(d) None of these.

97. Which region of the world has the largest concentration of inhabitants
(a) West Asia (b) North Asia
(c) East Asia (d) South Asia.

98. Demographic transition means
(a) Process of change of population in a given society
(b) Processs of change of only female population in a society
(c) A stage where death and birth rate is not taken under consideration
(d) None of these.

99. What is indicated by a population Pyramid.
(a) Indicates the distribution by male and female population of a region
(b) Indicates the percentage of the toal population in each five year age group or category
(c) Indicates the newly born male baby in a calendar years
(d) None of these.

100. Altogether the growth rate of population of the world has increased due to
(a) Advance medical science

(b) Advancement in technical field
(c) Rane floating of rivers
(d) None of these.

101. The reasons for the wide settlement of population in the Indo-Gangetic plain and Hwong-Ho Valley of China is
(a) The two rivers are fed by seasonal rainfall, flooding is caused and deposition of alluvial takes place
(b) Sufficient pernial water for agro activities is available
(c) Because of the plain land and long stretch of river, industries are set up
(d) All of the above.

102. When the cultural aspects of a region is taken into account, the process is termed as
(a) Cultural succession
(b) Norms and values succession
(c) Ecological succession
(d) None of these.

103. The open continental situation is largely known as
(a) Maritime situation (b) Middland situation
(c) Laurendian situation (d) None of these.

104. In the Northern hemisphere, the land and the sea ratio is
(a) 2 : 1 (b) 4 : 1
(c) 1 : 2 (d) 1 : 1.5.

105. When a considerable amount of labour force and other resources are put-in, in a piece of land to increase its productivity, it is termed as
(a) Shifting cultivation (b) Transhumane
(c) Insensitive farming (d) None of these.

106. What is Intra regional migrations
(a) Non-metropolitan to metropolitan immigration
(b) Rural to urban migration
(c) Urban to sub-urban migration
(d) All of the above.

107. There are several hundred varieties of pady, each is sown to suit local climatic and topographical conditions and they are raised in

(a) single cropping
(b) double cropping
(c) single, double or triple cropping
(d) only single cropping.

108. Heavy rainfall bewteen 50 and 200 inches without any prolonged drought or cold is needed for

(a) Silk cultivation (b) Flax cultivation
(c) Hemp fibre cultivation (d) Tea cultivation.

109. If the animal migration takes place in semi-arid steppes, it is better called

(a) Shifting herding (b) Nomadic herding
(c) Move herding (d) None of these.

110. If the concentration of the farm is on small fruits or horticultural crops the more appropriate term for this practice is

(a) Market gardening or truck farming
(b) Vegetable gardening
(c) Small scale farming
(d) horticultural farming.

111. The farming that concentrate on food crops grown on ploughed land, such as wheat, barley, oats, etc. are called

(a) cultivation farming (b) farming
(c) arable farming (d) None of these..

112. ------------ cultivation is practised in the tropical Andean highlands of South America

(a) fixed cultivation (b) sedentary cultivation
(c) permanent cultivation (d) shifting cultivation.

113. The area where the individual farm families decide to remain permanently in the area they have cleared for cultivation is termed as

(a) Permanent cultivation (b) Fixed cultivation
(c) Sedentary cultivation (d) Individual cultivation.

114. The solid is leached rapidly under tropical conditions and its fertility is soon exhausted. The people having no knowledge of solid maintenance and no domesticated animals to enrich the fields with manure, clears a new patch for cultivation and the families keep on shifting to the new fields. This type of practice is called
(a) Changing cultivation (b) New cultivation
(c) Shifting cultivation (d) None of these.

115. On tropical lowlands and hill-slopes local people clear small patches of the rain forests and cultivate with only primitive implements, sufficient for their own needs is called
(a) Tropical agriculture
(b) Highland difficult farming
(c) Outdated farming
(d) Primitive subsistence agriculture.

116. Dates can only be successfully grown in a
(a) lowland arid environment
(b) highland arid environment
(c) lowland wet environment
(d) highland wet environment.

117. An ltalian has a
(a) Dark hair, dark eyes (b) Olive skin
(c) Both (a) and (b) (d) None of these.

118. A Norwegian has a fair skin and fair hair and is usually
(a) Dark eyes (b) Blue eyes
(c) Black eyes (d) None of these.

119. Which is the index plant of the Mediterranean climate
(a) Oak (b) Teak
(c) Olive (d) Spruce.

120. By which name steppes are known in Hungary
(a) Pustaz (b) Topaz
(c) Bush-veld (d) None of these.

121. Which of the following tribes group is known as the Tartars

(a) Kazakhas (b) Kalonuck
(c) Kirghiz (d) None of these.

122. Which of the following grasslands become world's leading exporter of beef due to its pastoral industry

(a) Steppes (b) Downs
(c) Veld (d) Pampas.

123. Sirocco, a hot, dry dusty wind is known by the name -------- in Spain

(a) Khausin (b) Chili
(c) Ghibi (d) Leveche.

124. The houses made by bushmen, a hollow dug beneath a thorn free surrounded by bushes, is known as

(a) Wurilies (b) Igloo
(c) Sherms (d) None of these.

125. Which type of the climatic region is known as 'Gadle of world civilization'?

(a) Mediterranean (b) Laurentian
(c) China type climate (d) Temperate continental.

126. Wurlies, simple shelters made of branches and tufts and grass are made by

(a) Bushmen (b) Bindibu
(c) Masai (d) None of these.

127. Bushmen ram the

(a) Arizona desert (b) Antacama desert
(c) Kalahari desert (d) Mohave desert.

128. Hausa are the tribes of

(a) Kenya (b) Nigeria
(c) Uganda (d) Tanzania.

129. Which of the following statements is untrue about the Masais of Africa.

(a) Cattle are considered for more valuable than anything else

(b) They drink milk as well as blood of their animals
(c) They do not slaughter the cattle for meat
(d) They build conical huts.

130. Masi pastoralists are found in
(a) East Africa (b) West Africa
(c) South Africa (d) North Africa.

131. T.R. Malthus has provided an comprehensive theory regarding population. His theory at best can be termed as
(a) Economic theory (b) Cultural theory
(c) Biological theories (d) None of these.

132. Which is the highest city in the world
(a) La Paz (b) Bogota
(c) Ontario (d) Berne.

133. Which of the following is an example of tertiary concentration
(a) California
(b) Eastern Brazil
(c) South Eastern Australia
(d) Nicle Valley.

134. In Europe 11% of the world population occupy less than---- percent of the world land area
(a) 4 (b) 5
(c) 6 (d) 8.

135. South East Asia, Europe and north-eastern North America alone account for approximately what percent of world population
(a) 65 (b) 70
(c) 75 (d) 80.

136. Which is the most populated country of African continent?
(a) Nigeria (b) Sudan
(c) Egypt (d) Algeria.

137. Which of the following races is having the largest population?

(a) Negroids (b) Caucasoids
(c) Mongoloids (d) None of these.

138. 'Inverse Distance Law' of migration has been propounded by
(a) Ravenstein (b) D. Smith
(c) C.K. Zipf (d) None of these.

139. About how many million persons would be added to the world population according to a medium variant projection by the year 2000
(a) 88 millions (b) 83 millions
(c) 78 millions (d) 92 millions.

140. Over population leads to
(a) Low per capita income
(b) High levels of unemployment
(c) Pronounced outward migration
(d) All of the above.

141. Which of the following is not an example of under population
(a) Mexico (b) New Zealand
(c) Australia (d) Argentina.

142. Which of the following is not an outcome of high population growth
(a) Starvation (b) Higher income
(c) Malnutrition (d) Poverty.

143. Match the following

(a) 1650-1750 AD	1. Late Expanding
(b) 1950-2000	2. High Fluctuating
(c) 1900 -1950	3. Early expanding
(d) 1750 - 1900	4. Low fluctuating.

144. India is expected to attain net reproduction rate of 1.0 by the year
(a) 2001 (b) 2006
(c) 2011 (d) 2015.

145. A net reproduction rate of 1.0 will lead to
   (a) increase in population
   (b) decrease in population
   (c) static population growth
   (d) none of these.

146. Which of the following has put forward the "theory of vicious circle"
   (a) Rostow (b) G. Myrdal
   (c) H.W. Singer (d) D. Smith.

ANSWERS

1.	(b)	2.	(b)	3.	(d)	4.	(c)
5.	(b)	6.	(c)	7.	(a)	8.	(d)
9.	(b)	10.	(c)	11.	(a)	12.	(b)
13.	(c)	14.	(a)	15.	(b)	16.	(b)
17.	(a)	18.	(c)	19.	(d)	20.	(a)
21.	(a)	22.	(c)	23.	(b)	24.	(b)
25.	(c)	26.	(a)	27.	(d)	28.	(d)
29.	(d)	30.	(b)	31.	(c)	32.	(a)
33.	(c)	34.	(c)	35.	(c)	36.	(d)
37.	(c)	38.	(a)	39.	(c)	40.	(c)
41.	(d)	42.	(a)	43.	(c)	44.	(b)
45.	(d)	46.	(a)	47.	(d)	48.	(a)
49.	(b)	50.	(d)	51.	(c)	52.	(b)
53.	(d)	54.	(c)	55.	(a)	56.	(c)
57.	(b)	58.	(c)	59.	(b)	60.	(d)
61.	(a)	62.	(d)	63.	(a)	64.	(a)
65.	(b)	66.	(d)	67.	(c)	68.	(d)
69.	(d)	70.	(a)	71.	(c)	72.	(b)
73.	(c)	74.	(d)	75.	(c)	76.	(b)
77.	(d)	78.	(d)	79.	(b)	80.	(c)
81.	(c)	82.	(a)	83.	(d)	84.	(b)
85.	(a)	86.	(a)	87.	(c)	88.	(d)
89.	(a)	90.	(a)	91.	(b)	92.	(a)
93.	(c)	94.	(c)	95.	(c)	96.	(b)
97.	(c)	98.	(a)	99.	(b)	100.	(a)
101.	(d)	102.	(c)	103.	(b)	104.	(d)

105.	(c)	106.	(d)	107.	(c)	108.	(d)
109.	(b)	110.	(a)	111.	(c)	112.	(b)
113.	(c)	114.	(c)	115.	(d)	116.	(a)
117.	(c)	118.	(b)	119.	(c)	120.	(a)
121.	(c)	122.	(d)	123.	(d)	124.	(c)
125.	(a)	126.	(b)	127.	(c)	128.	(b)
129.	(d)	130.	(a)	131.	(c)	132.	(a)
133.	(d)	134.	(c)	135.	(b)	136.	(a)
137.	(b)	138.	(c)	139.	(a)	140.	(d)
141.	(a)	142.	(b)	143.	(b)	144.	(c)
145.	(c)	146.	(c)				

4
ECONOMIC GEOGRAPHY

1. Which of the following is not responsible for the depletion of fishing resources
   (a) Oil spills
   (b) Silviculture
   (c) Draining Industrial effluents into sea
   (d) Ocean Transport.

2. Which of the following countries are the main producers of copper in Africa
   (a) Zaire and South Africa (b) Zambia and Tanzania
   (c) Congo and Chad (d) Zaire and Zambia.

3. In which of the following Latin American countries lies the largest reserves of good quality iron ore
   (a) Argentina (b) Vanezuela
   (c) Brazil (d) Chile.

4. In India, which of the following states is richest in iron-ore reserves?
   (a) Orissa (b) Bihar
   (c) Madhya Pradesh (d) Karnataka.

5. Which of the following is not a producer of iron-ore in the African continent
   (a) Liberia (b) South Africa
   (c) Zaire (d) Algeria.

6. Sweden exports most of its iron-ores because
   (a) It does not have sufficient limestones reserves
   (b) It does not have sufficient coal reserves
   (c) It does not have appropriate technology
   (d) It specialies in other products.

7. In Europe, best quality iron-ores is found in which of the following country
   (a) USSR (b) Sweden
   (c) France (d) U.K.

8. Which of the following is the famous silver mines of Australia
   (a) Broken Hill (b) Kalgoorlie
   (c) Silverton (d) Both (a) and (c).

9. Which region of New Zealand has the highest density of milch cows
   (a) Taranaki plain (b) Otago plateau
   (c) Canterbury plain (d) None of these.

10. Fishing resources of the western and eastern coasts have been declining steadily mainly because of
    (a) Nuclear tests under the sea
    (b) Water pollution due to rapid industrialization of adjoining areas
    (c) Heavy Ocean Transport
    (d) Oil spills.

11. Fishes are a rich sources of
    (a) Fat (b) Minerals
    (c) Vitamins (d) Proteins.

12. Who holds the opinion that for developing countries theory of unbalanced growth is more apt and applicable
    (a) Gunnar Myrdal (b) A Hirschnan
    (c) A Lewis (d) Von. Thunen.

13. Which of the following has propounded the theory of balanced growth for a nation

(a) R. Nurkse (b) Lt. Leibeustein
(c) A Weber (d) A. Lasch.

14. Which of the following mode of transport is most cost-effective for long distance with large volume?
(a) Land transport (b) Railways
(c) Seaways (d) Airways.

15. The recently concluded GATT treaty was signed by how many nations?
(a) 110 (b) 115
(c) 112 (d) 117.

16. Which of the following items occupies the first place in international trade
(a) Foodstuffs (b) Manufactured goods
(c) Raw materials (d) Services.

17. The centre of gravity of the world trade is shifting to
(a) North Atlantic (b) Pacific Basin
(c) Western Europe (d) Middle East.

18. The most industrialized region of Japan is which of the following?
(a) Keihin Region (b) Ise Bay region
(c) Hanshin Region (d) Kitakyushu region.

19. Which of the following is the largest coal-field of China ?
(a) Tianjin-Bejing (b) Yangtze-Kiang Area
(c) Shanxi-Baotou (d) Manchuria.

20. Who has put forward the concept of diffusion of innovation
(a) Schumpeter (b) Hagerstrand
(c) Thunen (d) Larenz.

21. Sedimentary iron-ore deposits are not found in which of the African country?
(a) South Africa (b) Tunisia
(c) Algeria (d) Morocco.

22. Which of the following type of deposits are known as placer deposits?
    (a) Sedimentary ore deposits
    (b) Oceanic mineral deposits
    (c) Igneous ore bodies
    (d) Alluvial deposits.
23. Which of the following is not an economic influence on mining activity?
    (a) Demand of the ore
    (b) Size of reserves
    (c) Availability of capital
    (d) Availability of Transport system.
24. Which city has been most affected by mining of Uranium and is better known of "the first nuclear-age ghost town, and undoutedly the handsomest one anywhere in the world?
    (a) Alsace (b) Carnwall
    (c) Elliot Lake (d) Great Bear Lake.
25. What is/are the operating costs in the transport of goods
    (a) Overhead costs (b) Transfer costs
    (c) Line-haul costs (d) All of the above.
26. Trans Canadian Highway links
    (a) Halifax and Vancouver
    (b) St. John and Victoria
    (c) St. John and Vancouver
    (d) None of these.
27. According to D.M. Smith's theory of spatial margin to profitability theory important factors is/are
    (a) Demand only (b) Cost only
    (c) Both demand and cost (d) None of these.
28. Indonesia is the world's largest producer of
    (a) Rubber (b) Sugercane
    (c) Cinchona (d) Tea.

29. Which is most important drainage system in South America
    (a) Parana Parguay system
    (b) Amazon system
    (c) San Francisco
    (d) None of these.

30. How much distance has been reduced between Bombay and London due to Suez Canal
    (a) 8800 Kms (b) 9900 kms
    (c) 9600 kms (d) 10,720 kms.

31. Ismailia, an important town in the Suez area is located on the
    (a) Lake Timsa (b) Great Bitter Lake
    (c) Lake Manzale (d) None of these.

32. Due to opening of the Panama canal how much distance has been reduced from Liverpool and San Francisco
    (a) 600 kms (b) 8000 kms
    (c) 7000 kms (d) 9000 kms.

33. What is India's share in the total international trade?
    (a) 0.5 % (b) 1.0%
    (c) 2.0% (d) 5.0%.

34. What is India's share is in total forest area in the world?
    (a) 2% (b) 4%
    (c) 6% (d) 8%.

35. Which of the following country leads in the per capita arable hand
    (a) India (b) China
    (c) USA (d) Canada.

36. Which of the following countries has the highest percentage of cultivated area?
    (a) China (b) India
    (c) USA (d) Canada.

37. At which place an important copper reserve has been found in India.
(a) Malajkhand (b) Aguncha Rampura
(c) Ghatshila (d) Khetri.

38. Which of the following is not a product of Tizerra Templada Zone?
(a) Rice (b) Rubbey
(c) Sugar (d) Corn.

39. The Puna or Paramos Zone is also known as
(a) Selva (b) Conifers
(c) Alpine Meadow (d) None of the above.

40. Earl B. Shaw's classification of world agricultural regions does not take into congnizance the important of
(a) Location (b) Climate
(c) Landforms (d) Productivity.

41. Which of the following is not a required condition for the cultivation of suger beet?
(a) Cool and moderately moist climate dry weather before harvest
(b) Temperature in the range of 20-22^{0}C
(c) Fertile loamy soil, rich in lime
(d) Rainfall 100-150 cm.

42. Who pioneered the theory of location of agriculture land use zones
(a) Von Thunen (b) Mecklenburg
(c) A. Losch (d) H. Hotelling.

43. The cultivation of sugarcane cannot be successful if one of the following conditions comes into play
(a) Hot and humid climate
(b) 24°- 27° C temperature
(c) Frost
(d) 150 cm rainfall spread over 8 months.

44. Which of the following crops is not frost tolerant ?
    (a) Rye (b) Oats
    (c) Barley (d) Rubber.

45. Who has put forward the theory of 'Spatial margins to profitability'?
    (a) A. Weber (b) Hoover
    (c) Smith (d) A. Losch.

46. A. Weber has coine to be known of the pioneer of the theory of industrial location which of the following is not related to his theory
    (a) Concept of least transport cost
    (b) Concept of weight gaining and weight loosing industries
    (c) Critical Isodapanes
    (d) Spatial margins to profitability.

47. World Trade Organisation is to be set up for promotion of international trade world wide. It has been proposed after meeting at which place?
    (a) Seattle (b) Davos
    (c) Marrakesh (d) Marritania.

48. Which of the following is not conspicuous regarding international trade?
    (a) Manufactured goods trade occupies first place
    (b) BOP is in favour of UDCS
    (c) World trade has increasingly become trade blocs oriented
    (d) Pacific basin is taking place of north Altantic in volume as well as value of the world trade.

49. Which is the biggest port of the world?
    (a) New York (b) New Orlens
    (c) Rotterdam (d) Kobe.

50. Which country has the densest cargo traffic
    (a) USA (b) Former USSR or CIS
    (c) China (d) India.

51. Which of the following is the largest ship canal of the world
    (a) Suez Canal (b) Panama Canal
    (c) Kiel (d) Gota.

52. Which is the deepest ship canal of the world
    (a) Corinth (b) Suez
    (c) Panama (d) Princess Juliana.

53. The most important river of Britain is
    (a) Thames (b) Seven
    (c) Trent (d) Great Ouse.

54. Canada produces about 50% of the world's production of nickel and most of this comes from a single great nickle producing area of the world
    (a) Sudbury (b) Yellowknife
    (c) Southampton (d) Edmonton.

55. Which country is the leading producer of Titanium
    (a) USA (b) Canada
    (c) Australia (d) Norway.

56. Which of the following is the largest producer of mercury?
    (a) Spain (b) USSR
    (c) Italy (d) Mexico.

57. Which African country is the largest producer of Obact?
    (a) Zambia (b) Morocco
    (c) Zaire (d) South Africa.

58. Which country leads in the production of Molybdenum?
    (a) USSR (b) India
    (c) USA (d) Chile.

59. Which place was the venue of Earth Summit 92?
    (a) Rio D Janeiro (b) Manchester
    (c) Buenos Aires (d) Sao Paolo.

60. Which of the following countries has highest percentage area under forest?

(a) Brazil (b) Japan
(c) Zaire (d) Argentina.

61. "Oriental Agriculture" is the name given to which type of agriculture?
(a) Sedentary subsistence agriculture
(b) Plantation agriculture
(c) Intensive subsistence agriculture
(d) Mixed farming.

62. Which of the following regions of Australia is most industrialized?
(a) South Wales (b) Queensland
(c) Western Australia (d) South Australia.

63. Which of the following ironore fields of USA not situated on the Pacific coast?
(a) Seattle (b) San Francisco
(c) Atlant (d) Fontana.

64. Which of the following countries is the largest producer of cement, one of the most important inputs of spreading concrete jungle the world over?
(a) Japan (b) USA
(c) China (d) Former USSR or CIS.

65. Where is Dogger Bank, one of the largest fishing ground of the world situated?
(a) North-West Pacific (b) North-West Atlantic
(c) North Sea (d) Norwegian Sea.

66. Which is the world's largest fishing ground?
(a) North-West Pacific (b) North-West Atlantic
(c) North-East Atlantic (d) North Sea.

67. About how much areas of forest are being turned to agricultural and pastoral lands and for settlements for the rapidly growing population
(a) 60 million hectares (b) 70 million hectares
(c) 75 million hectares (d) 50 million hectares.

68. About what percent of land is not suitable for human use
(a) 50 (b) 60
(c) 40 (d) 70.

69. Forests accounts for how much percent of the market production of biomass in the territorial ecosystem?
(a) 45 (b) 50
(c) 60 (d) 70.

70. Which of the following countries is the largest producer of cocoa?
(a) Ivory coast (b) Brazil
(c) Ghana (d) Ecuador.

71. Which European country is the leading wheat producer in Europe?
(a) England (b) Germany
(c) France (d) Italy.

72. Which place is known as the "Wheat bowl of the world"?
(a) Winniepeg (b) Ukraine
(c) Dakota (d) Oklahama.

73. National Rice Research Institute is located at
(a) Jorhat (b) Cuttack
(c) Calcutta (d) Bhubaneshwar.

74. Which of the following is not an improved variety of rice?
(a) Jaya (b) Padma
(c) Hira Moti (d) Kanchan.

75. Where is International Rice Research Institute located?
(a) Bangkok (b) Tokyo
(c) Manila (d) Calcutta.

76. Which country has the highest productivity of Rice?
(a) Japan (b) China
(c) North Korea (d) South Korea.

77. About what percent of total area is under Rice cultivation in Asia

(a) 85 (b) 90
(c) 75 (d) 80.

78. It is known as 'Thuming" in N-E India, 'Lading' in Malaysia by which name it is known in Brazil?
(a) Milpa (b) Changin
(c) Roka (d) Konuko.

79. Who are the main producers of thorium, a mineral intensively used for harnessing nuclear energy?
(a) Srilanka and India
(b) India and Malasia
(c) Malasia and Srilanka
(d) None of these.

80. Which country is known as the land of thousand lakes
(a) Sweden (b) Greenland
(c) Iceland (d) Finland.

81. The Duars are famous for plantation of
(a) Tea (b) Coffee
(c) Rubber (d) Banana.

82. Dead sea is a source of
(a) Sulphur
(b) Common salt and Bromide
(c) Iodine
(d) Chlorin and fluorine.

83. Aswan dam has been built over the river
(a) Nile (b) Zambezi
(c) Niger (d) Orange.

84. Llanos, the tropical grassland is found in the
(a) Amazon basin (b) Orinoco basin
(c) Colorado basin (d) Parana basin.

85. The grasslands of South Africa is known as
(a) Downs (b) Steppes
(c) Pampas (d) Veldt.

86. At which place was oil first drilled in West Asia
(a) Gachsaran (b) Agasari
(c) Masjide Sulaiman (d) Rub-al-Khali.

87. In which country of African continent is the production of bauxite highest ?
(a) Guinea (b) Liberia
(c) Zambia (d) Zaire.

88. Chuqicamata is famous for its
(a) Copper mines (b) Iron-ore mines
(c) Gold mines (d) Oil fields.

89. Which of the following is not an ore of copper ?
(a) Cuprite (b) Malachite
(c) Siderite (d) Calchocite.

90. Which of the following continents has the maximum water power potential?
(a) Africa (b) North America
(c) Asia (d) Europe.

91. The middle East accounts for---------percent of world's crude oil reserves.
(a) 78 (b) 70
(c) 75 (d) 60.

92. Principal ore of tin is
(a) Cassiterite (b) Kaolin
(c) Carundum (d) None of these.

93. The chief sources of potassium are
(a) Dust of cement plants and blast furnaces
(b) Vegetable substances
(c) Sea water, salt lakes
(d) All of the above.

94. Major products of crude oil are
(a) Kerosene (b) Diesel
(c) Gasoline (d) All of the above.

95. The Lubuge project is in
    (a) North Korea (b) Italy
    (c) France (d) China.

96. The Huangni river is in
    (a) North Korea (b) Bhutan
    (c) China (d) Burma.

97. --------- has the world's largest reserve of crude oil among the following.
    (a) USA (b) India
    (c) Libya (d) Egypt.

98. Which of the following is the larget producer of chromium in the world?
    (a) Former USSR (b) USA
    (c) Canada (d) Kenya.

99. Which of the following countries is the largest producer of mica?
    (a) Bangladesh (b) Nepal
    (c) India (d) Burma.

100. Hoover dam which is one of the largest irrigational projects and power projects in the world is on the river
    (a) Mississipi (b) Nile
    (c) Amazon (d) Colorado.

101. The oil of--------field is highly potential for its low percentage of residue.
    (a) The Texas province (b) The Nevada
    (c) The Appalachian (d) The Yarmouth.

102. The ---------, only African country which has attained important petroleum production.
    (a) Egypt (b) Libya
    (c) Uganda (d) Somalia.

103. Mindanao in the Philippine island has deposits of high quality of

(a) Coal (b) Gold
(c) Iron-ore (d) Mica.

104. The role of Molybdenum in making steel is that, it increases
(a) Resistance
(b) Ductility
(c) Strength and toughness
(d) All of the above.

105. Which of the following statements is wrong?
(a) Gypsum is used in preparation of sulphuric acid
(b) Salt is in great use for livestock for treatment of water, controlling dust and ice on the highways and railways
(c) USA ranks first with more than 71% of native sulphur production
(d) None of these.

106. The concentration and smelting of copper-ore two examples of
(a) weight increasing industries
(b) weight reducing industries
(c) small scale cottage industries
(d) all of the above.

107. Which of the following districts in USA accounts for 80% of the country's total output of iron-ore?
(a) The lake superior district
(b) The North-eastern district
(c) The South-eastern district
(d) The Southern district.

108. The Lubuge project has been designed to expand the power generating capacity of China with the help of World Bank aid and
(a) Australia, Canada, Norway
(b) Germany, France, Norway
(c) USA, Italy, Sweden
(d) None of the above.

109. Which of the following countries is the largest producer of mica?
(a) USA (b) India
(c) China (d) Bangladesh.

110. Of the world's total forests coniferous accounts for
(a) 33% (b) 62%
(c) 42% (d) 16%.

111. Which soil is most ideal for coffee plantation?
(a) Sandy soil (b) Black soil
(c) Terra-Rosa soil (d) Loamy soil.

112. Subsistence agriculture is practised in
(a) Northern China (b) Peninsular India
(c) North Korea (d) All of the above.

113. Major fishing areas in the world include
(a) The North-West Atlantic coast of New foundland
(b) North East Atlantic region
(c) The North-West Pacific
(d) All of the above.

114. The temperate grasslands are known as
(a) Velt in Australia
(b) Prairies in North America
(c) Pampas in South Africa
(d) Downs in Argentina.

115. Mainly trees of which forest are used for ship building and heavy building materials
(a) Temperate deciduous hard wood forest
(b) Taiga forests
(c) Equatorial forests
(d) None of these.

116. Plantation is
(a) Characterised by large seasonal labour force important and provided with food, housing and other facilities

(b) A form of commercial agriculture found in the tropics and subtropics

(c) A large form that specialize in the production of one or two crops for sale

(d) All of the above.

117. U.S Government has adopted which of the following policies to attack the problem of excess productive capacity?

(a) By selling or donating excesss grain to foreign government

(b) Government buys surplus food production

(c) Farmers are encouraged to keep land out of production of crops that are in excess supply

(d) All of the above.

118. An industry practiced on a small scale in homes or villages prior to the industrial revolution is termed as

(a) Cottage industry

(b) Weight hampering industry

(c) Cottage corn industry

(d) None of these.

119. In no other farming region is agriculture so diverse and at the same time so specialised as in the

(a) Mediterranean lands

(b) Monsoon lands

(c) Low latitude high lands

(d) Tropical lands.

120. Which of the following energy sources are getting importance day by day for its easiness?

(a) Nuclear Energy (b) Thermal Energy

(c) Wind Energy (d) None of these.

121. -------- and -------- are one of the largest banana producing nations.

(a) India and Bangladesh (b) India and Brazil

(c) India and Burma (d) None of these.

122. According to Zimmerman's functional concept of resources whose role is supreme in the process of creation of resources

(a) Nature (b) Man
(c) Culture (d) None of these.

123. Japan is the leading fishing nation of the world. It accounts for------percent of the total fish catch in the world.

(a) 8 (b) 10
(c) 13.5 (d) 16.

124. Saudi Arabia has the highest proved reserves of petroleum but the highest refining capacity is of which of the following countries

(a) USSR or CIS (b) Italy
(c) Venezuela (d) USA.

125. Which country, leads in the reserves as well as production of natural gas?

(a) Former USSR or CIS (b) Iran
(c) Saudi Arabia (d) USA.

126. Former Soviet Union or CIS has estimated how much percent of iron-ore reserves

(a) 30 (b) 35
(c) 40 (d) 25.

127. Which of the following is not a characteristic of plantation agriculture?

(a) Estate farming
(b) Heavy capital outlay
(c) Scientific management of farms
(d) Intensive farming.

128. Which region is better known as the 'orchard lands of the world'?

(a) Lands of Mediterranean Agriculture
(b) Lands of plantation agriculture
(c) Lands of livestock ranching
(d) None of these.

129. D. Whittlesey has used certain parameters for characterization of agricultural landscape. Which of the following is not a parameter used by him?
   (a) Intensity of Landuse
   (b) Crop and Livestock Combination
   (c) Degree of Mechanization
   (d) Economic Rent.

130. Hammerfest is famous for
   (a) It is a leading cod-fishing centre
   (b) It is a famous lumbering station
   (c) It is the place full of igloos
   (d) None of the above.

131. Which is known as the loneliest island?
   (a) St. Helena Island (b) Tristan da Cunha Island
   (c) Ascension Island (d) McDonald's Island.

132. Which country is the largest producer of electricity ?
   (a) France (b) Germany
   (c) USA (d) Japan.

133. The general theory of location with the major emphasis on demand which sought to explain the size and shape of market areas. Who propounded this theory?
   (a) Weber (b) Hoover
   (c) H. Hotelling (d) Alosch.

134. According to Hirschman, poor countries are since deficient in capital they should go in for unbalanced growth so as to maximise backward and forward linkages by setting up an industry, which industry should be established first?
   (a) Chemical industry (b) Heavy & Basic Industry
   (c) Iron and Steel Industry (d) Automobile Industry.

135. In the Christaller's central place theory if K=3 network, how many hamlets does this central market serve (Where K = total no. of settlements of a certain order served by a central place of the next higher order).

(a) 9 (b) 27
(c) 6 (d) 81.

136. ASEAN has how many members

(a) 5 (b) 6
(c) 7 (d) 15.

137. Asia Pacific Economic Conference was held at Seattle it is situated on

(a) East Coast of Canada (b) West Coast of USA
(c) East Coast of USA (d) None of these.

138. Mesabi is the most important mine and contributes about------- percent of total iron-ore production of the USA.

(a) 60 (b) 65
(c) 70 (d) 75.

139. About half of the total iron-ore extracted in former USSR is obtained from which of the following region?

(a) Krivoy Rog Region
(b) Kwisk Magnetic Anomaly
(c) Nizhny Tagil
(d) Suerdolovsk.

140. Which of the following possess the highest water power potential

(a) Africa (b) North America
(c) Asia (d) Europe.

141. Which of the following has the largest production of Iron-ore ?

(a) France (b) Canada
(c) USA (d) Former USSR or CIS.

142. Gasoline is more preferable than coal as a fuel because

(a) It is of low price
(b) It is very light and very high powerd liquid
(c) Performance of oil driven ships is better than driven by coal
(d) None of these.

143. Total production of sulphur in the world is about
   (a) 79 million metric tones
   (b) 32 million metric tones
   (c) 80 million metric tones
   (d) None of these.

144. The total coal reserves in the U.K. have been estimated of about . . . per cent of the world coal.
   (a) 10.2 (b) 15.8
   (c) 22.1 (d) 3.4.

145. Which of the following is not a coal-field of Europe?
   (a) The west phalia yields
   (b) Silesian coal field
   (c) Saxony coal fields
   (d) Middle Appalachian coal field.

146. Which of the following countries leads the world in the export of soil?
   (a) Venezuela (b) Iran
   (c) Iraq (d) Saudi Arabia.

147. The largest tobacco . . . . producing countries in the world.
   (a) China and Korea (b) China and United States
   (c) India and Burma (d) France and China.

148. China produces -------- per cent of the total world production of tabacco.
   (a) 25 (b) 45
   (c) 32 (d) 60.

149. Turkey produces . . . per cent of total world tabacco production.
   (a) 6 (b) 3
   (c) 12 (d) 10.

150. Main characteristics of monsoonal agriculture are
   (a) Farming largely depends on animal energy
   (b) In river area, with irrigation, cash crops like sugarcane, tabacco, cotton are grown in bumper

(c) Both (a) and (b)
(d) All of the above.

151. Which of the following areas practise commercial grain farming?
(a) Illinois - Ohio-Indiana states
(b) Central Asia - Uzbekistan
(c) Region extending from Ukraine to West of Siberia
(d) All of the above.

152. Sedentary farming is practised in
(a) Africa
(b) Asia-mainland and south-eastern part
(c) Haiti
(d) All of the above.

153. Areas of plantation farming for the most part lie near the sea because
(a) Due to transport facility by ocean
(b) Water is rich in minerals
(c) These regions have low population and have shortage of human labour
(d) None of the above.

154. Which of the following agricultural practice is based only on human labour
(a) Truck farming
(b) Plantation farming
(c) Migratory primitive agriculture
(d) Cash crops.

155. The problem that faces the agricultural advanced countries like the Canada, Australia and USA is
(a) To secure or guarantee a wide market for their agri production
(b) Very high cost of production which they cannot bear
(c) Low yield production
(d) None of the above.

156. In intensive method of agriculture
    (a) Practised in those areas where the supply of land is limited and the pressure of population is more
    (b) Emphasis is made for the maximum production of per yield acre
    (c) Additional land under cultivation is restricted
    (d) All of the above.

157. Area where the rainfall is negligible for production of crops practises
    (a) Humid farming (b) Shifting farming
    (c) Double Crop farming (d) Intensive farming.

158. The chief characteristics of mixed commercial farming is
    (a) Major part of the income comes from the sale of livestock products
    (b) Crops and livestocks go together
    (c) Growing of maximum variety of crops
    (d) All of the above.

159. It is seen that in no other farming region is agriculture so diverse and at the same time so specialised as in the
    (a) Mediterranean lands (b) Monsoonal lands
    (c) Polar lands (d) Coastal lands.

160. In the hard red winter wheat belt of U.S.A.
    (a) Wheat is sown in peak winter
    (b) Winters are short and mild
    (c) Wheat is mainly used for processing
    (d) All of the above.

161. -------- of land is U.S.A. is under agriculture.
    (a) 24% (b) 32%
    (c) 12% (d) 16%.

162. The position of agriculture in the developing countries of Asia, Africa and Latin America is different from developed countries in that the
    (a) There lies a vast stock of one variety of cereal

(b) Production of food not competing properly with the growth of population
(c) Products are not profit-giving
(d) None of these.

163. Which of the following areas is the lowest density zone in the world?
(a) The dry belt of Latin America from Peru via Bolivia into south Argentina
(b) Mid-Western New Zealand
(c) Eastern part of Japan
(d) None of these.

164. Which of the following industries of Switzerland is renowned all over?
(a) Ship building industries
(b) Trawaler industries
(c) Watch industries
(d) None of these.

165. One of the best oil tankers of the world are manufactured in
(a) Hungary (b) India
(c) Pakistan (d) Japan.

166. The electronic items of which country is supposed to be most sophisticated and up to date?
(a) Germany (b) Yugoslavia
(c) Japan (d) Hungary.

167. Motor-cars of which of the following countries are of maximum demand in the world?
(a) China (b) Russia
(c) England (d) Japan.

168. In which of the following, the means of productions are owned individually?
(a) Socialist economies (b) Neo-Socialist economies
(c) Capitalist economies (d) None of these.

169. Which of the following types of forest mostly grows in the belt of land lying between 50° N to 70° N?
(a) Temperate coniferous type of forests
(b) Temperate softwood forests
(c) Temperate very hardwood forests
(d) None of these.

170. The important varieties of rice are
(a) Padma, Prabhat, Jaya (b) Jaishree, Tulsi, Sooraj
(c) Jaya, Meera, Sona (d) None of these.

171. What are the most common animals found in the semi-arid temperate grasslands
(a) Sheep and goats (b) Horses and donkeys
(c) Reindeers (d) Elephants and yaks.

172. Suitable soil for sugarcane cultivation is
(a) Clayey soil (b) Alluvial soil
(c) Rich loamy soil (d) All of the above.

173. The soil best suited for rice cultivation is
(a) Sandy soil (b) Clayey-loam soil
(c) Red soil (d) Black Chernozem

174. Which of the following countries leads in fish-hauling
(a) Japan (b) Finland
(c) Sweden (d) Australia.

175. Soft coniferous woods are preferred for making of pulp for paper manufacturing because
(a) It has high resin content
(b) It has low resin content
(c) It has tremendous resin content
(d) Both (a) and (c).

176. It is very difficult to work in the tropical forests, the reason being
(a) Very high temperature
(b) Lack of proper transportation

(c) Heavy rainfall
(d) All of the above.

177. Mechanised farming could not be practised in
(a) Vast agro-field
(b) Fragmented plot
(c) Vast land strech with proper fencing
(d) Not practised in (b) category of plot and undulated land surface.

178. Temperate grasslands are not suitable for livestock rearing because
(a) Grasses are thick, rough and tall
(b) Fewer trees and scattered nature
(c) Grains are very nutritious
(d) Rainfall is unpredictable.

179. In the temperate coniferous softwood forests
(a) Wood is of soft nature
(b) Trees are tall, straight and needle like leaves
(c) Under growth is not seen generally
(d) All of the above.

180. In India, Truck farming is of much importance because of
(a) Majority of Indian population is vegetarian, especially the rural ones
(b) It has a long growing season and grows in all parts of the country
(c) Vegetables are always cheaper compared to meat, fish etc.
(d) All of the above.

181. Commercial scale fishing have not developed in the tropics because of
(a) Plankton do not grow in the warm seas
(b) Tropical waters are not shallow and contain no banks
(c) Demand of marine food is not so high from the regional population
(d) All of the above.

182. Of the following which is the largest fishing grounds in the world
(a) North Sea (b) Bay of Bengal
(c) Arabian Sea (d) None of these.

183. Japan occupies a very favourable position for fishing due to
(a) The area of Japan's coastal fishing ground is around 9 lakh sq. miles
(b) Confluence of two major currents Kurashio-Warm and Oyoshio cold helps in the rapid growth of fish in the interland straits
(c) It has an approximate coastline of 1700 miles
(d) All of the above.

184. The fishing grounds of North West Pacific includes
(a) Korea
(b) Northern China
(c) Former north-eastern USSR
(d) All of the above.

185. Which of the following agricultural regions in Russia contains coniferous forests which have short summer and podzol soil?
(a) Taiga forest region
(b) Tundra region
(c) Sub-tropical agricultural region
(d) None of these.

186. A type of farming in which different crops are grown a particular field each year. So that different nutrients are removed from the soil in different years, is
(a) Agro intense farming
(b) Mixed commercial farming
(c) Shifting cultivation
(d) None of these.

187. In Russia which of the following agricultural regions have 'Sovkhozes' and 'Kolkhozes' mainly to increase the production of meat?

(a) Taiga region
(b) Tundra region
(c) Far eastern agricultural region
(d) None of these.

188. Khoisan language is mainly found in
(a) South Western Africa
(b) Britain
(c) Eastern China
(d) Hilly area of South Korea.

189. Farming under which two crops are raised simultaneously from the same plot of land during a year is known as
(a) Single crop farming (b) Double crop farming
(c) Multiple crop farming (d) All of the above.

190. The chief distinctive features of the Taiga region of Russia are
(a) The soil is not fertile
(b) The summer period is for only 60-80 days in a year
(c) The winter is long and very cold
(d) All of the above.

191. Which of the following statements is incorrect regarding the corn belt area in USA?
(a) Pigs are often bred directly on the forms while cattle are brought into the fetched on corn
(b) It is the most important and region of mixed farming where half of the farm land is planted with corn
(c) Both (a) and (b)
(d) None of these.

192. In Russia 'Kolkhozes' are defined as
(a) Collective farms of peasants
(b) Land not at all suitable for farming
(c) State owned farms
(d) None of these.

193. Which of the following statements is wrong?
   (a) The mixed farming belt of the north-east America produces wheat and maize along with rearing of animals
   (b) In the soft winter wheat belt of USA fruits like oranges, apples, grapes etc. are grown
   (c) Both (a) and (b)
   (d) None of these.

194. The tropical soils are after short in nitrogen due to
   (a) the burning of underbush humus is destroyed
   (b) the heavy rainfall and temperature throughout the year, the destruction of humus is quicker than its formation
   (c) both (a) and (b)
   (d) None of these.

195. Cryolite is
   (a) The compound where the alumina content being too low and silicate content being too high is not used in aluminium extraction
   (b) A primary alumina-aluminium oxide
   (c) A double fluoride of aluminium and soda
   (d) None of these.

196. Cryolite, Corundum, Kaolin and Bauxite refers to which of the following statement below
   (a) The natural compounds of aluminium
   (b) Compounds of lead and zinc
   (c) The ores of iron
   (d) None of these.

197. ---------- is the largest producer of tungsten in the world
   (a) USA (b) Canada
   (c) China (d) India.

198. Which of the following is the ferro alloy metal ?
   (a) Nickel (b) Copper
   (c) Lead (d) Tin.

199. The use of Tungsten in making steel is important, because
   (a) It is used for electroplating
   (b) It is able to retain hardness and toughness at high temperature
   (c) It increase resistance of shock
   (d) None of these.

200. Chief features of minerals are that
   (a) The quality and quantity of minerals are inversely correlated
   (b) Most of the minerals are exhaustible
   (c) Both (a) and (b)
   (d) All of the above.

201. Which of the following types of coal has largest amount of carbon content?
   (a) Anthracite (b) Lignite
   (c) Peat (d) Bituminous.

202. The largest fish exporting region in the world is
   (a) The North-West Pacific region
   (b) The North-East Pacific region
   (c) The South-East Asia region
   (d) The North-East Atlantic region.

203. Which of the following countries consume more fish than any other country in the world?
   (a) Great Britain (b) China
   (c) Japan (d) France.

204. Which of the following statements is worng?
   (a) Grimsky is the greatest fishing part of the world in the variety and huge bulk of ship landed
   (b) In the tropics commercial fisheries have much developed
   (c) Both (a) and (b)
   (d) None of these.

205. 'Bush-fallow' agriculture is referred as a type of agriculture practised where

(a) The farmers return back to the land where they used to do shifting cultivation in order to cultivate it temporarily in a gap of a 10 to 15 years
(b) The farmers practice high sophisticated agro implements
(c) Both (a) and (b)
(d) None of these.

206. Which of the following areas have a density varying from 25 to 30 inhabitants per square mile?
(a) The inland grazing area of South America
(b) Part of Malayan Archipelago
(c) The drier region of Central and Eastern Africa
(d) All of the above.

207. One of the most important coal fields of the world are the Appalachian coal fields, and located in
(a) Great Britain (b) USA
(c) China (d) Norway.

208. Savanna is a
(a) Tropical grassland in Africa
(b) Type of hilly farming region in Burma
(c) Temperate grassland in Australia
(d) The hill station in Switzerland.

209. The solar energy
(a) could be directly converted into electricity with the help of photo voltaic cells
(b) is most widely and non-exhaustible source of energy
(c) is sufficiently available in the tropical region for longer periods throughout the year
(d) All of the above.

210. The yield of mixed farming in North-West Europe yields fairly high returns due to
(a) Nearness to heavy demanding urban markets
(b) Highly mechanised methods of farming
(c) Good net work of transportation

(d) All of the above.

211. Commercial fishing is best developed in

(a) Japan (b) North Korea
(c) Italy (d) China.

212. The North-West Pacific fishing grounds of the world include

(a) Former North-eastern USSR
(b) Korea
(c) Northern China
(d) All of the above.

213. Which of the following statements is correct regarding the pigmies of the Zaire basin ?

(a) They have a tendency to settle on the banks of the river for easy transportation
(b) Pigmies make their abode on the huge branches of trees
(c) Pigmies are of short height some of them only 90 cms tall
(d) All of the above.

214. The main geographical factors responsible for the location of industries are

(a) Energy sources and sufficient labour
(b) Market and good mean of transport
(c) Raw materials
(d) All of the above.

215. The type of industries which are not related to any particular raw materials are said to be as

(a) Foot loose industries
(b) Heavy industries
(c) Primary industries
(d) Agro-based industries.

216. Britains share of world's steel output has declined because of

(a) Rising cost of iron-ore, labour and coal
(b) Its inefficiency for the conservative management
(c) Heavy fixed charges for excessive capitalization
(d) All of the above.

217. Lagoons are often found
(a) On the sea ward side of the fringing reef
(b) On the sea ward side of the offshore fringe
(c) Both (a) and (b)
(d) None of these.

218. Which of the following statements is incorrect?
(a) Water transport is cheaper than land transport
(b) Water ways provide a ready-made highways
(c) Both (a) and (b)
(d) None of these.

219. Inland waterways are used most extensively for carrying bulky goods in the
(a) South and Central China
(b) Mississippi basin
(c) North-West Europe
(d) All of these.

220. The geographical conditions necessary for the growth of rice is that it
(a) requires temperature not below 27° to 30° C during growth period
(b) requires warm and humid climate
(c) requires flooded field during the time of plantation
(d) all of the above.

221. The leading producer of bauxite is
(a) USA (b) Canada
(c) India (d) Australia.

222. What is Baku famous for
(a) Cork (b) Oil
(c) Wine (d) Oranges.

223. World silk production has declined due to
(a) Competition from manmade fibres
(b) Lack of demand
(c) Lack of remunerative prices
(d) Lack of skilled labour.

224. The largest quantity of barley is produced in
(a) India (b) China
(c) USA (d) Russia.

225. The most important activity of the tundra region
(a) cropping (b) hunting
(c) cattle rearing (d) fish farming.

226. The largest producers of mutton are
(a) USA and Australia
(b) India and Japan
(c) New Zealand and Australia
(d) Argentina and New Zealand.

227. Aluminium ore is known as
(a) Bauxite (b) Lignite
(c) Pyrite (d) Anthracite.

228. The largest producer of long staple cotton is
(a) Sudan (b) China
(c) USA (d) Egypt.

229. Leeds is well-known for
(a) Cotton textiles (b) Films
(c) Iron smelting (d) Woollen textiles.

230. Which country is the leading producer of automobiles?
(a) USA (b) Japan
(c) China (d) Russia.

231. The largest producer of magnese is
(a) Sudan (b) Egypt
(c) India (d) USA.

232. Which country is known as the sugar bowl of the world?
(a) Russia (b) USA
(c) Cuba (d) India.

233. Which country is the leading producer of Uranium
(a) India (b) China
(c) Japan (d) Canada.

234. Zaire is the leading producer of
(a) Oil (b) Steel
(c) Diamond (d) Coal.

235 The largest producer of phosphate is
(a). USA (b) Spain
(c) Mexico (d) France.

236. One of the leading producers of Chromium is
(a) Zaire (b) South Africa
(c) Brazil (d) India.

237. The largest producer of Mercury is
(a) Italy (b) USA
(c) Canada (d) Japan.

238. Which country is the largest producer of tabacco
(a) India (b) Russia
(c) China (d) Japan.

239. Which country has the largest cattle population
(a) India (b) Canada
(c) Australia (d) China.

ANSWERS

1. (b)	2. (d)	3. (c)	4. (a)
5. (c)	6. (b)	7. (b)	8. (d)
9. (a)	10. (b)	11. (d)	12. (b)
13. (a)	14. (c)	15. (d)	16. (b)
17. (b)	18. (a)	19. (c)	20. (b)

21. (a)	22. (d)	23. (b)	24. (c)
25. (d)	26. (c)	27. (c)	28. (c)
29. (a)	30. (c)	31. (a)	32. (b)
33. (a)	34. (a)	35. (d)	36. (b)
37. (b)	38. (b)	39. (c)	40. (d)
41. (d)	42. (a)	43. (c)	44. (d)
45. (c)	46. (d)	47. (c)	48. (b)
49. (c)	50. (b)	51. (d)	52. (c)
53. (b)	54. (a)	55. (c)	56. (a)
57. (c)	58. (c)	59. (a)	60. (c)
61. (c)	62. (a)	63. (c)	64. (d)
65. (c)	66. (a)	67. (b)	68. (b)
69. (c)	70. (a)	71. (c)	72. (a)
73. (b)	74. (c)	75. (c)	76. (d)
77. (d)	78. (c)	79. (c)	80. (d)
81. (c)	82. (b)	83. (a)	84. (b)
85. (d)	86. (c)	87. (a)	88. (a)
89. (c)	90. (a)	91. (d)	92. (a)
93. (d)	94. (d)	95. (d)	96. (c)
97. (a)	98. (a)	99. (c)	100. (d)
101. (c)	102. (a)	103. (c)	104. (d)
105. (a)	106. (b)	107. (a)	108. (a)
109. (b)	110. (a)	111. (c)	112. (a)
113. (d)	114. (b)	115. (a)	116. (d)
117. (d)	118. (a)	119. (a)	120. (c)
121. (b)	122. (b)	123. (c)	124. (d)
125. (a)	126. (c)	127. (a)	128. (a)
129. (d)	130. (a)	131. (b)	132. (c)
133. (d)	134. (c)	135. (b)	136. (b)
137. (b)	138. (c)	139. (b)	140. (a)
141. (d)	142. (d)	143. (b)	144. (d)
145. (d)	146. (a)	147. (b)	148. (a)
149. (b)	150. (d)	151. (d)	152. (d)
153. (a)	154. (c)	155. (a)	156. (d)
157. (a)	158. (d)	159. (a)	160. (b)
161. (a)	162. (b)	163. (a)	164. (c)
165. (c)	166. (d)	167. (d)	168. (c)
169. (a)	170. (a)	171. (b)	172. (d)
173. (b)	174. (a)	175. (b)	176. (d)
177. (d)	178. (c)	179. (d)	180. (d)
181. (d)	182. (a)	183. (d)	184. (d)

185. (a)	186. (b)	187. (b)	188. (a)
189. (b)	190. (d)	191. (d)	192. (a)
193. (b)	194. (c)	195. (c)	196. (a)
197. (c)	198. (a)	199. (b)	200. (d)
201. (a)	202. (d)	203. (c)	204. (b)
205. (a)	206. (d)	207. (b)	208. (a)
209. (d)	210. (d)	211. (a)	212. (d)
213. (d)	214. (d)	215. (a)	216. (d)
217. (a)	218. (d)	219. (d)	220. (d)
221. (d)	222. (a)	223. (a)	224. (b)
225. (b)	226. (c)	227. (a)	228. (c)
229. (d)	230. (a)	231. (c)	232. (c)
233. (a)	234. (b)	235. (a)	236. (c)
237. (a)	238. (c)	239. (a)	

5

REGIONAL STUDY OF IMPORTANT COUNTRIES

1. Which of the following is not a feature of coniferous forests?
   (a) They are of moderate density
   (b) They are conical in shape
   (c) Leaves are broad and thin
   (d) All of the above
2. Which of the following crop needs 200 days frost free for cultivation?
   (a) Rice (b) Cotton
   (c) Sugarcane (d) Wheat.
3. The cool temperate western margin (British type) climate has which type of forests?
   (a) Mountains
   (b) Desiduous
   (c) Alpine
   (d) None of these.
4. Which country is best known for terrace forming
   (a) China (b) Japan
   (c) Thailand (d) Indonesia.
5. Which of the following is not a temperate grassland
   (a) Steppes (b) Downs
   (c) Selvas (d) Prairies.

6. Which of the following is known as 'big game' country?
   (a) The Savanna or Sudan climate
   (b) Mediterranean climate
   (c) Warm temperate Eastern margin (China type climate)
   (d) None of the above.

7. Which of the following countries accounts for three-quarters of 'teak' wood
   (a) Indonesia (b) Burma
   (c) Thailand (d) India.

8. Which of the following statement is wrong regarding the Savanna or Sudan climate?
   (a) It is typified by tall grass and short tree
   (b) It is a region of tropical grassland
   (c) Many trees are umbrella shaped
   (d) Trees do not shed their leaves even once in year.

9. Which is largest country of Africa
   (a) Egypt (b) Sudan
   (c) South Africa (d) Nigeria.

10. Which of the following is the highest volcanic mountain wheather active or dormant
   (a) Acatenango (b) Fujiyama
   (c) Cotopaxi (d) Kilimanjaro.

11. Which of the following rivers drains into yellow sea?
   (a) Yanisei (b) Hwang Ho
   (c) Me Kung (d) Yangtze Kiang.

12. The volga rises in
   (a) Ural mountains (b) Stanavoy range
   (c) Valdai hills (d) None of these.

13. Match the following

A.	Orizaba	1.	USA
B.	Santa Maria	2.	Cango
C.	Lassen	3.	Mexico
D.	Karisimbi	4.	Guatemala

	A	B	C	D
(a)	1	2	3	4
(b)	3	1	4	2
(c)	3	4	1	2
(d)	2	3	1	4.

14. The highest waterfall of the world is Angel falls. It is situated on the tributary of which of the following river?
    (a) Magdalena (b) Caroni
    (c) Utshi (d) None of these.

15. The Great Barrier Reef is located in which sea
    (a) Timor sea (b) Banda sea
    (c) Tasman sea (d) Coral sea.

16. Which of the following rivers do not make a Estuarine filling delta
    (a) Mackenzie (b) Elbe
    (c) Mekong (d) Hudson.

17. Bermude triangle is situated in
    (a) North Atlantic (b) South Altantic
    (c) North-West Pacific (d) South-East Pacific.

18. River Rio Grande drains into
    (a) Atlantic (b) Pacific
    (c) Gulf of Mexico (d) None of these.

19. Which of the largest island in the pacific?
    (a) New Guinea (b) Borneo
    (c) Philipines (d) Japan.

20. Sonoran desert is found in
    (a) Peru (b) Turkmenistan
    (c) Arizona and California (d) Sinkiang.

21. The deepest point in Mariana Trench is
    (a) Vityez (b) Aldrich
    (c) Milne (d) Cape Johnson.

22. Lake Eyre, is the lowest point of
    (a) Asia (b) Africa
    (c) Oceania (d) None of these.

23. Alfalga grass is found in abundance in which of the following grasslands
    (a) Selvas (b) Llanos
    (c) Pampas (d) Campos.

24. Which of the following sea has the greatest depth
    (a) Carribbean Sea (b) Gulf of Mexico
    (c) Mediterranean Sea (d) Bering Sea.

25. The Canadian Pacific Railway, one of the longest railway lines of the world run from
    (a) Vancouver to St. John's
    (b) Seattle to Halifix
    (c) Vancouver to Halifix
    (d) Prince Rupert to St. John's.

26. Which of the following is the biggest waterfall by order of volumes
    (a) Sete Quedas (b) Niagra
    (c) Antarctica (d) Asia.

27. Rio Negro is the lowest point of
    (a) South America (b) North America
    (c) Asia (d) Antarctica.

28. Campos as the grassland of
    (a) Guyana highlands (b) Gran Chacco
    (c) Brazelian highlands (d) Amazonion besin.

29. Which of the following are the oldest mountains of Europe?
    (a) Apennines (b) Jura
    (c) Dinaric Alps (d) Urals.

30. Which of the following Latin American Country is the leading producer of tin?
    (a) Bolivia (b) Chile
    (c) Peru (d) Argentina.

31. Which of the following is a buffer state?
    (a) France (b) Holland
    (c) Switzerland (d) Belgium.

32. How many countries are located in the central America?
    (a) 4 (b) 5
    (c) 6 (d) 7.

33. Norrkoping is one of leading industrial centre of Sweden, which of the following industry is located here?
    (a) Paper (b) Iron and steel
    (c) Engineering (d) Ship building.

34. Hollick Kenyon Plateau is situated in which of the following continents.
    (a) North America (b) South America
    (c) Antarctica (d) Australia.

35. Which of the following country leads in ship building in Europe?
    (a) Germany (b) Sweden
    (c) U.K. (d) France.

36. Kiel Canal joins
    (a) Aegean sea and Baltic sea
    (b) Aegean sea and Adriatic sea
    (c) North sea and Baltic sea
    (d) Norwegian sea and Gulf of Bothnia.

37. Canterbury plains form a part of
    (a) North Island of New Zealand
    (b) South Island of New Zealand
    (c) Hungary
    (d) Australia.

38. Which of the following is the largest island of Japan?
    (a) Hokkaido (b) Honshu
    (c) Hyushu (d) Shikoku.

39. Hudson Mts is situated in
(a) North America (b) South America
(c) Europe (d) Antarctica.

40. Patagonia Plateau is situated in
(a) Argentina (b) Chile
(c) Bolivia (d) None of these.

41. Which of the following is the largest lake of Europe?
(a) Lake Onega (b) Lake Rudolph
(c) Lake Ladoga (d) None of these.

42. Which of the following is the highest peak of Antarctica ?
(a) Mt. Kosciousko (b) Mt. Vinson
(c) Communism peak (d) Mt. Lsick.

43. Paris is situated on the banks of
(a) Rhine (b) Rhone
(c) Loire (d) Seiene.

44. Which of the following is the largest river after Amazon in South America ?
(a) San Francisco (b) Parana
(c) Orinoco (d) Paranaiba.

45. Mt. Cook is the highest peak of
(a) Australian Alps (b) Pyreness
(c) Southern Alps (d) Apennines.

46. Which of the following the highest peak of Australian Alps ?
(a) Mt. Vinson (b) Kosciusko
(c) Mt. Blanc (d) None of these.

47. Which of the following is known as the 'desert state' of Australia
(a) South Wales (b) Western Australia
(c) South Australia (d) None of these.

48. The largest oil producing region in CIS is
(a) Baku (b) Volga-Ural region
(c) Central Asia (d) Sakhalin region.

49. The highest peak in South America is
(a) Chii borazo (b) Cotopaxi
(c) Aconcagua (d) None of these.

50. Elbruz mountains are in
(a) Iraq (b) South Arabia
(c) Jordan (d) Iran.

51. Baleric Islands are the part of which of the following countries?
(a) Denmark (b) France
(c) Spain (d) None of these.

52. Ustrut plateau lies between the
(a) Caspian and Ural sea
(b) Amu Darya and Syr Darya
(c) Amur and Usseri
(d) None of these.

53. Kimberley plateau is situated in
(a) Australia (b) Brazil
(c) Sweden (d) Italy.

54. Which of the following river crosses the equator twice?
(a) Limpopo (b) Zaire
(c) Paraguay (d) Amazon.

55. Fergana Valley is in
(a) East Siberia (b) West Siberia
(c) Northern Siberia (d) CIS's Central Asia.

56. Ural mountains form the bounday between
(a) Europe and Africa
(b) Asia and Africa
(c) Europe and Asia
(d) None of these.

57. Litto and Sungari river flows in
(a) Mongolia (b) Sinkiang
(c) Manchria (d) Gobi desert.

58. Mt. Albrus is the highest peak of which of the following mountain ranges.
(a) Caucasus (b) Alps
(c) Ural (d) Carpathian Mts.

59. Which mountain range separates Tranee and Spain?
(a) Alps (b) Andes
(c) Pyrenenes (d) Vosges.

60. Karun Valley is located in which of the following countries.
(a) Iraq (b) Iran
(c) Jordan (d) South Arabia.

61. The principle fishing grounds of world are located
(a) between 30° and 66° N
(b) between 20° and 50° N
(c) between 20° and 60° N
(d) None of the above.

62. The mackenzie river drains into
(a) The Atlantic (b) The Arctic
(c) The Pacific ocean (d) The Hudson Bay.

63. Where is the natal coast situated?
(a) South Africa (b) North Africa
(c) Philippines (d) Italy.

64. Habrin city is situated on
(a) Amur river (b) Singari rver
(c) Hwang-Ho river (d) None of these.

65. The U.S. is the largest exporter of
(a) Barley (b) Rice
(c) Corn (d) Wheat.

66. The Great Diving range is located in
(a) South Africa (b) North Africa
(c) Europe (d) Australia.

67. Low open scrub forest of Eastern corner of Brazil?
   (a) Bush forest (b) Calc cole
   (c) Golden forest (d) Catinga.

68. Kun-lun and Hanshan mountain lie in the north of
   (a) The Gobi desert
   (b) Tibetan Plateau and mountaineous region
   (c) Sinkiang region
   (d) None of these.

69. The Po Valley is famous for rice cultivation. It is situated in
   (a) France (b) Japan
   (c) North Africa (d) Itlay.

70. The Ob river drains into
   (a) Black Sea (b) Caspian Sea
   (c) Arctic Sea (d) Baltic Sea.

71. Brazil has become world's largest producer of coffee mainly because
   (a) The Brazilian Plateau is well drained land
   (b) The coffee plant is native of Brazil
   (c) The climate conditions are suitable
   (d) The terra-rosa are quite flexible.

72. Major oilfields of China are located in
   (a) Tiber (b) Yangtze basin
   (c) Yannan Plateau (d) Arid regions of the West.

73. Corner Brook in New foundland is famous for
   (a) fish catch
   (b) production of fruit
   (c) pulp and paper industry
   (d) industry.

74. Nile, the longest river, passes through
   (a) Libya (b) Chad
   (c) Sudan (d) Burma.

75. Which of the following rivers has a birds foot delta

(a) Niger (b) Amazon
(c) Mississipi (d) Nile.

76. Death valley is an area in

(a) North Africa (b) USA
(c) France (d) Europe.

77. Which of the following lakes is not located in a rift valley?

(a) Lake Rudolf
(b) Lake Albert
(c) Lake Victoria
(d) Lake Tangannayika.

78. Which country ranks first in producing teak?

(a) Japan (b) Burma
(c) Thailand (d) Sudan.

79. Which area is known as 'the fertile cresent'?

(a) The land of Ganges
(b) The land of Euphrates and Tigris
(c) The land of Nile
(d) None of these.

80. Victoria falls are across the river

(a) Zambezi (b) Nile
(c) Zaire (d) Niger.

81. Which of the following is a continental shelf sea?

(a) Arabian sea (b) Baltic sea
(c) North sea (d) Red sea.

82. Which part of Siberia is a relatively flat plan

(a) East (b) West
(c) North (d) South.

83. Which of the following ocean does not have a North-South Submarine ridge?

(a) Atlantic ocean (b) Pacific ocean
(c) Arctic ocean (d) Indian ocean.

84. Celebes is an island of

(a) Japan (b) Indonesia
(c) China (d) India.

85. The most densely populated island of the world is

(a) Greenland (b) Java
(c) Sri Lanka (d) Puerto Rico.

86. The longest island of Philippines is

(a) Mindano (b) Luzon
(c) Cabuleyte (d) Negroes.

87. Which of the following minerals is exported from S.E Asia in large quantities

(a) Lead (b) Iron Ore
(c) Tin (d) Copper.

88. The dense evergreen forests of the equatorial Africa is known as

(a) Pampas (b) Savannas
(c) Veldt (d) Salvas.

89. Manchuria and Korea belong to

(a) cool east margin region
(b) tropical monsoon region
(c) warm east margin region
(d) cool west margin region.

90. Extensive reserve of gold occur in Siberia in the basin of

(a) The Ob (b) The Lena
(c) The Amur (d) The Yenisay.

91. Coral Plateau is in

(a) Burma (b) China
(c) South Africa (d) Thailand.

92. A close growing monsoon forest in Indonesia, the dominent tree species of which is a type of acacia

(a) Plango (b) Pilang
(c) Moshav (d) Padang.

93. Duncan passage lies between
    (a) Andman and Nicobar Island
    (b) India and Sri Lanka
    (c) Malaysia and Indonesia
    (d) Sri Lanka and Maldives.

94. Mid Latitude grassland in Russia are used for
    (a) Nomadic harding of animals
    (b) Extensive agriculture
    (c) Commerical grazing of animals
    (d) Intensive subsistence agriculture.

95. The red river is an important river of
    (a) China
    (b) Malaysia
    (c) Vietnam
    (d) Iraq.

ANSWERS

1.	(c)	2.	(b)	3.	(b)	4.	(b)
5.	(c)	6.	(a)	7.	(b)	8.	(d)
9.	(b)	10.	(c)	11.	(b)	12.	(c)
13.	(c)	14.	(b)	15.	(d)	16.	(c)
17.	(a)	18.	(c)	19.	(a)	20.	(c)
21.	(d)	22.	(c)	23.	(c)	24.	(a)
25.	(c)	26.	(a)	27.	(a)	28.	(c)
29.	(b)	30.	(a)	31.	(c)	32.	(d)
33.	(a)	34.	(c)	35.	(b)	36.	(c)
37.	(b)	38.	(b)	39.	(d)	40.	(a)
41	(c)	42	(b)	43.	(d)	44.	(b)
45.	(c)	46.	(b)	47.	(c)	48.	(b)
49.	(d)	50.	(a)	51.	(c)	52.	(b)
53.	(a)	54.	(b)	55.	(d)	56.	(c)
57.	(b)	58.	(a)	59.	(c)	60.	(b)
61.	(a)	62.	(b)	63.	(a)	64.	(b)
65.	(a)	66.	(d)	67.	(c)	68.	(b)
69.	(d)	70.	(c)	71.	(d)	72.	(d)

73.	(c)	74.	(c)	75.	(c)	76.	(b)
77.	(c)	78.	(c)	79.	(b)	80.	(a)
81.	(c)	82.	(b)	83.	(d)	84.	(b)
85.	(b)	86.	(b)	87.	(c)	88.	(d)
89.	(a)	90.	(b)	91.	(d)	92.	(b)
93.	(a)	94.	(b)	95.	(c)		

6

INDIAN GEOGRAPHY

1. In the Deccan Plateau the natural vegetation is mainly controlled by--------
   (a) Soil conditions (b) Rainfall
   (c) Altitude (d) Irrigation.

2. Which of the following is the principle source of irrigation in India?
   (a) Wells and tubewells (b) Tanks
   (c) Canals (d) None of the above.

3. Water for irrigation is available from
   (a) Rain (b) Underground water
   (c) Rivers and springs (d) All of the above.

4. The water of which of the following rivers of India is used most extensively for irrigation?
   (a) Sutlej (b) Mahanadi
   (c) Ganges (d) Brahmaputra.

5. Cultural factors responsible for soil erosion are
   (a) Overgrazing (b) Deforestation
   (c) Over utilization of soil (d) All of the above.

6. Of the total irrigated area in India, Bhakra Canal system irrigates
   (a) 10.6 % (b) 5.8%
   (c) 3.6% (d) 1.4%.

7. Which of the following types of wood is specially used for railway sleepers?
   (a) Sarrah and Barvi
   (b) Mahogany
   (c) Norywood
   (d) Green heart wood.

8. In dry areas, wells are dug near ponds or in depression in order to
   (a) Get larger amount of water
   (b) Make use of pond water
   (c) Reduce the salinity of water
   (d) None of the above.

9. Mahogany is the name of a tree found in
   (a) Tropical evergreen forest
   (b) Tropical monsoon
   (c) Coniferous forest
   (d) Mediterranean forest.

10. In the uneven and relatively rockey plateau of peninsular India, where rainfall is also highly seasonal, people have sorted to
    (a) Canals (b) Tanks
    (c) Wells and tubewells (d) All of the above.

11. Kerala is famous in the cultivation of
    (a) Groundnut (b) Coconut
    (c) Black pepper (d) Rubber.

12. Which of the following rivers is known as India's river of sorrow?
    (a) Tista (b) Kosi
    (c) Sutlej (d) Narmada.

13. The cotton plant is highly sensitive of frost. How many frost free days does it require to mature
    (a) 100 days (b) 200 days
    (c) 300 days (d) None of these.

14. According to archaeological evidences the use of cotton in India has been known for the last

(a) 5,000 years (b) 2,500 years
(c) 3,000 years (d) 4,000 years.

15. Which of the following parts of India produces nearly 3/4 of total quantity of tea?

(a) Northern India (b) North-East India
(c) North-West India (d) Southern India.

16. Rubber is product of

(a) Plantation agriculture
(b) Mixed agriculture
(c) Mediterranean agriculture
(d) Specialised horticulture.

17. Water for irrigation is available from

(a) Rains (b) Rivers and Springs
(c) Underground water (d) All of the above.

18. The water from the wells is lifted for irrigation by

(a) Charsa (b) Dhingly
(c) Persian wheel (d) All of these.

19. Saline and alkaline soils are found in

(a). Rajmahal hills of Rajasthan
(b) Kerala and Bihar
(c) The Sunderban region of West Bengal
(d) Vindhya and Satpura ranges.

20. Sunderbans, a tidal forest is in

(a) Bangladesh (b) West Bengal
(c) Manipur (d) Assam.

21. Soils present in Vindhya and Satpura ranges the Nilgiri and Cardamom hills are termed as

(a) Peaty soils (b) Saline soils
(c) Mountain soils (d) Laterite soils.

22. To which of the following types does the natural vegetation of the western Ghats belong?
    (a) Evergreen (b) Mangrove
    (c) Deciduous (d) Alpine.

23. Which of the following are the typical monsoon forests?
    (a) Dry deciduous
    (b) Tropical moist deciduous
    (c) Montane (Southern)
    (d) Montane (Northern).

24. Mediterranean type of climate is best suited for the cultivation of
    (a) Pulse (b) Paddy
    (c) Fruits (d) Wheat.

25. Why is dry agriculture particulary suited to areas of Black cotton soils?
    (a) Moisture retentiveness (b) Cotton growing
    (c) Due to its texture (d) None of the above.

26. Laterite soils develop under which of the following types of climate
    (a) Hot and dry (b) Wet tropical
    (c) Mediterranean (d) Cold temperature.

27. The proble of leaching of the soil is more pronounced in the areas where the rainfall is
    (a) Scanty (b) Average
    (c) Heavy (d) Less than average.

28. Of the following commodities, the one which earns for India the largest amount of foreign exchange is
    (a) Coffee (b) Edible oils
    (c) Tea (d) Cashew karnels.

29. Which of the following soil grow forests?
    (a) Mountain soils (b) Alkaline soils
    (c) Khadar soils (d) Organic soils.

30. Which of the following is a tropical grassland?
(a) Pamps (b) Praines
(c) Savannah (d) Taiga.

31. Laterite soils are commonly found in which of the following states?
(a) Andhra Pradesh (b) Karnataka
(c) Punjab (d) Uttar Pradesh.

32. Which of the following soils has the characteristic of being generally clayey, deep and impermeable?
(a) Black (b) Desert
(c) Alluvial (d) Laterite.

33. Loam is regarded as the most suitable type of soil for crop production because
(a) It drains well
(b) It can hold enough water
(c) It contains adequate quantity of humus
(d) All of the above.

34. Which of the following statements is correct regarding alluvial soils?
(a) These are deficient in nitrogen and hume
(b) These have adequate potash
(c) It is gray, light brown or yellowish
(d) All of the above.

35. Which of the following states abound is Black soils?
(a) Gujarat (b) Andhra Pradesh
(c) Madhya Pradesh (d) All of the above.

36. Alpine meadow soil is
(a) sticky due to high proportion of clay
(b) a desert soil of a sandy texture
(c) a thin dark coloured soil which contains mostly decomposed plants
(d) all of the above.

37. Black soils cover
   (a) Maharashtra and Southern districts of Orissa
   (b) Southern and coastal Andhra Pradesh and Northern districts of Kerala
   (c) Central and Western M.P.
   (d) All of the above.

38. The saline soil contains
   (a) A lot of moisture
   (b) High concentration of salt
   (c) Hard rock
   (d) None of the above.

39. Which of the following soils is the most fertile?
   (a) Alluvial soils
   (b) Black soils
   (c) Red soils
   (d) Laterite soils.

40. Red soils cover almost whole of the
   (a) Andhra Pradesh (b) Tamil Nadu
   (c) Karnataka (d) All of the above.

41. The red soils develop a reddish colour due to
   (a) A wide diffusion of iron in ancient crystalline and metamorphia rocks
   (b) Deforestation and overgrazing
   (c) Tropical monsoonal conditions
   (d) The presence of potash and magnesia.

42. Black soil have a higher proportion of
   (a) Clay (b) Silt
   (c) Sand (d) All of the above.

43. Which of the following is most extensive soil group in India?
   (a) Red soil (b) Arid soil
   (c) Alluvium (d) Black soil.

44. Loam is mixture of
(a) Sand and clay (b) Sand, clay and silt
(c) Clay and silt (d) Sand and silt.

45. Alluvial soils are found in a greater part of
(a) Rajasthan (b) Punjab and U.P.
(c) Bihar and West Bengal (d) All of the above.

46. Which of the following statement is wrong?
(a) Red soil are less sandy and more clayey
(b) Black soils are strickly when wet and so difficult to plough
(c) Laterite is typical soil of tropical regions which receives heavy rainfall
(d) All of the above.

47. Black soils are best for growing
(a) Cereals (b) Oil seeds
(c) Cotton (d) All of the above.

48. 'Open Sky Policy' is related to
(a) Tourism
(b) Cango flights
(c) Agricultural aviation which is responsible for conducting aerial operation for fighting lowest invasion and breeding
(d) None of these.

49. Podzol soil is found in
(a) Mountains (b) Plains
(c) Deserts (d) All of the above.

50. The black cotton soil in India are otherwise called
(a) Khadar (b) Regur
(c) Bangar (d) Terai.

51. The high level soils where flood water cannot reach are formed of old alluvial and known as
(a) Bhangar (b) Khadar
(c) Bhur (d) Kankar.

52. New Alluvium is named as
   (a) Soils and Deccan plateau
   (b) Khadar
   (c) Bhanger
   (d) None of the above.

53. Bondla and Cotiago wildlife sanctuaries and Dr. Salim Ali bird sanctuary are present in
   (a) Kerala (b) Goa
   (c) Madhya Pradesh (d) Karnataka.

54. First postage stamp in India was issued in
   (a) 1852 (b) 1839
   (c) 1907 (d) 1911.

55. Indian Airlines was set up under the Air Corporations Act in
   (a) 1947 (b) 1963
   (c) 1951 (d) 1976.

56. Which of the following states of India was once named as Pragjyotisha and Kamrupa?
   (a) Kerala (b) Assam
   (c) Himachal Pradesh (d) Jammu and Kashmir.

57. Which of the following statement is correct?
   (a) Visakhapatnam is the deepest Port
   (b) Port of Mumbai is a natural harbour
   (c) Calcutta is a riverrine Port
   (d) All of the above.

58. Arunachal Pradesh, formerly a Union Territory of India was made a fullfledged state on
   (a) 12th Jan. 1981 (b) 15th Dec. 1950
   (c) 20th Feb. 1989 (d) 20th March 1976.

59. Which of the following rivers does not form any delta at its mouth?
   (a) Tapti (b) Godavari
   (c) Kaveri (d) Mahanadi.

60. With which of the projects listed below is Sardar Sarovar Dam associated?
(a) Bhakra Nangal
(b) Narmada river valley
(c) Tapti river valley
(d) Mahanadi river valley.

61. Project tiger, a centrally sponsored scheme to save tiger was launched in
(a) 1972 (b) 1973
(c) 1984 (d) 1980.

62. The character of vegetarian of place depends on its
(a) Rainfall
(b) Temperature
(c) Interference by man and soil
(d) All of the above.

63. Which of the following is not a sea port in India
(a) Cochin (b) Santa Cruz
(c) Jawahar Lal Nehru (d) Kandla.

64. The Indira Gandhi Rashtriya Uran Akadamy is located in
(a) Moradabad (b) Mumbai
(c) Fursatganj (d) Lucknow.

65. Pondicherry is a/an
(a) Port of France
(b) Centrally administered territory
(c) State in the Union of India
(d) Independent state.

66. Pong dam is on the river
(a) Sutlej (b) Rihand
(c) Beas (d) Penjar.

67. Srinagar is situated on the banks of the river
(a) Jhelum (b) Sutlej
(c) Chenab (d) Ravi.

68. The shipyard at Vishakhapatnam was set up
(a) 1947 (b) 1941
(c) 1972 (d) 1951.

69. Which one of the following cities does not lie on the banks of the Ganga?
(a) Kanpur (b) Haridwar
(c) Agra (d) Allahabad.

70. Indian Standard time is fixed on the mean time of
(a) 82° E longitude
(b) 72° E longitude
(c) 73° E longitude
(d) 62° E longitude.

71. Which of the following statements is false ?
(a) Mormagau is the deepest Port
(b) Kandla is a tidal Port
(c) Chennai is the oldest Port
(d) Mumbai is the biggest Port.

72. From which of the following places is the air route to Kathmandu the shortest?
(a) Varanasi (b) Patna
(c) Calcutta (d) Gorakhpur.

73. Which of the following states has different frontiers than the other three?
(a) West Bengal (b) U.P.
(c) Haryana (d) Rajasthan.

74. Why is the climate of Bombay equable
(a) It is located on the sea coast
(b) It is located at the fairly high altitude
(c) It receives heavy rainfall from South-West monsoon
(d) It receives vertical rays of the sun twice a year.

75. Haldia is famous for
(a) Oil refining (b) Gold refining
(c) Tea blending (d) Wine fermenting.

76. Which of the following is the most important raw material for generation of power in India
   (a) Mineral oil (b) Natural gas
   (c) Coal (d) Uranium.

77. Indian Standard time is the time of longitude that passes through
   (a) Delhi (b) Chennai
   (c) Mumbai (d) Allahabad.

78. In 'Telgu Ganga" project the water to Chennai will be supplied from
   (a) Krishna (b) Godavari
   (c) Kaveri (d) Ganga.

79. Dilwara is known for its
   (a) Wild life sanctuary (b) Monuments
   (c) Deer park (d) Water falls.

80. Which of the following rivers of India flow through a rift valley?
   (a) Narmada (b) Sutlej
   (c) Lum (d) Cauvery.

81. 'Diego Garcia' is an island in the --------- ocean.
   (a) Pacific (b) Indian
   (c) Arctic (d) Atlantic.

82. In which of the following states is the Dudhwa National Park situated?
   (a) M.P. (b) Karnataka
   (c) U.P. (d) Assam.

83. The deltas of the Mahanadi, the Godavari and the Krishna lie in the
   (a) Littoral of Andhra Pradesh and Orrisa
   (b) Goa and Littoral of Karnataka
   (c) Gujarat region
   (d) Tamil Nadu region.

84. The delta of Godawari and Krishna have enclosed between them a part of the sea now known as
(a) Kolleru lake (b) Chilka lake
(c) Bhahmani lake (d) None of the above.

85. Indian railway is divided into------- zones.
(a) 10 (b) 15
(c) 9 (d) 8.

86. Bela, Khedir and Pachkam island are in
(a) The Peninsula of Kutch
(b) The Rann of Kutch
(c) Rann of the Kathiawar
(d) None of the above.

87. Western Littoral region is divided into
(a) The Konkan
(b) Gujarat region north of Daman
(c) Goa and Littoral of Karnataka and Kerala
(d) All of the above.

88. The Meghalaya hills or Shillong Plateau includes
(a) Mukir hills (b) Garo hills
(c) Khas, Jaintia hills (d) All of these.

89. Coromandal coastal plain is present in the
(a) Karnataka region (b) Tamilnadu region
(c) Kerala region (d) Andhra Pradesh region.

90. 'Siachin Glacier' is in
(a) Kashmir (b) Pakistan
(c) China (d) Tibet.

91. Mt. Abu a small hilly block is separated from the Aravalli range by
(a) The Narmada Valley
(b) The Guru Sikhar Valley
(c) The Banas Valley
(d) The Malwa Plateau.

92. The Patkai Buin and Naga ranges of Purvaneha from water shed between
(a) India and Burma (b) India and Nepal
(c) Burma and Nepal (d) India and Pakistan.

93. Guru Sikhar is the highest peak of the
(a) Sivalik range (b) Satpura range
(c) Aravalli range (d) Malwa plateau.

94. Dhaola Dhar, the Pir Panjal and Nag Tiba ranges are included in the
(a) Sivalik range (b) Lesser Himalayas
(c) Great range (d) None of these.

95. Which of the following are the highest hills of South Indian?
(a) Nilgiri hills (b) Rajmahal hills
(c) Cardamom hills (d) None of these.

96. Kayals are the
(a) Deserts of Rajasthan
(b) Mountain ranges in Kerala
(c) Lagoon in the South of Kerala state
(d) None of the above.

97. Mt. Everest the highest peak of the world is situated in which of the following ranges of Himalayas?
(a) The Sivalik range (b) The Lesser Himalayas
(c) The Great Himalayas (d) None of these.

98. Which of the following is the range of Himalayas?
(a) The Great Himalayas (b) The Lesser Himalayas
(c) The Sivalik range (d) All of the above.

99. The highest peak of the Nilgiri hills is known as
(a) Doda betta (b) Mahendra Giri
(c) Saramati (d) None of these.

100. Nokrek is the highest peak of the
(a) Khasi Jaintia hills (b) Garo hills
(c) Rajmahal hills (d) None of the above.

101. The Kaimur Hills belong to the
   (a) Vindhya range (b) Satpura range
   (c) Aravalli range (d) Bhanrer range.

102. In the eastern highlands, Saramati is the highest peak of
   (a) Dapha Bum (b) Patkin Bum
   (c) Naga range (d) None of these.

103. The Karakoram range lie in
   (a) Arunachal Pradesh
   (b) Northern Parts of Jammu and Kashmir
   (c) Uttar Pradesh
   (d) North-eastern part of Sikkim.

104. Goa, Daman and Diu along the West Coast became a part of India in
   (a) December 1961 (b) November 1974
   (c) August 1947 (d) January 1950.

105. In 1975 Sikkim was integrated with India as her
   (a) 25th State (b) 18th State
   (c) 22nd State (d) 21st State.

106. Which of the following is not a Union Territory of India?
   (a) Arunachal Pradesh (b) Pondicherry
   (c) Chandigarh (d) Daman and Diu.

107. Sri Lanka is separated from India by a narrow channel of sea formed by the
   (a) Palk Strait (b) Gulf of Mannar
   (c) Both (a) and (b) (d) None of these.

108. The Thaga La, the Nitle Pass and the Lipu Lekh Pass of the Himadri range lie in
   (a) Uttar Pradesh (b) Sikkim
   (c) Jammu and Kashmir (d) Tibet.

109. All of the following are renewable abiotic resources in nature except
   (a) Iron ore (b) Manganese
   (c) Cobalt (d) Copper and nickel.

110. Sulphur may be derived from
   (a) Natiue Sulphur
   (b) Sulphides of metals
   (c) Sulphide ores such as copper, zinc and silver
   (d) All of the above.

111. A dense, hard radioactive; nickel-white metal with the highest atomic weights
   (a) Thorium (b) Copper
   (c) Uranium (d) Aluminium.

112. Some abiotic resources are renewable and are continuously being formed in noddles
   (a) inside the earth (b) one the ocean floors
   (c) in the air (d) on the land.

113. Coal fields of tertiary beds occur in-------
   (a) Andhra Pradesh and Madhya Pradesh
   (b) Madhya Pradesh and Bihar
   (c) Assam and Rajasthan
   (d) Bihar and West Bengal.

114. The base of all the following fuels is organic materials except that of
   (a) Uranium (b) Petroleum
   (c) Coal (d) Natural gas.

115. Sabarmati and Jamuna are two new varieties of
   (a) Rice (b) Maize
   (c) Wheat (d) Jowar.

116. The important well irrigated states are
   (a) Tamil Nadu (b) U.P. and Punjab
   (c) Maharashtra (d) All of the above.

117. Which of the following is not a cash crops?
   (a) Sugarcane (b) Cotton
   (c) Ground nut (d) Tabacco.

118. U.P. is a well irrigated area because
   (a) Here water table is high
   (b) Here wells are easily sunk
   (c) Here soil is soft
   (d) All of the above.

119. It is easier to irrigate undulation land through
   (a) Tanks (b) Tubewells
   (c) Trickle irrigation (d) Sprinklers.

120. Saline water is good for
   (a) Drinking
   (b) Irrigation
   (c) Both drinking and irrigation
   (d) Neither drinking nor irrigation.

121. Canal may be classified as
   (a) Inundation, Perennial and Storage work canals
   (b) Inundation and Perenaial canals
   (c) Perennial and Storage work canals
   (d) Inundation and Storage work canal.

122. India leads the world in the production of
   (a) Jute (b) Tea
   (c) Cotton (d) Both (a) and (b).

123. Tube-wells are used for irrigation in U.P. and Bihar because here
   (a) There is ample sub-soil water
   (b) Water table is high
   (c) Soil is not soft
   (d) All of the above.

124. Sabarmati and Jamuna are new varieties of rice which were released for cultivation in
   (a) 1954 (b) 1960
   (c) 1970 (d) 1945.

125. The important irrigation sources in India are

(a) Tanks (b) Wells
(c) Canals (d) All of the above.

126. Production of food and non-food crops can be stepped up by the application of

(a) Use of improved seeds
(b) Plant nutrient
(c) Timely irrigation
(d) All of the above.

127. In eastern India east of 80° east meridian and in the coastal lowlands is dominant crop

(a) Wheat (b) Jute
(c) Rice (d) Sugarcane.

128. About 23% of the total cropped areas in India is used in producing

(a) Maize (b) Rice
(c) Jowar (d) Wheat.

129. The centrally sponsored command area development programme was launched in

(a) 1968-69 (b) 1981-82
(c) 1989-90 (d) 1974-75.

130. Well irrigation is an important type of irrigation in India because

(a) Well are suitable for small farms
(b) They are more useful than canals
(c) There is no danger of water logging as in the case of cannals
(d) Of all the above reasons.

131. High yielding of warf varieties PV 18 and Sonora 64 were first developed in

(a) India (b) Japan
(c) Mexico (d) Malaysia.

132. The canals in the dry areas of Madhya Pradesh and Deccan are mostly of which type
(a) Inundation (b) Perennial cannals
(c) Storage work canals (d) Both (a) and (c).

133. Which of the following is not an example of exhaustible resources of the earth available to man
(a) Petroleum (b) Coal
(c) Natural gas (d) Water.

134. In India only--------per cent of the total areas under cultivation receives irrigational facilities.
(a) 12 (b) 22
(c) 29 (d) 45.

135. Eastern M.P., Orissa, Interior areas of Tamil Nadu and Andhra Pradesh have more land under
(a) Well irrigation (b) Canal irrigation
(c) Tank irrigation (d) None of the above.

136. All of the following are renewable biotic resources in nature except
(a) Agricultural crops
(b) Iron-ore
(c) Animals
(d) Forests and their products.

137. In India salt is obtained from
(a) Beeds of rocks salt
(b) Sea water
(c) Lake and sub-soil water
(d) All of the above.

138. All of the following are non-metallic minerals except
(a) Graphite (b) Platinum
(c) Asbestos (d) Sulphur.

139. Vast deposits of coal of Gondwara formation occur in
(a) Madhya Pradesh (b) Andhra Pradesh
(c) Bihar (d) All of the above.

140. Which of the following are non-metallic minerals?
(a) Cobalt (b) Thorium
(c) Gypsum (d) Uranium.

141. Haematite, Limonite and Magnetite are
(a) Different varieties of iron
(b) Iron-ores
(c) Iron qualities with varying carbon content
(d) All of the above.

142. Which of the following coal fields has the deepest mines in India?
(a) Girdih
(b) Raniganj
(c) Bokaro
(d) All of the above.

143. Ankleshwar is known for
(a) Gas (b) Coal
(c) Gold (d) Oil.

144. Significant reserves of Lignites are in
(a) Bikaner
(b) South Arcot of Tamil Nadu
(c) Gujarat and Kashmir
(d) All of the above.

145. The first newsprint paper mill in the public sector was set up in
(a) Andhra Pradesh (b) Maharashtra
(c) M.P. (d) Bihar.

146. Heavy Engineering Equipment Industries are located at
(a) Ranchi (b) Nasik
(c) Bangalore (d) All of the above.

147. Which of the following is the biggest oilfield in India?
(a) Kolal (b) Digboi
(c) Masimpur (d) Badarpur.

148. India's most important oil bearing area is the
   (a) Assam (b) Bihar
   (c) Arunachal Pradesh (d) Nagaland.

149. Locomotive industries in India are at
   (a) Tiruchirapalli (b) Koraput
   (c) Chittaranjan (d) Perambur.

150. Important oil-fields of Assam include
   (a) Digboi (b) Moron
   (c) Naharkatiya (d) All of the above.

151. Rourkela Iron and Steel plant is located near the river
   (a) Brahmani (b) Khorkal
   (c) Subarnarekha (d) Bhadra.

152. High grade steam coal is found in
   (a) Raniganj
   (b) Bokaro
   (c) Karanpura and Singauli fields
   (d) All of the above.

153. The first cotton mill was started in Mumbai in
   (a) 1854 (b) 1846
   (c) 1947 (d) 1962.

154. Which of the following is not an xample of inexhaus.ible resources of the earth available tc nan?
   (a) Air (b) Fossil fuels
   (c) Solar energy (d) Forests and wildlife.

155. The low heating capacity of which of the following types of coal reduces its value as an industrial fuel?
   (a) Lignite (b) Anthracite
   (c) Peat (d) Bituminous coal.

156. About 30 per cent of India's production of coal comes from
   (a) Raniganj and Jharia
   (b) Singrauli and Girdih
   (c) Girdih
   (d) Bokaro and Karanpura.

157. Bhilai steel plant was set up in collaboration with

(a) USSR (b) USA

(c) Germany (d) U.K.

158. Apsara is the name associated with a

(a) Lake (b) Satellite

(c) Nuclear reactor (d) Thermal Power station.

159. According to future plans, new steel plants are to be set up at

(a) Vijay Nagar

(b) Visakhapatnam

(c) Salem

(d) All of the above.

160. Indian Coal reserves are estimated to be ------- per cent of world's total coal reserves.

(a) 1.6 (b) 1.1

(c) 8.4 (d) 2.7.

161. Copper may be found native, that is, impure state, but is more often found in chemical combination with

(a) Iron lead and sulphur

(b) Iron, gold and silver

(c) Gold, silver and lead

(d) All of the above.

162. Main sources of nitrogen are

(a) By products of blast furnaces

(b) Natural nitrates

(c) Coke ovens and synthetic nitrates

(d) All of the above.

163. Which of the following places in India has uranium deposits of great economic importance?

(a) Singhbhum (b) Jharia

(c) Keonjhar (d) Siliguri.

164. Gangue is referred to the
  (a) Iron-Sulphur compounds
  (b) Iron-Manganese compounds
  (c) Iron-Oxygen compounds
  (d) Iron-Carbon compounds.

165. Aeroplane industries in India are located at
  (a) Nasik
  (b) Kanpur
  (c) Bangalore
  (d) All of the above.

166. Which of the following is a private sector oil refinery?
  (a) Assam oil Company (b) Koyali
  (c) Oil India Ltd. (d) All of the above.

167. The production of steam locomotives for broad gauge lines commenced in India for the first time in
  (a) 1952 (b) 1946
  (c) 1950 (d) 1956.

168. When was Iron and Steel industry on a large scale established in India?
  (a) 1911 (b) 1919
  (c) 1853 (d) 1975.

169. Which of the following Iron and Steel plants is known as Visvesvaraya Iron and Steel Works Ltd. ?
  (a) Jamshedpur (b) Bhilai
  (c) Bhadravati (d) Rourkela.

170. The first large scale modern factory for the production of machine tools in India was set up at
  (a) Bangalore (b) Pinjore
  (c) Ranchi (d) Secunderabad.

171. The headquarters of Geological Survey of India is located in
  (a) Mumbai (b) Calcutta
  (c) Dehradun (d) New Delhi.

172. From which of the following ports we have the highest percentage export trade
(a) Marmagao (b) Mumbai
(c) Calcutta (d) Vishakhapatnam.

173. The Central or the Himalayan zone of isoclinal folds incorporate parts of lesser as well as the great Himalayas. This zone is mainly composed of
(a) Metamorphic and crystalline rock
(b) Sedimentary rock
(c) Igneous rocks
(d) None of these.

174. Which of the following is not a natural harbour
(a) Mumbai (b) Cochin
(c) Manglore (d) Chennai.

175. Which of the four language families occupies first place in India
(a) Austric (b) Sino-Tibetan
(c) Indo-Aryan (d) Dravidian.

176. Which of the following groups of minerals, India produces in sufficient surplus for exports
(a) Coal and Bauxite
(b) Asbestos and Borax
(c) Phosphates and Nickel
(d) None of the above.

177. The outer or the sub-Himalayan zone, corresponding to the Sivaliks is composed of
(a) Igneous rocks (b) Sedimentary rocks
(c) Metamorphic rocks (d) None of the above.

178. Which of the following dialect is related to Munda branch of Austric languages
(a) Karku (b) Santhal
(c) Brahur (d) Ho.

179. The Tibetan zone consist of

(a) Igneous rocks (b) Metamorphic rocks
(c) Schists and gneisses (d) Sedimentary rocks.

180. Which of the following states have the largest acreage under rubber cultivation

(a) Kerala (b) Maharashtra
(c) Andhra Pradesh (d) Karnataka.

181. The section of Himalayas between the Sutlej and the Kali is known as

(a) Nepal Himalayas (b) Assam Himalayas
(c) Kumaon Himalayas (d) Punjab Himalayas.

182. Rachna doab is situated between the rivers

(a) Beas and Sutlej (b) Chenab and Jhelum
(c) Ravi and Chenab (d) Beas and Ravi.

183. Which of the following states does not have a common boundary with Bangladesh

(a) Manipur (b) Tripura
(c) Mizoram (d) West Bengal.

184. Which of the following rivers does not drain Malwa plateau

(a) Kein (b) Chambal
(c) Sone (d) Betwa.

185. I.A.F Paratrooper's training school is in

(a) Agra (b) Delhi
(c) Jawalapur (d) Trivandrum.

186. Which is the fastest growing million city

(a) Bangalore (b) Mumbai
(c) Jaipur (d) Delhi.

187. Vikram Sarabhai space centre is located at

(a) Trombay (b) Sriharikota
(c) Trivandrum (d) Bangalore.

188. Who deltaic plain is most extensive

(a) Indus (b) Godavari
(c) Ganga (d) Krishna.

189. Which of the following is wrongly match

(a) HMT-Bangalore
(b) IOC-Mathura
(c) BCCL-Ranchi
(d) BHEL-Tiruchirrapalli.

190. Which of the following states is the largest producer of tabacco

(a) Uttar Pradesh (b) Gujarat
(c) Andhra Pradesh (d) Maharashtra.

191. What is the literacy rate of India

(a) 48 (b) 52
(c) 55 (d) 61.

192. Which of the following is not a Dravidian language

(a) Korku (b) Gondi
(c) Kannada (d) Brahur.

193. Which of the following is the longest dam in the world

(a) Aswan Dam (b) Bhakra Nangal
(c) Hirakud (d) None of these.

194. Tropic of cancer passes through how many no. of states

(a) 6 (b) 7
(c) 8 (d) 9.

195. About what percent of total sheep population is found in Rajasthan, Andhra Pradesh and Tamil Nadu

(a) 45 (b) 55
(c) 50 (d) 60.

196. Which of the following administrative unit of Pondicherry is situated on the eastern coast

(a) Yanam (b) Kakaikal
(c) Mahe (d) Both (a) and (b).

197. How many no. of states do have common boundary with Bangladesh
(a) 5 (b) 6
(c) 7 (d) 8.

198. Antibiotics are manufactured at
(a) Pimpri (b) Alwar
(c) Rishikesh (d) Hyderabad.

199. Find the odd one out
(a) Tripura (b) Chandigarh
(c) Lakshdweep (d) Pondicherry.

200. Andaman and Nicobar islands have been inhabited by
(a) Alpo-Dinanics (b) Proto-Australoids
(c) Paleo Mongoloids (d) Negritos.

201. Which state accounts for 63% production and therefore ranks first in the production of dolomite ?
(a) Bihar (b) Orissa
(c) Andhra Pradesh (d) Madhya Pradesh.

202. India's best quality sheeps are found in which of the following states
(a) Tamil Nadu (b) Rajasthan
(c) Andhra Pradesh (d) Himachal Pradesh.

203. Zinc and lead occur in association enclosed either among the crystalline or as veins and pockets in the ---------rocks.
(a) Pre cumbrian (b) Permian
(c) Archean system (d) Cretaceous.

204. Soliga tribes are the inhabitants of which part of India
(a) Andhra Pradesh (b) Karnataka
(c) Maharashtra (d) Kerala.

205. Which of the following milch breeds gives maximum will gield per lactation period?
(a) Sahewal (b) Red Sindhi
(c) Gir (d) Deoni.

206. Paraffin is a by-product of

(a) Kerosene (b) Coke
(c) Petroleum (d) Gasoline.

207. What are the main objectives of CADP?

(a) deveopment of infrastructure
(b) on farm development works
(c) construction of link roads, godowns and market places
(d) All of the above.

208. Hill Area Development Programme does not cover which of the following hills.

(a) Darjeeling hill (b) Mahadeo hills
(c) Mikir hills (d) Nilgiris.

209. What has been VIIIth plan outlay for the North Eastern Council to expedite the progress of development in the state of seven sisters?

(a) 1000 cr. (b) 1240 cr.
(c) 1160 cr. (d) 1100 cr.

210. Which of the following rivers fall into the Arabian sea?

(a) Mondoki (b) Sabarmati
(c) Tapti and Narmada (d) All of the above.

211. Which of the following is not a commercial crop?

(a) Coffee (b) Sugarcane
(c) Rubber (d) Tea.

212. Which state leads in the production of manganese?

(a) Orissa (b) Bihar
(c) Karnataka (d) Madhya Pradesh.

213. Which state ranks first in the density of cattle population?

(a) M.P. (b) U.P.
(c) Haryana (d) Punjab.

214. Which of the following river was once known as "Sorrow of Bengal"?

(a) Meghna (b) Padma
(c) Damodar (d) Kamla.

215. Operation flood was launched during
(a) Vth plan (b) IVth plan
(c) VIth plan (d) Annual plans.

216. Which of the following will not have sun overhead even once in a year
(a) Bolangir (b) Nagpur
(c) Gwalior (d) Indore.

217. Which of the following crops is not a cash crop?
(a) Jute (b) Tea
(c) Tabacco (d) Cotton.

218. The National Flood Control Programme was launched in
(a) 1954 (b) 1962
(c) 1958 (d) 1964.

219. Western Ghats Development Programme covers the area from
(a) Mouth of Sabarmati to KanyaKumari
(b) Mouth of Narmada to Trivandrum
(c) Mouth of Tapi river to Kanya Kumari
(d) Mouth of Tapi to Cochin.

220. Mahatma Gandhi Power Station is in
(a) Gujarat (b) Kerala
(c) Maharashtra (d) Karnataka.

221. Desert Development Programme covers
(a) Hot desert regions of Gujarat, Rajasthan and Haryana
(b) Cold desert regions of H.P. and J & K.
(c) Drought affected areas of different states
(d) Both (a) and (b).

222. Cauvery, one of the most important east flowing river of Peninsular India rises in
(a) Sahyadris (b) Cardamon hills
(c) Brahmagiri hills (d) None of the above.

223. Western Ghats Development Programme covers the length of

(a) 1200 kms (b) 1400 kms
(c) 1600 kms (d) 1000 kms.

224. Which is the second biggest west flowing river?

(a) Tapti (b) Mondovi
(c) Periyar (d) Periyar.

225. What has been the outlay for CASP in the VIIIth plan?

(a) 1680 cr. (b) 1580 cr.
(c) 1650 cr. (d) 1750 cr.

226. Jog falls, the highest waterfall of India is on which river

(a) Netravati (b) Tadri
(c) Sharavati (d) Tungabhadra.

227. North Eastern Council Development Programme was initiated in

(a) 1971 (b) 1975
(c) 1980 (d) 1972.

228. Which of the folllowing rivers do not make an I-shaped valley in the Himalaya?

(a) Beas (b) Indus
(c) Sutlej (d) Brahmaputra.

229. In India which of the following states has the largest population?

(a) Punjab (b) Bihar
(c) Uttar Pradesh (d) Madhya Pradesh.

230. Which of the following states is not covered under the Desert Development Programme?

(a) Punjab (b) Haryana
(c) Gujarat (d) Himachal Pradesh.

231. Border Area Development Programme was started in

(a) VIth Plan (b) Vth Plan
(c) VIIth Plan (d) VIIIth Plan.

232. About what percent of Narmada basin is in Madhya Pradesh

(a) 80 (b) 82
(c) 87 (d) 78.

233. The Secretariat of the North Eastern Council is situated at

(a) Silchar (b) Shillong
(c) Tezpur (d) Jorhat.

234. Kulu hills is the source of which of the following rivers?

(a) Chenab and Indus
(b) Ravi and Beas
(c) Chenab and Jhelum
(d) Jhelum and Sutlej.

235. Bhils are mainly confined to

(a) Bihar, Assam and Meghalaya
(b) Madhya Pradesh, Rajasthan and Gujarat
(c) Sikkim, Arunachal Pradesh and Chota Nagpur Plateau
(d) None of the these.

236. Which of the following language families is predominat in India?

(a) Austric languages (b) Dravidian languages
(c) Aryan languages (d) Sino-Tibetan languages.

237. The rural settlements in India may be classified into

(a) Dispersed type (b) Clustered type
(c) Semi-clustered type (d) All of the above.

238. In India which of the following states has a largest population?

(a) Punjab (b) Bihar
(c) Uttar Pradesh (d) Madhya Pradesh.

239. A distinguishing feature of the Indian house type is the

(a) Gali
(b) Courtyard
(c) Double roofs
(d) Separate space for storing agricultural produce.

240. Settlements have developed due to
(a) Religious purposes
(b) Economic purposes
(c) Cultural, political and military purposes
(d) All of the above.

241. Which of the following was the original home land of Mongoloid race?
(a) Tibet (b) China
(c) Burma (d) Baluchistan.

242. Lushai is the name given to the tribal population living in
(a) Manipura (b) Manipur
(c) Tripura (d) Meghalaya.

243. The tribal communities in India include major groups like
(a) Santhals (b) Bhils
(c) Gonds (d) All of the above.

244. Which of the following is the predominant occupation of rural settlement?
(a) Hunting
(b) Agriculture
(c) Gathering
(d) None of the above.

245. Which of the following states has the largest percentage of Buddhist population?
(a) Maharashtra (b) Karnataka
(c) West Bengal (d) Manipur.

246. In the Bhotiya tribe the graziers are called
(a) Andwal (b) Bugiyal
(c) Kharaks (d) Payar.

247. Khasi and Garo tribes belong to
(a) Nagaland (b) Meghalaya
(c) Arunachal Pradesh (d) Sikkim.

248. Which of the following states stands first regarding the literacy rate?
(a) Kerala (b) Karnataka
(c) Delhi (d) Mumbai.

249. The most important occupation of the Bhotiyas
(a) Trade with Tibet (b) Agriculture
(c) Dairy farming (d) None of the above.

250. Indo-Aryan languages include
(a) Tamil (b) Ladakhi
(c) Oriya (d) Lushai.

251. Khasi and Garo tribes mainly live in
(a) Meghalaya (b) Kerala
(c) Chota Nagpur (d) Tamil Nadu.

252. The basic unit of residence is
(a) Settlement (b) House
(c) Village (d) Metropolis.

253. Which of the following is the leading state of India in respect of the production of the Lac?
(a) Orissa (b) Bihar
(c) Assam (d) Madhya Pradesh.

254. Steel manufacturing plant is located in
(a) Bhadravati (b) Digboi
(c) Kola (d) Panna.

255. Which of the following states account for the largest share of Industrial growth and capital investment?
(a) Uttar Pradesh (b) West Bengal
(c) Maharashtra (d) Tamil Nadu.

256. Which of the following racial groups constitues the bulk of the population?
(a) The mongoloids (b) The Negritos
(c) The Proto Australoids (d) The Mediterraneans.

257. Kadars in habit the
(a) Nilgiri hills
(b) Annaimalai hills
(c) Tirunelvelli and Palni hills
(d) Travancore and Cochin hills now in Kerala.

258. Clusters of houses make a
(a) Street (b) Village
(c) Settlement (d) None of the above.

259. Loktak is the only major power project in
(a) Meghalaya (b) Haryana
(c) Manipur (d) West Bengal.

260. Which of the following industries was affected most due to partition?
(a) Steel industries
(b) Cotton and jute
(c) Tea and coton
(d) Small scale industries.

261. Apart from Calcutta, Jute industry is also located at
(a) Assam and Haryana
(b) Katihar and Kanpur
(c) Jamshedpur and Cuttak
(d) None of the above.

262. Suitable site of a cement plant requires proximity to
(a) Lime stone and Gypsum
(b) Coal and Gypsum
(c) Coal and Iron
(d) Lime stone and Manganese.

263. Wagads, Kumpta, Uppan, Broach and Lalios are local names of
(a) Cotton (b) Chemical
(c) Wool (d) Jute.

264. India has large deposits cf bauxite ores in
(a) Gujarat
(b) Ranchi district of Bihar
(c) Jabalpur and Katni regions of Madhya Pradesh
(d) All of the above.

265. The Paleolithic population moved into India from the
(a) Southern passes (b) Western passes
(c) North-eastern passes (d) South-western passes.

266. Maithon dam is built on the river
(a) Damodar (b) Bokaro
(c) Barakar (d) Konar.

267. The Narimanam oil field is located in
(a) Godavari delta (b) Kauveri delta
(c) Krishna delta (d) Mahanadi delta.

268. In Madhya Pradesh, Dewas is famous for its
(a) Aluminium plant
(b) Alkaloid factory
(c) Currency printing press
(d) None of the above.

269. Which of the following pairs is not correctly matched?
(a) Nangal : Haryana (b) Sindri : Bihar
(c) Sholapur : Maharashtra (d) Rourkela : Orissa.

270. Which of the following ports is a free trade zone?
(a) Mumbai (b) Manglore
(c) Kandla (d) Visakhapatnam.

271. ...... Per cent of out of total population lives in rural areas.
(a) 76 (b) 80
(c) 35 (d) 38.

272. The fiist hydro-power plant was installed at
(a) Pyakara (b) Darjeeling
(c) Mandi (d) Shivasamudram.

273. Which is the best reason for concentration of pulp industry in West Bengal?
(a) Good market
(b) Nearness to coal reserves
(c) Availability of raw material
(d) More number of rivers in the area.

274. Shivasamudram hydro electricity project is located in
(a) Karnataka (b) Kerala
(c) Andhra Pradesh (d) Tamil Nadu.

275. In terms of Sine of population, India stands------- in the world.
(a) First (b) Second
(c) Third (d) Fourth.

276. The first woollen mill in India was set up at
(a) Amritsar (b) Dhariwal
(c) Kanpur (d) Haryana.

277. Which of the following states produces more than half of vegetable tanned hides produced in India ?
(a) Tamil Nadu (b) West Bengal
(c) U.P (d) Maharashtra.

278. In India the first Census was held in
(a) 1947 (b) 1872
(c) 1950 (d) 1956.

279. Rihand hydro-electricity project is located in
(a) M.P. (b) Rajasthan
(c) Punjab (d) U.P.

280. Racial differences are based on
(a) Physical attributes to the humans
(b) Languages of the humans
(c) Cultural attributes of the humans
(d) None of the above.

281. Giri irrigation scheme is largest in the state of
   (a) Gujarat (b) Himachal Pradesh
   (c) Jammu and Kashmir (d) Uttar Pradesh.

282. Which of the following rivers has changed its affiliation as a tributary of Ganga to Brahmaputra?
   (a) Tista (b) Kosi
   (c) Manas (d) Subansiri.

283. Which of the two rivers joins to form one of the most fertile deltas of the world ?
   (a) Krishna and Tungabhadra
   (b) Godavari and Wardha
   (c) Ganga and Brahmaputra
   (d) Ravi and Beas.

284. In Trewartha's scheme of classification of climates, India has been divided into how many regions ?
   (a) 5 (b) 7
   (c) 6 (d) 8.

285. The Himalyan oregeny started in miocene and continued upto.
   (a) Pleistocene (b) Eocene
   (c) Oligocene (d) None of these.

286. The Montane sub-tropical forests are not found in
   (a) Satpuras (b) Palni hills
   (c) Mikir hills (d) Khassi hills.

287. Which of the following states has the largest percentage area covered by forests?
   (a) Arunachal Pradesh (b) Himachal Pradesh
   (c) Meghalaya (d) Madhya Pradesh.

288. Indian Lac Research Institute is located at
   (a) Sambhalpur (b) Gumla
   (c) Numkum, Ranchi (d) Lohardaga.

289. Which type of the forest are economically most important?
   (a) Tropical Evergreen forests
   (b) Deciduous forests
   (c) Sub-tropical evergreen forests
   (d) Wet temperate forests.

290. The Forest Research Institute is located at
   (a) Shimla (b) Jorhat
   (c) Dehradun (d) Shillong.

291. Which type of forests are called 'Sholas"?
   (a) Sub-tropical wet temperate forests
   (b) Deciduous forests
   (c) Mangrove forests
   (d) Tropical wet evergreen forests.

292. Which wood is extensively used for doors, beams, carriage and wagon building?
   (a) Khair (b) Sal
   (c) Teak (d) Deodar.

293. Red soils generally develop on
   (a) Igneous rocks
   (b) Metamorphic rocks
   (c) Sedimentary
   (d) None of these.

294. Brahmaputra, one of the longest river of the Indian sub-continent, is known as Tsangpo in Tibet and as Dihang in Arunachal Pradesh, by what name it is known as after it joins Ganga in Bangladesh
   (a) Padma (b) Jamuna
   (c) Meghna (d) None of these.

295. Which of the following states has the highest percentage area of the total area covered by rice cultivation?
   (a) Orissa (b) West Bengal
   (c) Uttar Pradesh (d) Andhra Pradesh.

296. Which state has the highest density of population according to 1991 census?
(a) Haryana (b) Bihar
(c) West Bengal (d) Kerala.

297. Which of the following soils cover largest area in India?
(a) Laterite and Lateritic soils
(b) Red soil
(c) Black soil
(d) Alluvial soil.

298. According to the historical classification of Indian cities, which of the following is not an ancient Indian city?
(a) Pune (b) Cochin
(c) Haridwar (d) Cuttack.

299. How many of Indian Islands lie in the Arabian sea?
(a) 28 (b) 37
(c) 43 (d) 33.

300. Which state occupies the first place in area as percentage of total area under Jowar?
(a) Karnataka (b) Madhya Pradesh
(c) Rajasthan (d) Maharashtra.

301. Of the total coal production of India about 30% comes from the Jharia coal-field and the coal-bearing rocks there occupy an area of only about
(a) 312 Kms (b) 272 Kms
(c) 360 Kms (d) 292 Kms.

302. Which of the following is a volcanic island situated north of Port Blair, in the Andaman and Nicobar group of Islands?
(a) Tillanchong (b) Narcondum
(c) Trinkant (d) Camarta.

303 Match of the following

A.	Dhuvaran	1.	Gujarat
B.	Tawa	2.	Kerala
C.	Idikki	3.	Karnataka

D Malaprabha 4. Madhya Pradesh
5. Andhra Pradesh

	A	B	C	D
(a)	3	2	1	5
(b)	4	1	2	3
(c)	1	2	5	4
(d)	1	4	2	3.

304. The population density of India has increased by percent during 1981-1991?
(a) 24.8 (b) 23.6
(c) 23.2 (d) 24.2.

305. On the average 33% of the flood damages in India is accounted far by which of the following states
(a) West Bengal
(b) Uttar Pradesh
(c) Assam
(d) Bihar.

306. Which of the following cities does not have a lake front location?
(a) Patan (b) Udaipur
(c) Hyderabad (d) Ajmer.

307. Which of the following is not associated with the alluvial soil?
(a) Kallar (b) Kankar
(c) Bhangar (d) Khadar.

308. At which of the following cities, Sikhs have the highest contribution of religious group in total population?
(a) Bhatinda (b) Ludhiana
(c) Patiala (d) Amritsar.

309. Which of the following states occupies second position in areas percentage of total area under cultivation of cotton
(a) Madhya Pradesh (b) Gujarat
(c) Karnataka (d) Maharashtra.

310. The Prevention of Pollution of Water Act was promulgated in

(a) 1981 (b) 1977
(c) 1974 (d) 1972.

311. Which city is located on the banks of Godavari

(a) Wardha (b) Madurai
(c) Nagpur (d) Nasik.

312. The Kalleru lake is situated between the

(a) mouth of Krishna and Godavari
(b) mouth of Subernarekha and Mahanadi
(c) mouth of Krishna and Cauvery
(d) mouth of Mahanadi and Godavari.

313. Which of the following islands is not a part of Andaman and Nicobar group of Islands?

(a) Katchall (b) Teressa
(c) Nancowry (d) Pamban Island.

314. Which Union territory experienced least population growth during 1981-1991?

(a) Dadra and Nagar Haveli
(b) Daman and Diu
(c) Pondicherry
(d) Lakshadweep.

315. According to 1991 census how many million cities are in India?

(a) 15 (b) 18
(c) 23 (d) 20.

316. Which is the southern-most point of India?

(a) Indira point (b) Rajeev point
(c) Tuticorin (d) Kanya Kumari.

317. The Peaty Saline are called Kari in which state?

(a) Kerala (b) Andhra pradesh
(c) Karnataka (d) Orissa.

318. Which of the following is not a tertiary coal-field
(a) Garo hills (b) Khasi hills
(c) Daphla hills (d) Mikir hills.

319. What is the difference between the densest state of India and the state of least density?
(a) 746 (b) 737
(c) 756 (d) 726.

320. Nathu La pass is located in which of the following states
(a) Sikkim (b) Arunachal Pradesh
(c) Himachal Pradesh (d) Uttar Pradesh.

321. Bombay, the most populous city of India ranks as----- largest city in world?
(a) 9th (b) 7th
(c) 6th (d) 5th.

322. The southern most limit of India (main land) is
(a) 6° 4' N latitude (b) 7° 4' N latitude
(c) 8° 4' N latitude (d) 8° 6' N latitude.

323. When were the states of India organised on a linguistic basis ?
(a) 1950 (b) 1952
(c) 1954 (d) 1956.

324. Which one of the following is the smallest state of India?
(a) Bihar (b) Sikkim
(c) Nagaland (d) Meghalaya.

325. Of which major river system is the Sutlej a part ?
(a) Ganga (b) Yamuna
(c) Indus (d) Brahmaputra.

326. Which of the following has the oldest rocks in the country?
(a) The Aravallis
(b) The Himalayas
(c) The Siwaliks
(d) The Indo-Gangetic Plain.

327. The monsoon starts retreating from India in
   (a) mid-March (b) mid-December
   (c) mid-September (d) late October.

328. Which soil swells when wet and develops cracks when dry?
   (a) Black (b) Alluvial
   (c) Red (d) Laterite.

329. Which place receives the maximum solar energy in December
   (a) Chennai (b) Delhi
   (c) Patna (d) Amritsar.

330. Which area of India receives the least rainfall?
   (a) The Western Ghats (b) Eastern Rajasthan
   (c) Western Tamil Nadu (d) Heh.

331. Which area in India gets the summer monsoon first?
   (a) The Western Ghats
   (b) The Eastern Ghats
   (c) The Himalayas
   (d) The Indo-Gangetic Plains.

332. Which river forms its delta is Orissa?
   (a) Tapti (b) Mahanadi
   (c) Godavari (d) Ganga.

333. One of the regions that receives rainfall from the North-easterly monsoon is
   (a) Kerala (b) Punjab
   (c) Bihar (d) Tamil Nadu.

334. In which area does the Sabarmati rise?
   (a) The Aravallis (b) The Vindhyas
   (c) The Satpuras (d) The Western Ghats.

335. In which climatic region are Haryana and Punjab included?
   (a) Steppe
   (b) Alpine
   (c) Humid sub-tropical, with dry winters
   (d) tropical evergreen forest.

336. The Aravallis fail to cause orographic precipitation in Rajasthan because
   (a) the monsoons do not reach them
   (b) they are not sufficiently high
   (c) they lie parallel to the direction of the winds
   (d) they do not support any vegetation.

337. Through which states does the river Chambal flow between the Satpuras and the Vindhyas?
   (a) Narmade (b) Ganga
   (c) Tapti (d) Gandak.

338. Through which states does the river Chambal flow?
   (a) M.P. Jharkand, Bihar
   (b) Rajasthan, M.P. , Bihar
   (c) U.P., M.P., Rajasthan
   (d) M.P., Gujarat, U.P.

339. The climate around Bikaner can be decribed as
   (a) Hot desert (b) Tropical monsoon
   (c) Semi-arid steppe (d) Mediterranean type.

340. During the period of the south west monsoon, Tamil Nadu remains dry because
   (a) the temperature is too high to led the winds cool down
   (b) there are no mountains in this area
   (c) the winds do not reach this area
   (d) it lies in the rain-show area.

341. Matatilla multipurpose project is in
   (a) Tamil Nadu (b) Bihar
   (c) Uttar Pradesh (d) West Bengal.

342. Copper-gold-iron-coal are connected with
   (a) Kolar-Khetri-Jharia-Kudremukh
   (b) Kudremukh-Kolar-Khetri-Jharia
   (c) Kolar-Kudremukh-Khetri-Jharia
   (d) Khetri-Kolar-Kudremukh-Jharia.

343. Which state has the largest area under canal irrigation in terms of the total acreage?

(a) Punjab (b) Haryana
(c) Uttar Pradesh (d) Jammu and Kashmir.

344. The most important resin producing state is

(a) Karnataka
(b) Madhya Pradesh
(c) Andhra Pradesh
(d) Himachal Pradesh.

345. Which is one of the most important items of Indian exports among marine products?

(a) Crabs (b) Whole oil
(c) Lobsters (d) Shrimps.

346. Which state in India has the largest area under irrigation in terms of total acreage?

(a) Uttar Pradesh (b) Tamil Nadu
(c) Haryana (d) Punjab.

347. Wheat crop is susceptible to

(a) smut (b) mosaic
(c) rust (d) brown leaf spot.

348. Th Mehsana breed of Buflalo is found mainly in

(a) Bihar (b) Gujarat
(c) Punjab (d) Haryana.

349. To which disease is sugarcane especially prone

(a) red rot (b) smut
(c) rust (d) bunchy top.

350. Which crop is affected by the disease called blast

(a) Wheat (b) Bajra
(c) Rice (d) Sugarcane.

351. Which crop is most susceptible root knot

(a) Cotton (b) Banana
(c) Tomato (d) Potato.

352. Which of the following are the major characteristics of intensive forming
   (i) Low capital
   (ii) High density of population
   (iii) Small size of holding
   (iv) Emphasis on machinery
   (a) i, ii, iii (b) i, iii
   (c) ii, iii, iv (d) i, ii, iv.

353. The highest peak in India territory is K^2, in which range is it located?
   (a) Trans - Himalayas (b) Central Himalayas
   (c) Kumaun Himalayas (d) Karakoram Range.

354. The rocks in the Himalayan system are mainly
   (a) igneous (b) pluronic
   (c) sedimentary (d) none of these.

355. Which of the following rivers flow through a rift valley?
   (a) Narmada (b) Ganga
   (c) Krishna (d) Brahmaputra.

356. Where is the maikal range located?
   (a) Bihar (b) Tamil Nadu
   (c) Madhya Pradesh (d) Jammu and Kashmir.

357. The exact height of Mt. Everest is
   (a) 8788 metres (b) 8782 metres
   (c) 8848 metres (d) 8868 metres.

358. Which part of the islands in the Arabian Sea is known as Minicoy islands
   (a) Northern (b) Western
   (c) Eastern (d) Southern.

359. An important cash crop of Punjab is
   (a) Jute (b) Manila hemp
   (c) Bajra (d) Cotton.

360. The erosion of soil by winds can be controlled by
   (a) Continuous tilling
   (b) Afforestation
   (c) The removal of vegetation
   (d) The creation of wind breaks.

361. What is the chief characteristic of the soil of the Indo-Gangetic Plain?
   (a) It is derived from local rocks
   (b) It is derived from Himalayan rocks
   (c) It is formed of Peninsular rocks
   (d) It is rich in humus.

362. Alluvial soil is fertile mainly because
   (a) It is rich in lime
   (b) It contains minerals in fine particles which can be absorbd easily by plants
   (c) It is rich in humus
   (d) It can be used for both rabi and kharib cropping.

363. What kind of soil predominates in the Sunderbans area
   (a) Alluvial
   (b) Red
   (c) Black
   (d) Laterite.

364. Winter rains in north western India are caused by
   (a) Trade winds
   (b) Retreating Monsoon
   (c) Westerly depressions
   (d) South-westerly monsoons.

365. Most rivers flowing west from the Western Ghats do not form deltas because of
   (a) the high gradient
   (b) lack of eraded material
   (c) lack of vegetation-free area
   (d) low velocity.

366. Rajasthan receives very little rain because
   (a) the monsoons fail to reach this area
   (b) it is too hot
   (c) the winds do not come across any barrier to cause the necessary uplift to cool the winds
   (d) there is no water available and thus the winds remain dry.

367. Which one is a land-locked state?
   (a) Bihar (b) West Bengal
   (c) Gujarat (d) Andhra Pradesh.

368. In which area does the Sabarmati rise?
   (a) the Satpuras (b) the Aravallis
   (c) the Vindhyas (d) the Western Ghats.

369. The maximum daily range of temperature can be observed at
   (a) Delhi (b) Patna
   (c) Lucknow (d) Mumbai.

370. Which state has very little alluvial soil area?
   (a) Bihar (b) West Bengal
   (c) Haryana (d) Tamil Nadu.

371. Most plantations of tea, coffee and fruit are laid out on
   (a) black soil (b) delta soil
   (c) mountain soil (d) alluvial soil.

372. Which crop is specially prone to the disease called smut
   (a) rice (b) wheat
   (c) bajra (d) sugarcane.

373. Nili is a breed of buffalo found mainly in
   (a) Uttar Pradesh and Bihar
   (b) Gujarat and Maharashtra
   (c) Bihar and Jharkhand
   (d) Punjab and Haryana.

374. One area in which peary soil is found is
(a) Bihar (b) Rajasthan
(c) Kerala (d) Madhya Pradesh.

375. Mountain soil contains a lot of
(a) Coarse material
(b) Clay
(c) Humus
(d) Iron and aluminium salts.

376. Which is the western most limit of the Siwalik Hills?
(a) River Kosi (b) Morni Hills
(c) Pir Panjal (d) Potwar Basin.

377. Where is the greatest variety of flowers found?
(a) Assam
(b) Uttar Pradesh Himalayas
(c) Sikkim
(d) Kerala.

378. Where is the Forest Research Institute located?
(a) Patna (b) Dehradun
(c) Delhi (d) Lucknow.

379. What is a water hyacinth?
(a) A medicinal plant
(b) A weed
(c) A decorative plant
(d) A highly sought after plant.

380. One method of controlling soil erosion in mountains is by
(a) clearing the land of large trees
(b) ploughing fields regularly
(c) laying roads
(d) terrace cultivation.

381. Which state has more than 90 per cent of its area under forests
(a) Arunachal Pradesh (b) Kerala
(c) West Bengal (d) Bihar.

382. Which is not on of the most important characteristics of Himalayan rivers?
(a) They have a perennial flow
(b) They have a great capacity for erosion
(c) They do not form gorges
(d) Many of them have their sources in the inner Himalayas.

383. Which states of India have a common boundary with Pakistan?
(a) Punjab, Jammu and Kashmir, Rajasthan, Gujarat
(b) Jammu and Kashmir, Himachal Pradesh, Punjab, Rajasthan
(c) Jammu and Kashmir, Punjab, Haryana, Rajasthan
(d) Punjab, Himachal Pradesh, Gujarat, Rajasthan.

384. India and its neighbouring countries are together called the Indian sub-continent because of the
(a) typical economic links between the various member states
(b) vast size of the area
(c) region's aloofness from the rest of the world
(d) political dominance of India.

385. Where can one expect dry winters in India ?
(a) Bengal plain
(b) Jammu and Kashmir
(c) Tamil Nadu
(d) Punjab and Haryana plains.

386. In which state are the Aravalli ranges located
(a) Rajasthan (b) Himachal Pradesh
(c) Orissa (d) Maharashtra.

387. Where is the Gulf of Mannar located?
(a) East of Tamil Nadu
(b) West of Kerala
(c) West of Gujarat
(d) South of Kanyakumari.

388. Which one of the following joins the Ganga from the south?
   (a) Gandak (b) Teesta
   (c) Sone (d) Gomti.

389. Which is the largest state of India
   (a) Madhya Pradesh (b) Rajasthan
   (c) Orissa (d) Bihar.

390. The territorial waters of India extend up to
   (a) 6 nautical miles (b) 12 nautical miles
   (c) 15 nautical miles (d) 10 nautical miles.

391. One of the states not bisected by the tropic of Cancer is
   (a) West Bengal (b) Bihar
   (c) Orissa (d) Rajasthan.

392. On which river is the Nagarjunasagar project located?
   (a) Tapti (b) Cauveri
   (c) Ganga (d) Krishna.

393. The largest production of coal comes from
   (a) Gujarat (b) West Bengal
   (c) Madhya Pradesh (d) Jharkhand.

394. Which river has been harnessed under the Bhakra Nangal project?
   (a) Sutlej (b) Ravi
   (c) Ganga (d) Beas.

395. Kothagudam thermal power project is a project in
   (a) Bihar (b) Madhya Pradesh
   (c) West Bengal (d) Andhra Paradesh.

396. Which state is the leading producer of ginger?
   (a) Madhya Pradesh (b) Kerala
   (c) West Bengal (d) Uttar Pradesh.

397. Which state has the largest area under tank irrigation?
   (a) West Bengal (b) Orissa
   (c) Uttar Pradesh (d) Tamil Nadu.

398. How long is the average gestation period of goat?

(a) 110 days (b) 120 days
(c) 240 days (d) 260 days.

399. In which part of India are thorn forests commonly found?

(a) Terai region of Uttar Pradesh
(b) Assam and Meghalaya
(c) Malabar coast
(d) Rajasthan and Gujarat.

400. Which animals are prone to the disease called rinderpest

(a) Cattle, buffaloes, sheep, goats and pigs
(b) Cattle and buffaloes
(c) Sheep and goats
(d) Poultry birds.

401. Where does teak grow most abundantly

(a) The Western Ghats (b) The Himalayas
(c) Central India (d) Assam and Meghalaya.

402. John's disease affects

(a) Poultry (b) Cattle
(c) Sheep and goats (d) All animals.

403. The total area covered by the Himalayas is about

(a) 5,00,000 sq. kms. (b) 6,00,000 sq. kms.
(c) 1,00,000 sq. kms. (d) 4,00,000 sq. kms.

404. Which river of India is called Tsangpo in one of its reaches?

(a) Kosi (b) Brahmaputra
(c) Teesta (d) Ganga.

405. Which area in India has an internal type of drainage?

(a) Rajasthan (b) Tamil Nadu
(c) Central Himalayas (d) Chhota Nagpur plateau.

406. One of the states through which the tropic of Cancer passes is

(a) Uttar Pradesh (b) Bihar
(c) Himachal Pradesh (d) Rajasthan.

407. The northernmost limit of India is

(a) 36° 4' latitude (b) 36° 12' N latitude
(c) 37° 8' N latitude (d) 37° 6' N latitude.

408. India is the seventh largest country in the world. It occupies about ------% of the area.

(a) 4.2 % (b) 3.4 %
(c) 2.4 % (d) 5.4 %.

409. What percentage of the total number of Indian cattle constitute good breeds?

(a) about 25 (b) about 30
(c) about 35 (d) about 40.

410. Which state has the lowest area under forests?

(a) Haryana (b) Uttar Pradesh
(c) Gujarat (d) Bihar.

411. Which is an area of tropical evergreen forests?

(a) Madhya Pradesh (b) Western Himalayas
(c) Western Ghats (d) The Eastern Ghats.

412. There are ------ species of birds in India.

(a) 500 - 600 (b) More than 1200
(c) about 300 (d) less than 400.

413. John's disease affects

(a) Sheep and goats (b) Cattle
(c) Poultry (d) All animals.

414. What kind of vegetation is usually found in river estuaries?

(a) Grass (b) Deciduous forests
(c) Littoral forests (d) Thorn forests.

415. In which state is the Kundah hydro electric project located?

(a) Tamil Nadu (b) Orissa
(c) West Bengal (d) Tamil Nadu.

416. Which state is the leading producer of bauxite?

(a) Jharkhand (b) Orissa
(c) Kerala (d) Rajasthan.

417. Which of the following is not important in tea processing ?
(a) fermeting (b) drying
(c) rolling (d) freezing.

418. The most important resin-producing state is
(a) Andhra Pradesh (b) Bihar
(c) Madhya Pradesh (d) Himachal Pradesh.

419. Which state irrigates largest percentage of land?
(a) Punjab (b) Uttar Pradesh
(c) Haryana (d) Madhya Pradesh.

420. Which state has the largest proportion of its net irrigated area under well irrigation?
(a) Haryana (b) Bihar
(c) Gujarat (d) West Bengal.

421. Rabbies affects
(a) Polutry (b) Cattle
(c) Goats (d) All animals.

422. The disease, green ear, affects
(a) Coffee (b) Rice
(c) Bajra (d) Wheat.

423. Which crop is specially prone to bacterial blight?
(a) Wheat (b) Cotton
(c) Rice (d) Sugarcane.

424. Cattle belonging to the famous Gir breed are found mainly in
(a) Gujarat, Rajasthan and Maharashtra
(b) Haryana, Bihar and Punjab
(c) Punjab, Uttar Pradesh and Maharashtra
(d) Gujarat, West Bengal and Jharkhand.

425. About what percentage of the total cattle population of the world is accounted for by India
(a) 15 (b) 20
(c) 25 (d) 30.

426. How long is the gestation period of a cow?
(a) 260 days (b) 270 days
(c) 280 days (d) 290 days.

427. Which crop is specially prone to the disease called smut?
(a) Rice (b) Sugarcane
(c) Wheat (d) Bajra.

428. What is the quality of basic snag, a by-product of steel plants ?
(a) It is a potassic fertiliser
(b) It is a mixed fertiliser
(c) It is a nitrogenous fertiliser
(d) It is a phosphatic fertiliser.

429. What is the chief characteristic of the soil of the Indo-Gangetic plain?
(a) It is formed of peninsular rocks
(b) It is derived from local rocks
(c) It is derived from Himalayan rocks
(d) It is rich in humus.

430. The disease called black arm affects
(a) Cotton (b) Wheat
(c) Bajra (d) Sugarcane.

431. Which soil requires the least tilling?
(a) laterite (b) black
(c) alluvial (d) red.

432. Which soil needs only little irrigation as it remains soil water
(a) red (b) black
(c) laterite (d) alluvial.

433. Most of the precipitation in India is--------in nature.
(a) Stormy (b) Orographic
(c) Cyclonic (d) Convectional.

434. Which part of the country receives precipitation from the Bay of Bengal branch of the monsoons as well as the Arabian Sea branch?

(a) Maharashtra (b) Bihar plateau
(c) West Bengal (d) Punjab plains.

435. What is the major cause of 'October heat'?

(a) Hot dry weather
(b) Very low velocity of winds
(c) High temperature associated with high humidity
(d) low pressure systems over the Indo-Gangetic plains.

436. The amount and intensity of monsoon rains in India are affected by

(a) Tropical depressions
(b) Wave cyclones
(c) Westerly disturbances
(d) Rain-shadow effects.

437. The climate around Bikaner can be described as

(a) Mediterranean type (b) Semi-arid steppe
(c) Hot desert (d) Tropical monsoon.

438. In which state is the Dhuvaran thermal power station located?

(a) Gujarat (b) Maharashtra
(c) Madhya Pradesh (d) Andhra Pradesh.

439. From which river has the Rajasthan canal (Indira Gandhi canal) been taken out

(a) Chambal (b) Ganga
(c) Sutlej (d) Yamuna.

440. Which state in India is most important for antimony?

(a) Punjab (b) Bihar
(c) Orissa (d) Tamil Nadu.

441. In which state is the Korba thermal power station located?

(a) Gujarat (b) Bihar
(c) Madhya Pradesh (d) Uttar Pradesh.

442. One of the major aims of the Koyna project has been
   (a) Hydro electricity generation
   (b) Flood control
   (c) Conservation of wildlife
   (d) Thermal power generation.

443. How much is the density of population as per census of India 1991?
   (a) 214 (b) 267
   (c) 282 (d) 298.

444. Where is sandalwood commonly found?
   (a) Tropical deciduous forests
   (b) Tropical evergreen forests
   (c) Alpine forests
   (d) Tropical scrubland areas.

445. The largest amount of saffron comes from
   (a) Tamil Nadu (b) Kerala
   (c) Jammu and Kashmir (d) Jharkhand.

446. Which state has the largest cattle population?
   (a) Bihar (b) Punjab
   (c) Madhya Pradesh (d) Haryana.

447. Which state is a major producer of copper?
   (a) Orissa (b) Jharkhand
   (c) Kerala (d) Madhya Pradesh.

448. Where is Kalpakkam?
   (a) Maharashtra (b) Gujarat
   (c) Tamil Nadu (d) Bihar.

449. Which is the southernmost unit of India?
   (a) Lakshadweep
   (b) Kanyakumari
   (c) Daman and Diu
   (d) Great Nicobar Island.

450. Why does India have droughts despite ample precipitation?
   (a) The amount of rainfall is inadequate
   (b) Rainfall does not coincide with the dry season
   (c) The absence of forests results in rapid run-off and thus droughts
   (d) Most of the rainfall occurs within a few months.

451. In which of the following areas is maximum precipitation received from the summer monsoon?
   (a) The Western Himalayas
   (b) The Coromandel coast
   (c) The North-eastern hilly region
   (d) The Coromandel coast.

452. Which is an important red soil area?
   (a) Karnataka
   (b) Jammu and Kashmir
   (c) Bihar
   (d) Maharashtra.

453. The country has ------- national parks.
   (a) 58 (b) 63
   (c) 53 (d) 68.

454 What is the estimated drought-prone area?
   (a) 185 m. hectares (b) 275 m. hectares
   (c) 260 m. hectares (d) 230 m. hectares.

455. National Institute of Port Management is located at
   (a) Madras (b) Mumbai
   (c) Tuticorin (d) Kolkatta.

456. In India, dependency ratio is about
   (a) 70% (b) 75%
   (c) 68 % (d) 83%.

457. India possesses about ------ different species of plants.
   (a) 15,000 (b) 35,000
   (c) 30,000 (d) 45,000.

458. In Kashmir, the river Indus flows between
   (a) Ladakh and Karakoram ranges
   (b) Ladakh and Zaskar ranges
   (c) Karakoram and Zaskar ranges
   (d) Kunlun and Karakoram ranges.

459. Every post office in India serves on an average a population of
   (a) 5200 persons (b) 4500 persons
   (c) 4800 persons (d) 5400 persons.

460. Of which region is rice the most important crop
   (a) Steppes (b) Equatorial
   (c) Mediterranean (d) Tropical monsoon.

461. Where are iron ore mines located?
   (a) Jaduguda, Singhbhum, Kudremukh, Jharia
   (b) Singhbhum, Bastar, Mayurbhanj, Keeonjhar
   (c) Neyveli, Bastar, Jharia, Khetri
   (d) Bhadravati, Barauni, Nayveli, Singhbhum.

462. The Silent Valley project has been abandoned due to
   (a) Indifference of the state government
   (b) Its non-feasibility from the economic point of view
   (c) The danger of ecological imbalance in the region
   (d) Inaccessibility of the area.

463. In which state is Silent Valley located ?
   (a) Tamil Nadu (b) Kerala
   (c) Assam (d) Arunachal Pradesh.

464. Which kind of power accounts for the largest share of power generation in India?
   (a) Hydro electricity (b) Thermal
   (c) Nuclear (d) Solar.

465. Which state is the leading producer of thorium?
   (a) Kerala (b) Bihar
   (c) Orissa (d) Madhya Pradesh.

466. Of which mineral is Kerala one of the leading producers?
(a) Limestone (b) Uranium
(c) Zinc (d) Graphite.

467. One of the leading producers of lead is
(a) Madhya Pradesh (b) Tamil Nadu
(c) Kerala (d) Rajasthan.

468. The Indian Space Research Organisation is in----
(a) Trivandrum (b) Bangalore
(c) Thumba (d) Sriharikota.

469. Where is the National Physical Laboratory?
(a) New Delhi (b) Bombay
(c) Bangalore (d) Hyderabad.

470. Where are ships manufactured in India?
(a) Cochin Shipyard, Cochin
(b) Hindustan Shipyard, Visakhapatnam
(c) Mazagaon, Docks, Bombay
(d) Marmago Shipyard.

471. Where are ambassador cars manufactured?
(a) Bombay (b) Delhi
(c) Kolkatta (d) Bangalore.

472. In which states is Batanagar located?
(a) Uttar Pradesh (b) West Bengal
(c) Tamil Nadu (d) Maharashtra.

473. For what is Sindri known?
(a) Aluminium plant (b) Cement plant
(c) Fertiliser plant (d) Paper plant.

474. An important pesticides unit of the Hindustan Insecticides Ltd. is located at
(a) Bhopal (b) Alwaye
(c) Visakhapatnam (d) Madras.

475. The first paper mill of the country was started in 1832, where was it located?
(a) Nepanagar in Madhya Pradesh
(b) Mumbai
(c) Behrampore in West Bengal
(d) Yamunanagar in Haryana.

476. Which state leads in the production of cement?
(a) Rajasthan (b) Tamil Nadu
(c) Bihar (d) West Bengal.

477. Which state is the leading producer of glass?
(a) Madhya Pradesh (b) Bihar
(c) Uttar Pradesh (d) Tamil Nadu.

478. Where is the Hindustant Antibiotics plant located?
(a) Delhi (b) Rishikesh
(c) Bombay (d) Faridabad.

479. A pharmaceutical plant of India is
(a) IDPL, Hyderabad (b) IDPL, Kanpur
(c) HSL, Bhilai (d) HIL, Delhi.

480. Name the Public Sector company manufacturing aluminium products
(a) INDAL Co., Hirakud
(b) INDAL Co., Alpuram
(c) HINDAL Co., Mathura
(d) BAL Co., Karba.

481. Which state has the largest number of sugar mills?
(a) Maharashtra (b) Bihar
(c) Uttar Pradesh (d) Haryana.

482. For what is Rupnarainpur known?
(a) Hindustan Copper Plant
(b) Hindustan Cable Factory
(c) Bharat Aluminium Factory
(d) Indian Telephone Industry.

483. Where is security paper mills?
(a) Nasik (b) Bangalore
(c) Hoshangabad (d) Ozar.

484. Where was the first fertiliser plant in the public sector set up?
(a) Nangal (b) Cochin
(c) Trombay (d) Sindri.

485. For what is Ozar known?
(a) Newsprint factory (b) Cement factory
(c) MIG aircraft factory (d) HMT Watch factory.

486. Where is the oldest oil refinery of India?
(a) Haldia (b) Digboi
(c) Barauni (d) Cochin.

487. Where is the share-based steel plant located?
(a) Tuticorin (b) Salem
(c) Visakhapatnam (d) Mangalore.

488. Which state is the leading producer of sulphur?
(a) Tamil Nadu (b) Assam
(c) Punjab (d) Maharashtra.

489. What is Talchar important for?
(a) Hydro electricity generation
(b) Atomic reactor
(c) Heavy water plant
(d) Cable industry.

490. Where is the largest amount of manganese produced?
(a) Madhya Pradesh (b) Orissa
(c) Bihar (d) Assam.

491. In which state is lignite most abundantly found?
(a) Gujarat (b) Maharashtra
(c) Uttar Pradesh (d) Tamil Nadu.

492. Where are Diamonds mined in India?
   (a) Golkunda in Andhra Pradesh
   (b) Panna in Madhya Pradesh
   (c) Neyveli in Tamil Nadu
   (d) Kolar in Karnataka.

493. Who prepares the topographical maps of India?
   (a) Geological Survey of India
   (b) Survey of India
   (c) Defence Ministry
   (d) Geographical Survey of India.

494. Which of the following is not matched correctly?
   (a) Farakka-West Bengal
   (b) Nagarjunasagar-Andhra Pradesh
   (c) Tawa-Gujarat
   (d) Kobra-Madhya Pradesh.

495. What is Raniganj famous for?
   (a) Iron Ore (b) Coal
   (c) Manganese (d) Mica.

496. The most important producer of tin in India is
   (a) Bihar (b) Rajasthan
   (c) Karnataka (d) Andhra Pradesh.

497. Which state has deposits of lead, copper and zinc
   (a) Orissa (b) Madhya Pradesh
   (c) Karnataka (d) Rajasthan.

498. Which item is the most important among the exports of India in terms of total value?
   (a) Cotton textiles (b) Iron Ore
   (c) Tea (d) Engineering goods.

499. The largest number of cotton textile mills is in
   (a) Maharashtra (b) Gujarat
   (c) Tamil Nadu (d) Karnataka.

500. Which industry provides jobs to the maximum number of people?

(a) Iron and Steel (b) Cotton textile
(c) Sugar industry (d) Tea processing.

501. Which iron and steel plant has been located without giving importance to the availability of coal?

(a) TISCO, Jamshedpur (b) USL, Bhadravati
(c) HSL, Bhilai (d) HSL, Durgapur.

502. The first modern iron and steel plant of India was established at

(a) Bokaro (b) Durgapur
(c) Bhilai (d) Jamshedpur.

503. Which iron and steel plant has been established with German collaboration?

(a) TISCO, Jamshedpur (b) HSL Rourkela
(c) HSL, Bhilai (d) HSL, Durgapur.

504. Which two iron and steel plants have been established with Soviet collaboration?

(a) Jamshedpur and Rourkela
(b) Durgapur and Bokaro
(c) Bhilai & Dugapur
(d) Bokaro & Bhilai.

505. HSL, Durgapur has been established with the help of

(a) USSR (b) Sweden
(c) U.K. (d) Germany.

506. What has had the maximum influence on localisation of the woollen textile industry in India?

(a) Market factor (b) Raw material
(c) Skilled labour (d) Means of transport.

507. A major plant of Hindustan Machine Tools Ltd. is in

(a) Bhopal (b) Visakhapatnam
(c) Pinjore (d) Kolkatta.

508. Where are broad gauge railway engines manufactured ?
(a) Gorakhpur (b) Jamshedpur
(c) Chittaranjan (d) Varanasi.

509. Where are electric locomotives manufactured ?
(a) Chittaranjan (b) Varanasi
(c) Bhopal (d) Jamshedpur.

510. Where is the Integral Coach Factory located?
(a) Madras (b) Perambur
(c) Jamshedpur (d) Hyderabad.

511. What is abra known for?
(a) A new refinery
(b) Thermal power station
(c) An upcoming aluminium plant
(d) Bird sanctuary.

512. Which of the following can be called a non-conventional source of energy?
(a) Hydro Power (b) Thermal Power
(c) Solar Power (d) Water Power.

513. In which state is Tarapur located?
(a) Tamil Nadu (b) West Bengal
(c) Uttar Pradesh (d) Maharashtra.

514. What means of transport accounts for the largest proportion of passenger traffic in India?
(a) Railways (b) Roads
(c) Airways (d) Waterways.

515. Which zone of the Indian Railways accounts for the maximum route length?
(a) Western Railway (b) Southern Railway
(c) Northern Railway (d) North-Eastern Railway.

516. Where are the headquarters of the North-Eastern Railway?
(a) Kolkatta (b) Gorakhpur
(c) New Jalpaiguri (d) Guwahati.

517. The head quarters of the South Central Railway are at
(a) Nagpur (b) Madras
(c) Secundrabad (d) Hyderabad.

518. How far apart are rails in a broad gauge line system ?
(a) 1.676 metres
(b) 1.576 metres
c) 1.845 metres
(d) 1.453 metres.

519. Thr broad gauge accounts for about ----- of the total route length of the Indian railways.
(a) 65% (b) 75%
(c) 50% (d) 40%.

520. What is the total length of roads in India?
(a) about 2 lakhs kms
(b) between 2 and 3 lakhs kms
(c) about 4 lakh kms
(d) more than 5 lakh kms.

521. Which state has the maximum length of roads?
(a) Madhya Pradesh (b) Uttar Pradesh
(c) Karnataka (d) Punjab.

522. Which national highway (NH) connects Agra and Mumbai?
(a) NH1 (b) NH7
(c) NH3 (d) NH5.

523. Which places are connected by NH1?
(a) Delhi and Amritsar via Ambala and Jalandhar
(b) Delhi and Amritsar via Fazilka
(c) Delhi and Kolkata via Mathura and Varanasi
(d) Delhi and Mumbai via Jaipur.

524. Which national highway connects Delhi and Kolkatta via Mathura and Varanasi?
(a) NH4 (b) NH2
(c) NH10 (d) NH6.

525. How many public sector shipping companies are there in India?
(a) 5 (b) 4
(c) 1 (d) 6.

526. Which one is not a major part on the east coast?
(a) Paradeep (b) Kolkatta
(c) Cochin (d) Visakhapatnam.

527. With what is 'blue revolution' concerend?
(a) Agriculture (b) Iron and Steel industry
(c) Irrigation (d) Fishing.

528. Where is the Civil Aviation Training centre?
(a) Kolkatta (b) Delhi
(c) Madras (d) Allahabad.

529. Where is the Manambakkam air port located?
(a) Bangalore (b) Madras
(c) Hyderabad (d) Bhubaneshwar.

530. Where is the Indira Gandhi Air port located ?
(a) Delhi (b) Allahabad
(c) Ahmedabad (d) Mumbai.

531. The first postal stamp of India was released in 1837, where was it released ?
(a) Mumbai (b) Dhaka
(c) Karachi (d) Rangoon.

532. When was the postal department set up in India ?
(a) 1837 (b) 1854
(c) 1911 (d) 1921.

533. In which state has the petro-chemical industry developed most in India?
(a) West Bengal (b) Bihar
(c) Gujarat (d) Tamil Nadu.

534. How many PIN Zones has India been divided into?

(a) 5 (b) 6
(c) 7 (d) 8.

535. When was the national telex service started?

(a) 1954 (b) 1982
(c) 1974 (d) 1963.

536. Where are teleprinters manufactured in India?

(a) Madras (b) Bangalore
(c) New Delhi (d) Kolkatta.

537. When and where was the first telephone exchange with automatic lines established?

(a) 1940, Delhi (b) 1913, Kolkatta
(c) 1913, Shimla (d) 1918, Mumbai.

538. When was the OYT scheme introduced?

(a) 1964 (b) 1949
(c) 1960 (d) 1956.

539. When was the 'on demand' trunk service started by the telephone department?

(a) 1949 (b) 1960
(c) 1964 (d) 1961.

540. Which artificial harbour is located on the east coast?

(a) Cochin (b) Calcutta
(c) Kandla (d) Madras.

541. How much is the total population of India as per 1991 census?

(a) 84.39 crore (b) 88.36 crore
(c) 83.79 crore (d) 85.74 crore.

542. An important feature of the balance of India's foreign trade is that

(a) It is usually negative
(b) It is usually positive
(c) It keeps changing from positive to negative
(d) It is always in favour of India.

543. What is the most important item of Indian imports in terms of total value?

(a) Petroleum and petroleum products
(b) Food grains
(c) Fertilisers
(d) Non-electric machinery and apparatus.

544. The life expectancy in India is

(a) more in the case of males
(b) more in the case of females
(c) equal in the case of males and females
(d) not comparable in the case of males and females as it keeps changing.

545. Which area has the highest density of population among the states and the Union territories?

(a) Delhi (b) Kerala
(c) Chandigarh (d) Goa, Daman and Diu.

546. Which state has the lowest density?

(a) Jammu and Kashmir (b) Rajasthan
(c) Nagaland (d) Sikkim.

547. Which area has the lowest density of population among the states and Union territories?

(a) Sikkim (b) Arunachal Pradesh
(c) Himachal Pradesh (d) Mizoram.

548. An area with density of less than 50 persons per sq. km. is

(a) Rajasthan (b) Manipur
(c) Mizoram (d) Jammu and Kashmir.

549. In which state do women outnumber men?

(a) Tamil Nadu (b) Kerala
(c) Nagaland (d) Maharashtra.

550. During which decade did the population record a negative growth rate?

(a) 1921-31 (b) 1911-21
(c) 1941-51 (d) 1931-41.

551. In which area are Zoroastrians concentrated?

(a) Tamil Nadu (b) Andhra Pradesh
(c) Maharashtra (d) Madhya Pradesh.

552. Where can a significant concentration of christians be found in India?

(a) Sikkim (b) Arunachal Pradesh
(c) Madhya Pradesh (d) Nagaland.

553. Which is the group of languages spoken by the largest number of people in India?

(a) Indo-Aryan (b) Dravidian
(c) Austro-Asiatic (d) Sino-Tibetan.

554. To which group do the tribals of central and southern India belong?

(a) Negritoes
(b) Proto-Australoids
(c) Mongoloids
(d) Western Brachycephals.

555. Among the mediterraneans are included the people of

(a) Andaman and Nicobar Islands
(b) West Bengal and Orissa
(c) Punjab and Uttar Pradesh
(d) The mountaineers zone in the north.

556. Who are believed to be the oldest inhabitants of India?

(a) Mediterraneans (b) Negritoes
(c) Nordics (d) Mongoloids.

557. Where are the Angamis found?

(a) Madhya Pradesh (b) Andhra Pradesh
(c) Tamil Nadu (d) Manipur.

558. Where are the Todas found?

(a) Madhya Pradesh (b) Tamil Nadu
(c) Rajasthan (d) Arunachal Pradesh.

559. Who are the Moplahs?
(a) Tribals of Madhya Pradesh
(b) Tribals of Assam
(c) Muslims of Kerala
(d) Tribals of West Bengal.

560. Where do Birhors live?
(a) Madhya Pradesh (b) Assam
(c) Nagaland (d) Tamil Nadu.

561. How many villages exist in India?
(a) about 3.8 lakh (b) about 5.6 lakh
(c) about 10.0 lakh (d) about 4.9 lakh.

562. Which state has the largest numbers of urban units?
(a) Tamil Nadu (b) Maharashtra
(c) Uttar Pradesh (d) West Bengal.

563. Which state has the distinction of having no uninhabited villages?
(a) Uttar Pradesh (b) Kerala
(c) West Bengal (d) Tamil Nadu.

564. Which city has the largest population?
(a) Greater Bombay (b) Delhi
(c) Kolkatta (d) Chennai.

565. What is the term used to describe cultivation on hill slopes with small patches of land in descending order?
(a) Truck farming (b) Slope cultivation
(c) Hill farming (d) Contour farming.

566. What is meant by 'reserved' forest?
(a) A forest reserved exclusively for grazing
(b) A forest reserved for hunting
(c) a forest reserved for commercial exploitation with restrictions on grazing
(d) A forest reserved for the use of tribal people.

567. Where is the Bandipur National Park?
(a) Rajasthan (b) Andhra Pradesh
(c) Assam (d) Karnataka.

568. Corbett National Park is in
(a) Bihar (b) Madhya Pradesh
(c) Uttar Pradesh (d) Himachal Pradesh.

569. Where is the home of the Asiatic lion?
(a) Gir National Park (b) Dudhwa National Park
(c) Kanha National Park (d) Corbett National Park.

570. Where is the wild ass sanctuary?
(a) Uttar Pradesh (b) Assam
(c) Rajasthan (d) Gujarat.

571. Kaziranga National Park is in
(a) Uttar Pradesh (b) Tamil Nadu
(c) Assam (d) Kerala.

572. For what is the Manas Sanctuary in Assam known?
(a) Bear (b) Tiger
(c) Wild ass (d) Birds.

573. Which national park is known for the Great Indian cone horned Rhinoceros?
(a) Dudhwa (b) Corbett
(c) Kaziranga (d) Gir.

574. The famous Ghana Bird Sanctuary is located in
(a) Jorhat (b) Barpeta
(c) Nainital (d) Bharatpur.

575. Which sanctuary in Kerala is known for elephants?
(a) Parkal (b) Periyar
(c) Chandraprabha (d) Kanha.

576. What is Jhoom?
(a) A type of cultivation
(b) A type of swinging basket
(c) A river valley in a dry region
(d) None of these.

577. Most of India's cultivated area is under
   (a) Shifting cultivation (b) Sedentary cultivation
   (c) Tribal cultivation (d) Dry zone cultivation.

578. One of the most prominent crops of dry farming in India is
   (a) Paddy (b) Wheat
   (c) Bajra (d) Cotton.

579. The growing of crops one after the other successively to maintain soil fertility is called
   (a) Crop rotation (b) Crop succession
   (c) Intensive farming (d) Extensive farming.

580. The cultivation of rice in West Bengal is an example of
   (a) Commercial grain farming
   (b) Subsistence grain farming
   (c) Commercial plantation agriculture
   (d) Mechanised multiple cropping for commerce.

581. Which crop requires water logging for its cultivation?
   (a) Tea (b) Coffee
   (c) Rice (d) Mustard.

582. What kind of soil is ideal for rice cultivation?
   (a) clayey
   (b) sandy
   (c) clayey loams of the deltas
   (d) rich regur.

583. Jaya is the name of a high yielding variety of
   (a) Wheat (b) Rice
   (c) Bajra (d) Cotton.

584. What is the ideal temperature for the cultivation of wheat?
   (a) 20° to 25° C (b) 15° to 20° C
   (c) 10° to 15° C (d) 25° to 30° C.

585. Which is the leading producer of wheat?
   (a) Madhya Pradesh (b) Maharashtra
   (c) Punjab (d) Uttar Pradesh.

586. Which state is the leading producer of maize?
(a) Punjab (b) Uttar Pradesh
(c) Kerala (d) Rajasthan.

587. Of which crop is Gujarat one of the chief producers?
(a) Wheat (b) Sugarcane
(c) Bajra (d) Coconut.

588. In an area with annual rainfall of more than 200 cm and sloping hills which crop will be ideal?
(a) Jute (b) Cotton
(c) Maize (d) Tea.

589. Where are tea and coffee both grown?
(a) North-Western India
(b) North-Eastern India
(c) Central India
(d) Southern India.

590. Which state after West Bengal leads in Jute production?
(a) Assam (b) Meghalaya
(c) Uttar Pradesh (d) Bihar.

591. Which state is the leading producer of coconut?
(a) Assam (b) Kerala
(c) Tamil Nadu (d) Karnataka.

592. Sugarcane in India matures in about
(a) 5 months (b) 3 months
(c) 7 months (d) 12 months.

593. From which part of the plant is jute obtained?
(a) Flower (b) Fruit
(c) Stem (d) Leaf.

594. From which part of the plant is coffee fibre obtained?
(a) Seed (b) Flower
(c) Stem (d) Leaf.

595. Which state produces the bulk of natural rubber produced in India?
   (a) Tamil Nadu (b) Karnataka
   (c) Andhra Pradesh (d) Kerala.

596. The temperature needed for cultivation of rubber is
   (a) about 25^0 C (b) about 30^0 C
   (c) about 35^0 C (d) about 45^0 C.

597. Which state is called the 'sugarbowl' of India ?
   (a) Uttar Pradesh (b) Punjab
   (c) Andhra Pradesh (d) Bihar.

ANSWERS

1.	(b)	2.	(a)	3.	(d)	4.	(c)
5.	(d)	6.	(a)	7.	(a)	8.	(c)
9.	(a)	10.	(b)	11.	(a)	12.	(b)
13.	(b)	14.	(c)	15.	(b)	16.	(a)
17.	(d)	18.	(d)	19.	(c)	20.	(b)
21.	(c)	22.	(a)	23.	(b)	24.	(c)
25.	(a)	26.	(b)	27.	(c)	28.	(c)
29.	(a)	30.	(c)	31.	(b)	32.	(c)
33.	(d)	34.	(d)	35.	(d)	36.	(c)
37.	(d)	38.	(a)	39.	(d)	40.	(d)
41.	(a)	42.	(a)	43.	(c)	44.	(b)
45.	(d)	46.	(a)	47.	(d)	48.	(b)
49.	(a)	50.	(c)	51.	(a)	52.	(b)
53.	(b)	54.	(a)	55.	(c)	56.	(b)
57.	(d)	58.	(c)	59.	(a)	60.	(b)
61.	(b)	62.	(d)	63.	(b)	64.	(c)
65.	(b)	66.	(c)	67.	(a)	68.	(b)
69.	(c)	70.	(a)	71.	(a)	72.	(b)
73.	(a)	74.	(a)	75.	(a)	76.	(c)
77.	(d)	78.	(a)	79.	(b)	80.	(a)
81.	(b)	82.	(c)	83.	(a)	84.	(a)
85.	(c)	86.	(b)	87.	(d)	88.	(d)
89.	(b)	90.	(a)	91.	(c)	92.	(a)
93.	(a)	94.	(b)	95.	(a)	96.	(d)
97.	(c)	98.	(d)	99.	(a)	100.	(b)

101. (a)	102. (c)	103. (b)	104. (a)
105. (c)	106. (a)	107. (c)	108. (a)
109. (a)	110. (d)	111. (c)	112. (b)
113. (c)	114. (a)	115. (a)	116. (d)
117. (c)	118. (d)	119. (d)	120. (d)
121. (a)	122. (d)	123. (a)	124. (c)
125. (d)	126. (d)	127. (c)	128. (b)
129. (d)	130. (d)	131. (c)	132. (c)
133. (d)	134. (a)	135. (c)	136. (b)
137. (d)	138. (b)	139. (d)	140. (c)
141. (b)	142. (b)	143. (d)	144. (d)
145. (c)	146. (b)	147. (b)	148. (a)
149. (c)	150. (d)	151. (a)	152. (d)
153. (a)	154. (b)	155. (c)	156. (a)
157. (a)	158. (c)	159. (d)	160. (a)
161. (d)	162. (d)	163. (a)	164. (c)
165. (d)	166. (a)	167. (c)	168. (a)
169. (c)	170. (a)	171. (b)	172. (a)
173. (a)	174. (c)	175. (c)	176. (a)
177. (b)	178. (c)	179. (d)	180. (a)
181. (c)	182. (c)	183. (a)	184. (c)
185. (c)	186. (a)	187. (c)	188. (a)
189. (c)	190. (c)	191. (b)	192. (a)
193. (c)	194. (a)	195. (b)	196. (d)
197. (a)	198. (c)	199. (a)	200. (d)
201. (c)	202. (d)	203. (a)	204. (c)
205. (b)	206. (c)	207. (d)	208. (b)
209. (c)	210. (d)	211. (b)	212. (a)
213. (b)	214. (c)	215. (a)	216. (c)
217. (b)	218. (a)	219. (c)	220. (d)
221. (d)	222. (c)	223. (c)	224. (a)
225. (a)	226. (c)	227. (d)	228. (a)
229. (c)	230. (a)	231. (c)	232. (c)
233. (b)	234. (b)	235. (b)	236. (c)
237. (d)	238. (c)	239. (b)	240. (d)
241. (b)	242. (c)	243. (d)	244. (b)
245. (a)	246. (a)	247. (b)	248. (a)
249. (a)	250. (c)	251. (a)	252. (b)
253. (d)	254. (a)	255. (c)	256. (c)
257. (b)	258. (c)	259. (c)	260. (b)
261. (b)	262. (d)	263. (a)	264. (d)
265. (b)	266. (a)	267. (b)	268. (c)

269. (a)	270. (c)	271. (a)	272. (d)
273. (c)	274. (a)	275. (d)	276. (c)
277. (c)	278. (b)	279. (d)	280. (a)
281. (a)	282. (a)	283. (c)	284. (b)
285. (a)	286. (d)	287. (a)	288. (c)
289. (b)	290. (c)	291. (a)	292. (d)
293. (b)	294. (c)	295. (c)	296. (c)
297. (a)	298. (a)	299. (c)	300. (d)
301 (b)	302 (b)	303 (d)	304 (b)
305 (b)	306 (a)	307 (a)	308 (c)
309 (b)	310 (c)	311 (d)	312 (a)
313 (d)	314 (d)	315 (c)	316 (a)
317 (a)	318 (c)	319 (c)	320 (a)
321 (b)	322 (c)	323 (d)	324 (b)
325 (c)	326 (a)	327 (c)	328 (a)
329 (a)	330 (d)	331 (a)	332 (b)
333 (d)	334 (a)	335 (a)	336 (c)
337 (a)	338 (c)	339 (a)	340 (d)
341 (c)	342 (a)	343 (c)	344 (d)
345 (d)	346 (a)	347 (c)	348 (b)
349 (a)	350 (c)	351. (c)	352. (a)
353. (d)	354. (c)	355. (a)	356. (c)
357. (c)	358. (d)	359. (d)	360. (d)
361. (a)	362. (b)	363. (a)	364. (c)
365. (a)	366. (c)	367. (a)	368. (b)
369. (a)	370. (c)	371. (c)	372. (c)
373. (d)	374. (c)	375. (a)	376. (d)
377. (b)	378. (b)	379. (b)	380. (d)
381. (a)	382. (c)	383. (a)	384. (c)
385. (a)	386. (a)	387. (a)	388. (c)
389. (b)	390. (b)	391. (c)	392. (d)
393. (b)	394. (a)	395. (d)	396. (b)
397. (d)	398. (b)	399. (d)	400. (a)
401. (c)	402. (b)	403. (a)	404. (b)
405. (a)	406. (b)	407. (d)	408. (c)
409. (a)	410. (a)	411. (c)	412. (b)
413. (b)	414. (c)	415. (d)	416. (b)
417. (a)	418. (d)	419. (d)	420. (c)
421. (d)	422. (b)	423. (c)	424. (a)
425. (b)	426. (c)	427. (d)	428. (d)
429. (b)	430. (a)	431. (b)	432. (b)
433. (b)	434. (d)	435. (c)	436. (a)

437.	(c)	438.	(a)	439.	(c)	440.	(d)
441.	(c)	442.	(a)	443.	(b)	444.	(a)
445.	(c)	446.	(c)	447.	(c)	448.	(c)
449.	(d)	450.	(d)	451.	(c)	452.	(a)
453.	(c)	454.	(c)	455.	(a)	456.	(d)
457.	(d)	458.	(b)	459.	(b)	460.	(d)
461.	(b)	462.	(c)	463.	(b)	464.	(b)
465.	(a)	466.	(b)	467.	(d)	468.	(d)
469.	(a)	470.	(b)	471.	(c)	472.	(b)
473.	(c)	474.	(b)	475.	(c)	476.	(b)
477.	(c)	478.	(b)	479	(a)	480	(d)
481	(c)	482	(b)	483	(c)	484	(a)
485	(d)	486	(c)	487	(c)	488	(a)
489.	(c)	490.	(a)	491.	(d)	492.	(b)
493.	(b)	494.	(b)	495.	(c)	496.	(b)
497.	(a)	498.	(d)	499.	(d)	500.	(c)
501.	(b)	502.	(b)	503.	(d)	504.	(b)
505.	(d)	506.	(c)	507.	(a)	508.	(c)
509.	(c)	510.	(b)	511.	(b)	512.	(c)
513.	(d)	514.	(a)	515.	(c)	516.	(b)
517.	(c)	518.	(a)	519.	(c)	520.	(d)
521.	(c)	522.	(c)	523.	(a)	524.	(b)
525.	(c)	526.	(c)	527.	(b)	528.	(d)
529.	(d)	530.	(b)	531.	(a)	532	(c)
533.	(b)	534.	(c)	535.	(b)	536.	(a)
537.	(c)	538.	(b)	539.	(c)	540.	(d)
541.	(a)	542.	(a)	543.	(a)	544.	(a)
545.	(a)	546.	(b)	547.	(a)	548.	(d)
549.	(b)	550.	(c)	551.	(b)	552.	(b)
553.	(c)	554.	(d)	555.	(a)	556.	(b)
557.	(d)	558.	(a)	559.	(b)	560.	(c)
561.	(a)	562.	(b)	563.	(c)	564.	(b)
565.	(d)	566.	(c)	567.	(d)	568.	(c)
569.	(a)	570.	(d)	571.	(c)	572.	(b)
573.	(c)	574.	(d)	575.	(b)	576.	(a)
577.	(b)	578.	(c)	579.	(a)	580.	(b)
581.	(c)	582.	(c)	583.	(b)	584	(b)
585.	(c)	586.	(b)	587.	(c)	588.	(d)
589.	(d)	590.	(d)	591.	(b)	592.	(d)
593.	(c)	594.	(a)	595.	(d)	596.	(c)
597.	(c)						

7
CARTOGRAPHY

1. We can determine the north direction by
   (a) The sun
   (b) With a gyrocompass
   (c) Pole star which shines vertically above the geographical North Pole
   (d) All of the above.

2. A slope which curves inwards with its lower part rising gently but its upper part abruptly is said to be
   (a) Concur scope (b) Convex scope
   (c) Oval scope (d) Uniform scope.

3. Atmospheric pressure is measured by instrument known as
   (a) Thermometer (b) Altimetre
   (c) Barometre (d) Anemometer.

4. --------are used to present the output of mining and industrial centres.
   (a) Circles (b) Block piles
   (c) Dots (d) None of the above.

5. Absolute Humidity is defined as
   (a) The amount of water vapour actually present in one cubic metre of air at a certain temperature
   (b) The degree of saturation of air
   (c) Total saturation of air
   (d) None of the above.

6. The mean monthly rainfall of a specified month is that
   (a) Total amount of rainfall for some years divided by the number of years
   (b) Average rainfall of that month over a period of atleast 15 years
   (c) Average rainfall of that month divided by the mean annual rainfall
   (d) Total rainfall for that month received by adding the rainfall for every day of the month.

7. Six's thermometer is used to measure
   (a) Minimum temperature of the day
   (b) Maximum temperature of the day
   (c) Both the maximum and minimum temperatures of the day
   (d) Mean temperature of the day.

8. Geodetic surveying
   (a) Forms the basis of topographic surveying
   (b) Is a survey of a large area
   (c) Takes into account the sphirical nature of the surface of the earth
   (d) All of the above.

9. Anemometer is used to measure
   (a) The velocity of wind
   (b) Depth of the sea-level
   (c) The velocity of light
   (d) None of the above.

10. Roads, Railways, narrow river valleys and international boundaries running in the east-west direction from long distance can be shown on
    (a) Simple conical projection with one standard parallel
    (b) Bonne's projection
    (c) Mercatar's projection
    (d) Sinusoidal projection.

11. For the countries situated away from the equator and for big countries such as Brazil crossing the equator, the sinusoidal projection is more suitable because
    (a) The scale along the parallels is correct
    (b) The shapes are preserved satisfactarily if the meridias passing through that middle part of the area is selected as the contral meridian
    (c) The distance between the parallel are also correct
    (d) All of the above.

12. Water, whether in liquid or solid forms which actually falls from the atmosphere to the surface of the earth is called
    (a) Snow (b) Precipitation
    (c) Hail storm (d) Flakes.

13. Charochromatic maps are defined as
    (a) Maps showing non-quantitative areal distributions by shading or tinting the areas
    (b) Maps showing non-quantitative areal distribution by dots
    (c) Maps showing quantitative areal distribution by shading or tinting the areas
    (d) None of the above.

14. A line which shows the rise and fall of the surface of the ground along a chosen line on a map is termed as a
    (a) Contour line (b) Terrace line
    (c) Profile (d) Isohel.

15. A small area is surveyed with the help of
    (a) Plane table
    (b) Prismatic compass
    (c) Chain and a measuring tape
    (d) All of the above.

16. Loxodrome or rhumbline is a line of constant bearing and is associated with
    (a) Bonne's projection (b) Orthomorphic projection
    (c) Mercator's projection (d) None of the above.

17. Bonne's projection is a form of
    (a) Zenithal map projection
    (b) Conical map projection
    (c) Cylindrical map projection
    (d) Equi distant map projection.

18. Which of the following is most useful for measuring the shortest distance?
    (a) Globe (b) Wall maps
    (c) Thematic maps (d) None of the above.

19. The length of 1° latitude on the ground is equal to
    (a) 111 kms. (b) 76 kms.
    (c) 222 miles (d) 24 miles.

20. Which of the following globes show temperature, atmospheric pressure and rainfall of different seasons?
    (a) Relief globes (b) Political globes
    (c) Haphazard globes (d) Climatic globes.

21. The mapping of which of the following is most difficult?
    (a) Interior of the Earth
    (b) Ocean and their depth
    (c) Mountains
    (d) Plateaus and plains.

22. Types of surface on which the parallels and meridians of a globe are transferred are
    (a) A cone (b) A plane
    (c) A cylinder (d) All of the above.

23. In Conical map projection
    (a) The distance between the meridians decrease towards the poles
    (b) The standard parallel is correct to the scale
    (c) The central meridian is a straight line
    (d) All of the above.

24. For representing the population distribution of a city, the population maps consists of
    (a) Only dots to represent both rural and urban population
    (b) Dots to represent the rural population
    (c) Spheres to represent the population of urban centres
    (d) Both (b) and (c).

25. For enlargement and reduction of maps, instruments used are
    (a) Episcope (b) Pantograph
    (c) Photo camera (d) All of the above.

26. A climate graph in which data pertaining to two climatic elements of a place are plotted against each other is known as
    (a) Climograph (b) Hythergraph
    (c) Erograph (d) All of the above.

27. Main short comings of the scale for representing the ground distance is
    (a) That the fractional distance involve mathematical calculations
    (b) That since different countries have different units of length in use, the statement of scale may not be understood by the foreigners
    (c) Both (a) and (b)
    (d) None of the above.

28. A Hythergraph is defined as
    (a) A graph representing the nature of work done during the various periods of time of a year
    (b) A graph which means monthly temperature is plotted against the monthly rainfall
    (c) A graph in which data pertaining to two climatic elements of a place are plotted against each other
    (d) None of the above.

29. In topographic map direction is usually measured
   (a) Anti-clockwise from north
   (b) Anti-clockwise from south
   (c) Clockwise from north
   (d) Clockwise from south.

30. In an Orthomorphic projection
   (a) The scale along the parallel and meridians is same at a point
   (b) The parallels and the meridians intersect each other at a right angles
   (c) Both (a) and (b)
   (d) None of the above.

31. Large scale maps are
   (a) Topographical maps (b) Plans
   (c) Padastral maps (d) All of the above.

32. Maps used for air and marine navigation are better known as
   (a) Plans (b) Details
   (c) Chart (d) Perune maps.

33. the axis of our earth is inclined at an angle of ------- to that plane of ecliptic and passes through the centre of the earth.
   (a) 72-1/2° (b) 66-1/2°
   (c) 49-1/2° (d) 23-1/2°.

34. A scale may be expressed as
   (a) A fraction
   (b) A line divided into certain parts
   (c) In words
   (d) All of the above.

35. The globe which represents the earth is
   (a) Terrestrical globe (b) Operational globe
   (c) Operational globe (d) None of the above.

36. Planimeter is an instrument used to measure

(a) The area of the given map
(b) The lengthwise distance on the map
(c) The height of an undulated area in the map
(d) None of the above.

37. Short disconnected lines drawn in the direction in which the water would flow that is down the direction of the steepest slope are termed as
(a) Hachures (b) Bench marks
(c) Contour (d) Markers.

38. A line on a map connecting all points of the same depth below the mean sea level is called on
(a) Isobath (b) Isobar
(c) Isotherm (d) None of the above.

39. Isopleths are used
(a) To prepare maps showing density of population per square kilometre
(b) To show percentage e.g. percentage of area under what to the total cropped area
(c) For showing the distribution of temperature, rainfall and atmospheric pressure
(d) All of the above.

40. Which of the following statements is incorrect?
(a) Anti cyclones develop in India during the winter season
(b) A thermal cyclone develops in north-western India during the summer season
(c) In a weather map 'cal' in an area lying between two cyclones and two anticyclones
(d) None of the above.

41. Diagramatic maps are those distribution maps on which the regional variations in distribution of an element are shown by
(a) Squares and circles
(b) Bars
(c) Cubes, block piles and spheres
(d) All of the above.

42. A gunturs chain has a length of
   (a) 66 feet (b) 106 feet
   (c) 115 feet (d) 92 feet.

43. Points marked north, south, east and west on a mariner's compass are known as
   (a) Relative points (b) Intermediate points
   (c) Cardinal points (d) Central locus points.

44. The maps showing variations in the distribution of the value of an element by symbols such as dots, lines, a range of shading squares, circles and spheres are called
   (a) Quantitative areal distribution maps
   (b) Choropleth maps
   (c) Diagrammatic maps
   (d) Maps showing non-quantitative areal distribution by dots.

45. A contour may be defined as
   (a) A line on a map connecting all adjacent points of the same height above the mean sea level
   (b) A line on a map connecting all points of the same depth below the mean sea level
   (c) A line on a map connecting all points of different depths below the mean sea level
   (d) A line on a map connecting all points of different height above the mean sea level.

46. Projection in which the surface a plane placed tangentially at a pole of the globe and the 'view point' at the centre of the globe is termed as
   (a) Gromonic projection
   (b) Stenographic projection
   (c) Orthomorphic projection
   (d) None of the above.

47. A bearing is described as
   (a) An angle measured clockwise from a north-south line to a line connecting the observer's position with the object

(b) An angle measured anticlockwise from a east-west line to a line connecting the observer's position with the object
(c) An angle measured linear way from east-west line to a line opposite connecting the observer's position with the object
(d) None of the above.

48. Relief features are represented on maps by
(a) Hill shading and layer
(b) Statures
(c) Contours and formliness
(d) All of the above.

49. The mapping of which of the following is supposed to be most difficult?
(a) Mountains (b) Plateaus and plains
(c) Interior of the earth (d) Ocean and its depth.

50. A Zenithal projection is defined as a projection developed on a
(a) Plane (b) Rhombus
(c) Square (d) Rectangle.

ANSWERS

1.	(d)	2.	(a)	3.	(c)	4.	(b)
5.	(a)	6.	(a)	7.	(c)	8.	(d)
9.	(a)	10.	(a)	11.	(d)	12.	(b)
13.	(a)	14.	(c)	15.	(d)	16.	(c)
17.	(b)	18.	(a)	19.	(a)	20.	(d)
21.	(a)	22.	(d)	23.	(d)	24.	(d)
25.	(d)	26.	(a)	27.	(c)	28.	(b)
29.	(c)	30.	(c)	31.	(d)	32.	(c)
33.	(b)	34.	(d)	35.	(a)	36.	(a)
37.	(a)	38.	(a)	39.	(d)	40.	(d)
41.	(d)	42.	(a)	43.	(c)	44.	(a)
45.	(a)	46.	(a)	47.	(a)	48.	(d)
49.	(c)	50.	(a)				

SET 1
ASSESS YOURSELF

1. Between which one of the following pairs of Ports does Panama canal shorten the distance to the maximum?
   (a) New York and San Francisco
   (b) Liverpool and Sydney
   (c) New York and Honolulu
   (d) Liverpool and Shanghai.

2. Two states were locked in dispute over the installation of creat gates in the Almatti Dam. The states in question include
   (a) Karnataka and Maharashtra
   (b) Tamil Nadu and Kerala
   (c) Andhra Pradesh and Karnataka
   (d) Andhra Pradesh and Maharashtra.

3. Which one of the following statements concerning weathering and erosion is correct?
   (a) Both erosion and weathering are static processes
   (b) Weathering is a static process while erosion is not
   (c) Weathering as a process follows the process of erosion
   (d) Erosion is a static process while weathering is not.

4. The production of rubber tree is better adapted to areas where the climate is
   (a) warm and dry (b) warm and humid
   (c) cool and dry (d) cool and moist.

5. The planets are kept in motion in their respective orbits by the
   (a) Rotation of the sun on its axis
   (b) Great size and spherical shape
   (c) Gravitation and centrifugal forces
   (d) Rotation and the density of the planets.

6. The doubling period of population is the lowest in
   (a) Iran (b) Egypt
   (c) Pakistan (d) Bangladesh.

7. The correct sequence in the decending order of given countries in terms of life expectancy at birth is
   (a) Sri Lanka, India, China, Pakistan
   (b) Sri Lanka, China, Pakistan, India
   (c) China, India, Sri Lanka, Pakistan
   (d) China, Sri Lanka, Pakistan, India.

8. Human activities are conditioned and sometimes determined by biophysical environment is related to the doctrine of
   (a) Possibilism
   (b) Neo-determinism
   (c) Determinism
   (d) Humanism.

9. Which one of the following geographical conditions makes hunting and fishing the principal means of livelihood in the Tundre region?
   (a) Harsh climate
   (b) Sparse population
   (c) Infertile dissected terrain
   (d) Scarcity of vegetation.

10. The term 'Megalopolis' for the description of urban pattern of north-eastern seaboard of the USA was first introduced by
    (a) Jean Guttman (b) C.D Harris
    (c) David Harvey (d) Brian Berry.

11. The development of synclinal ridges and anticlinal valleys in a folded region is named as
    (a) abrasion platform
    (b) mentle and core
    (c) parallel belt of valleys and ridges
    (d) ridge and valley landscape.

12. The correct sequence (from the oldest to the youngest) of different periods of tertiary epoch is
    (a) Pliocene, Miocene, Eocene, Oligocene
    (b) Ecocene, Oligocene, Miocene, Pliocene
    (c) Ecocene, Oligocene, Pliocene, Miocene
    (d) Pliocene, Eocene, Miocene, Oligocene.

13. Radiolarian oozes occur in depths of
    (a) 2000 to 5000 fathoms
    (b) 5000 to 6000 fathoms
    (c) 600 to 1200 fathoms
    (d) 1500 to 200 fathoms.

14. The state of inactivity adopted by desert animals during the hottest and driest season is known as
    (a) hibernation
    (b) dormancy
    (c) aestivation
    (d) basal metabolism.

15. The first scholar to formulate the laws of migration was
    (a) Lee, E. (b) Kosinski, G.A.
    (c) Revenstein, E.G. (d) Zenkiusky, W.

16. Location of sugar industry in India is shifting from north to south because of
    (a) Cheap labour
    (b) Expanding regional market
    (c) Cheap and abundant supply of power
    (d) High yield and high sugar content in sugarcane.

17. Which one of the following statements about KOYALI is correct?

    It is a/an/the

    (a) Hydroelectric plant in Uttar Pradesh
    (b) Historic-cultural tourist centre in Rajasthan
    (c) Oil Refinery located in Gujarat
    (d) Site of steel plant under corporation in M.P.

18. Give one word that can be used for the geography of areas above sea level and their mapping

    (a) Oceanography (b) Oceanology
    (c) Hypography (d) Hydrology.

19. By what name we refer to the write spot or streak of the surface of the sun?

    (a) Facula (b) Flora
    (c) Flarica (d) Face.

20. Noho discontinuity is found between the

    (a) Mantle and core
    (b) Crust and mantle
    (c) Inner core and Outer core
    (d) Upper mantle and lower mantle.

21. Which one of the following pairs of lands is separated from each other by the ten degree channel?

    (a) Andman and Nicobar
    (b) Nicobar and Sumatra
    (c) Maldives and Lakshadweep
    (d) Sumatra and Java.

22. The correct sequence (in descending order) of exports of the given commodities from South-east Asia region is

    (a) Palm oil, rubber, copra, sugar
    (b) Rubber, Copra, palm oil, sugar
    (c) Rubber, palm oil, sugar, copra
    (d) Palm oil, sugar, rubber, copra.

23. The Dichotomy of general geography and special geography was advocated by
    (a) Alexander Von Humbol
    (b) Alfred Hettner
    (c) Elisee Reclus
    (d) B. Varenius.

24. While explaining the relation between nature and man, Blache cited the instance of the tradition of a regional concept of France known as
    (a) Pays (b) Functional region
    (c) Formal region (d) Compage.

25. The term 'Anthropogeographic' coined by Ratzel and was used by him for the
    (a) Geography of man and his works in relation to earth's surface
    (b) Geography of man in terms of individuals and races
    (c) Organic theory of society and state
    (d) Study of harmonious reciprocal relation of man and nature.

26. India's Eastern Ghats and Western Ghats met at the
    (a) Cardomom hills (b) Annamalai hills
    (c) Nilgiri hills (d) Palani hills.

27. During winter, north-western part of India gets rainfall from
    (a) Thunder storm (b) Tropical cyclones
    (c) Western disturbances (d) Retreating monsoon.

28. Which one of the following characteristics is not relevant to Ganga river?
    (a) It is a broaded river with numerous channels
    (b) It has multiple inter-twined sand bars
    (c) It deposits enormous sediments annually into the Bay of Bengal
    (d) It has extensive gullf erosion.

29. Which one of the following problems is NOT encountered in Indira Gandhi Canal command area?
    (a) Progressive waterlogging
    (b) Increase in soil salinity
    (c) Aeolian silting of the canal
    (d) Decline of water supply.

30. Which hill-tract in India receives the maximum rainfall?
    (a) Jayanti Hills (b) Khasi Hills
    (c) Aravali Hills (d) Nilgiri Hills.

31. Chandigarh is located at the foot of the
    (a) Khasi hills (b) Nilgiri hills
    (c) Shivalik hills (d) Greater Himalyas

32. From land-mass point of view India's position in the world is
    (a) Sixth (b) Seventh
    (c) Fifth (d) Fourth.

33. The maximum percentage of tribal population in India consists of
    (a) Urano (b) Munde
    (c) Santhals (d) Khasi.

34. The Line demarcating the boundary between India and China is the
    (a) Mac Mohan Line (b) Red Cliff Line
    (c) 17th Parallel Line (d) 18th Parallel Line.

35. The Hirakud project on Mahanadi is located in state of
    (a) Orissa (b) M.P.
    (c) U.P. (d) Karnataka.

36. The Bhakra Nangal project is built on the river
    (a) Vyas (b) Sutlej
    (c) Ravi (d) Jhelum.

37. Through which Indian state does river Chenab pass
    (a) Punjab (b) Bihar
    (c) Jammu and Kashmir (d) Uttar Pradesh.

38. Rocks formed inside the earth as a result of solidification of lava are called
    (a) Igneous rock (b) Metamorphic rock
    (c) Plurtonic rock (d) Volcanic rock.

39. Nepanagar in Madhya Pradesh is famous for
    (a) Watch (b) Newsprint paper
    (c) Fertilizer (d) Cloth.

40. The Gondwana coalfields are found in
    (a) Madhya Pradesh (b) Uttar Pradesh
    (c) Himachal Pradesh (d) Punjab.

41. The South-West Monsoon end in India in
    (a) October (b) November
    (c) December (d) September.

42. The 'Khetri Project' in Rajasthan is for the production of
    (a) Dimond (b) Gold
    (c) Copper (d) Silver.

43. Mt. Abu in Rajasthan is famous for
    (a) Dilwara temple (b) Ganesh tample
    (c) Goddess temple (d) Borobudur temple.

44. The Ghana Bird sanctuary is located in
    (a) Kerala (b) Assam
    (c) Rajasthan (d) Uttar Pradesh.

45. Ferozabad is famous for
    (a) Glass bangles (b) Leather goods
    (c) Cotton cloth (d) Toys.

46. The potential oil sources in India are in
    (a) Assam and Gujarat
    (b) Gujarat and Maharashtra
    (c) Tamil Nadu, Assam and Gujarat
    (d) None of the above.

47. In jute production India occupies the
    (a) First position (b) Second position
    (c) Third position (d) Fourth position.

48. The most developed industry in Bihar is
    (a) Steel (b) Iron
    (c) Coal (d) Copper.

49. Jog falls is associated with river
    (a) Mahanadi (b) Narmada
    (c) Brahmaputra (d) Sharavati.

50. Black Pagoda is situated in
    (a) Konark (b) Agra
    (c) Mahabalipuram (d) Goa.

ANSWERS

1.	(a)	2.	(c)	3.	(a)	4.	(b)
5.	(c)	6.	(a)	7.	(b)	8.	(b)
9.	(c)	10.	(a)	11.	(b)	12.	(b)
13.	(a)	14.	(c)	15.	(c)	16.	(d)
17.	(c)	18.	(c)	19.	(a)	20.	(b)
21.	(a)	22.	(b)	23.	(d)	24.	(a)
25.	(b)	26.	(c)	27.	(c)	28.	(d)
29.	(d)	30.	(b)	31.	(c)	32.	(b)
33.	(c)	34.	(a)	35.	(a)	36.	(b)
37.	(c)	38.	(c)	39.	(b)	40.	(a)
41.	(b)	42.	(c)	43.	(a)	44.	(b)
45.	(a)	46.	(c)	47.	(b)	48.	(a)
49.	(d)	50.	(a)				

SET 2
ASSESS YOURSELF

1. The Amul cooperative diary is located in
   (a) Punjab (b) Haryana
   (c) Anand (d) None of the above.
2. The direction of the monsoons of the Arabian sea branch is from
   (a) Southern trip (b) Southern trip to east
   (c) Both (a) and (b) (d) None of the above.
3. The biggest oil refinery in India is located in
   (a) Barauni (b) Koyali
   (c) Assam (d) Bombay High.
4. Lines joining places experiencing a Thunderstorm at the same time are known as
   (a) Isobront (b) Isobar
   (c) Isotop (d) Isotherm.
5. Anglo-Nubion is a breed of
   (a) Sheep (b) Goat
   (c) Poultry (d) Cattle.
6. Where is Lake superior, the largest freshwater lake in the world located?
   (a) Canada (b) France
   (c) USA (d) Brazil.

7. The term "Petroleum" owes its origin to which of the following pair of words ?
   (a) Petrol and Oil (b) Petro and Oil
   (c) Petro and Oleum (d) None of the above.

8. Petroleum is ----- than water and ----- in it.
   (a) heavier, soluble (b) heavier, insoluble
   (c) lighter, insoluble (d) lighter, insoluble.

9. Ankleshwar oilfield in Gujarat was discovered in the year
   (a) 1950 (b) 1952
   (c) 1955 (d) 1958.

10. Natural Gas consists mainly of
    (a) Methane (b) Burane
    (c) Propane (d) Ethane.

11. A device used for measuring the depth of the sea is called
    (a) Hydrometer (b) Manometer
    (c) Fathometer (d) Altimeter.

12. The process in which is solid substance on being heated, changes directly into gaseous state is known as
    (a) Evaporation (b) Sublimation
    (c) Dissolution (d) Dissociation.

13. One Astronomical unit is the average distance between
    (a) Earth and the Sun
    (b) Earth and the Moon
    (c) Jupiter and the Sun
    (d) Pluto and the Sun.

14. The order of layers in the atmosphere upwards from below is
    (a) Troposphere, stratosphere, ionosphere and exosphere
    (b) Stratosphere, troposphere, ionosphere and exosphere
    (c) exosphere, ionosphere, troposphere and stratosphere
    (d) troposphere, magnetosphere, stratosphere and exosphere.

15. Which one of the following types of erosion is responsible for the formation of Chambal Ravines?
    (a) Splash (b) Rill
    (c) Sheet (d) Gully.

16. The variety of coffee largely grown in India is
    (a) Old chicks (b) Kents
    (c) Coorgs (d) Arabica.

17. The asteroids revolve round the sun is between
    (a) Earth and Mars (b) Mars and Jupiter
    (c) Saturn and Uranus (d) Jupiter and Saturn.

18. A rare and endangered animal is silent valley is
    (a) Lion-tailed macaque (b) Rhinoceros
    (c) Tiger (d) Musk deer.

19. What is the Mascot of World Wild lLife found?
    (a) Tiger (b) Bear
    (c) Deer (d) Panda.

20. The sun appears deep orange-red before it sets because
    (a) It is hotter at the end of the day
    (b) It emits only orange-red light
    (c) Is contains more helium in the evening
    (d) Its light has to travel a thicker atmosphere therefore, other colours get scattered and do not reach us.

21. The oil refineries at Digboi (Assam), Barauni (Bihar), Haldia (West Bengal) and Mathura (Uttar Pradesh) are owned by
    (a) Indo-Burma Petroleum
    (b) Bharat Petroleum Corporation
    (c) Indian Oil Corporation
    (d) None of these.

22. Which of the following districts is on the international border of India?
    (a) West Khasi hills (b) Kinnaur
    (c) Gorakhpur (d) Kullu.

23. Laterite soil develops as a result of
   (a) deposits of alluvial
   (b) deposits of loess
   (c) leaching
   (d) continued vegetation cover.

24. The foodchains refers to the transfer of energy from
   (a) The interior of the earth to the surface
   (b) Lower to higher latitudes
   (c) One organism to another
   (d) Organism of the/and to those of the sea by means of river.

25. In which year the first refinery was set up in India?
   (a) 1877 (b) 1883
   (c) 1888 (d) 1892.

26. In which year the Oil and Natural Gas Commission, which has now been rechristened as Oil and Natural Gas Corporation, was created?
   (a) 1956 (b) 1958
   (c) 1960 (d) 1961.

27. The gross import of crude oil and petroleum products during the year 1998-99 was
   (a) 54.024 million metric tonnes
   (b) 56.40 million metric tonnes
   (c) 57.65 million metric tonnes
   (d) 58.59 million metric tonnes.

28. In which year the Mathura Refinery was commisioned?
   (a) 1978 (b) 1980
   (c) 1982 (d) 1984.

29. Nunmati Refinery near Guwahati was set up by the Indian Refineries Limited in the year ?
   (a) 1958 (b) 1960
   (c) 1962 (d) 1970.

30. Koyali Oil refinery is situated in the State of
    (a) Rajasthan (b) Bihar
    (c) Gujarat (d) None of these.

31. Which of the following pairs is NOT the products of the fractional distillation of crude petroleum oil
    (a) Fuel oil and Lubricating oil
    (b) Kerosene oil and Diesel oil
    (c) Wax and Asphalt
    (d) Gypsum and Carbon lumps.

32. Which of the following is not a petrochemical?
    (a) Ethylene (b) Benzene
    (c) Butadiene (d) None of the above.

33. The petroleum resources are found primarily in
    (a) Sedimentary rocks (b) Red sandstone
    (c) Metamorphic rocks (d) None of these.

34. In which region can be the phenomenon of Midnight Sun be observed
    (a) In the Arctic and Antarctic regions
    (b) Anywhere at the time of solar eclipse
    (c) In warm temperate regions
    (d) In the tropical zone.

35. The caloritic value at Natural Gas is
    (a) 58 KJ/gm (b) 59 KJ /gm
    (c) 55 KJ/gm (d) 15 KJ /gm.

36. The Hindustan Petroleum Corporation Limited (HPCL) was setup on
    (a) August 15, 1974 (b) July 15, 1974
    (c) August 15, 1976 (d) None of these.

37. Petroleum gas is a mixture of which of following combinations of hydrocarbons
    (a) Methane, Ethane and Methane
    (b) Butane, Ethylene and Propane
    (c) Butane, Propane and Ethane
    (d) None of these.

38. The Gas Authority of India (GAIL) has set up a state-of-art Gas Technology Institute, in collaboration with DANIDA, at
   (a) Gandhar (b) Usar
   (c) Vaghtiodia (d) Noida.

39. In which year the Government of India did introduce the parallel marketing of LPG and kerosene by private parties?
   (a) 1993 (b) 1994
   (c) 1995 (d) 1996.

40. The Indian Oil Corporation was set up by amalgamating Indian Refinery Limited with Indian Oil Company in the year
   (a) 1964 (b) 1965
   (c) 1966 (d) 1967.

41. The production of natural gas in 1998-99 was
   (a) 28,298 billion cubic metres
   (b) 38,314 billion cubic metres
   (c) 37,724 billion cubic metres
   (d) 27,427 billion cubic metres.

42. Which one is an anticyclone
   (a) Low pressure system with clockwise winds in the southern hemisphere
   (b) Low pressure system with clockwise winds in the northern hemisphere
   (c) High pressure system with clockwise winds in the northern hemisphere
   (d) None of these.

43. Name of most tropical country of Africa Continent
   (a) Zaire
   (b) Botswana
   (c) Rawanda
   (d) Tanzania.

44. What is Chromosphere?
    (a) Middle of the earth
    (b) Middle region of earth atmosphere
    (c) Middle region of sun's atmosphere
    (d) Outer region of moon.

45. Name the part of the earth where rice diet is believed to be originated
    (a) East India (b) Southern India
    (c) Central India (d) Eastern India.

46. Which ones are wrongly matched?
    1. Typhoons - China Sea
    2. Hurricanes - Indian Ocean
    3. Cyclones - West Indies
    4. Tornadoes - Australia
    (a) 1, 2 and 3 (b) 2, 3 and 4
    (c) 1, 2 and 4 (d) 1, 3 and 4.

47. Which of the alternatives is/are correctly matched?
    (a) Gonds - Africa
    (b) Lapps India
    (c) Oran - Norway
    (d) Eskimo - Canada.

48. During the period of the South-West Monsoon, Tamil Nadu remains dry because
    (a) The winds do not reach this area
    (b) There are no mountains in this area
    (c) It lies in the rain-shadow area
    (d) The temperature is too high to let the winds cool down.

49. Which one of the natural regions is known as the "Breadbasket of the world"?
    (a) The Steppe region
    (b) The Monsoon region
    (c) The Mediterranean region
    (d) The Equatorial region.

50. Which of the following is not true regarding production of tea in India?
    (a) The east and the north-east states account for 82% of the total tea growing area in India
    (b) India is the largest producer of tea in the world
    (c) Indian tea is not found suitable for export as the quality is far inferior to the Kenyan tea
    (d) The total production of tea in India was about 76000 tonnes during 1995.

ANSWERS

1.	(c)	2.	(a)	3.	(b)	4.	(a)
5.	(a)	6.	(c)	7.	(c)	8.	(d)
9.	(d)	10.	(a)	11.	(c)	12.	(b)
13.	(a)	14.	(a)	15.	(d)	16.	(d)
17.	(b)	18.	(a)	19.	(d)	20.	(d)
21.	(c)	22.	(a)	23.	(d)	24.	(c)
25.	(b)	26.	(a)	27.	(d)	28.	(c)
29.	(c)	30.	(a)	31.	(d)	32.	(d)
33.	(a)	34.	(c)	35.	(c)	36.	(b)
37.	(c)	38.	(d)	39.	(a)	40.	(a)
41.	(d)	42.	(c)	43.	(a)	44.	(c)
45.	(b)	46.	(b)	47.	(d)	48.	(c)
49.	(a)	50.	(c)				

SET 3
ASSESS YOURSELF

1. Which among the following is known as the 'King of Fibre' ?
   (a) Jute (b) Cotton
   (c) Silk (d) Wool.

2. In the monsoonal agriculture, the yield per acre is remarkably low due to the
   (a) Inadequate use of fertilizers, chemicals and high variety of seeds
   (b) Uncertainty of rainfall and inadequate irrigational facilities
   (c) Traditional method of agriculture on small plots of land
   (d) All of the above.

3. In Japan only 15 to 17% of the total land area is available for agriculture because
   (a) Most of the land in Japan is used for setting up industries
   (b) Agriculture is not encouraged in Japan
   (c) Both (a) and (b)
   (d) The mountain terrain highlands and unfavourable topographical features greatly restricts agricultural practices.

4. Crops like tea and coffee thrive best on the
   (a) low lands (b) plain lands
   (c) coastal grounds (d) elevated grounds.

5. Wool, flax, silk come under the category of
   - (a) Cereals
   - (b) Raw materials
   - (c) Beverages
   - (d) Fibres.

6. Malaya is the biggest producer of ------in the world.
   - (a) Copper
   - (b) Bronze
   - (c) Tin
   - (d) Silver.

7. Which of the following are the principal pastoral nomadic tribes of Central Asia?
   - (a) Kazakhs
   - (b) Kirghiz
   - (c) Both (a) and (b)
   - (d) None of these.

8. Khosisan language family is found only in
   - (a) North Africa
   - (b) South Western Africa
   - (c) Parts of South America
   - (d) Madagascar Island.

9. Human population is very much limited in
   - (a) Cold deserts
   - (b) Marshy lands
   - (c) Hot deserts
   - (d) All of the above.

10. Which island is most densely populated in the world
    - (a) Madagascar
    - (b) Kurile
    - (c) Bermuda
    - (d) Java.

11. Which of the following is known as leading steel production district of Great Britain?
    - (a) Birmingham
    - (b) South Wales
    - (c) Sheffield
    - (d) Dover.

12. Which of the following leads in the world's total production of rubber?
    - (a) India
    - (b) Sri lanka
    - (c) Malaysia
    - (d) Burma.

13. The best example of a large scale rehabilitation become of the soils is provided by the
    (a) D.V.C. (b) T.V.A.
    (c) G.V.C. (d) T.A.
14. A porous, sandy, well aerated soil is essential for the cultivation of
    (a) Ground nuts (b) Maize
    (c) Millets (d) Mustard.
15. Jutes are grown best in the
    (a) Deltas (b) Swampy Deltas
    (c) Sea-Shore (d) Flooded-river.
16. Which among the following south-east Asian countries has the highest density of population?
    (a) Burma (b) Singapore
    (c) Indonesia (d) Malaysia.
17. Though the cast iron is quite hard and tough but breaks easily because of
    (a) It contains many types of impurities like carbon, silicon
    (b) Coke composition is very low
    (c) Both (a) and (b)
    (d) None of these.
18. The Ruhr basin, which is very rich in coal fields is located in
    (a) France (b) Germany
    (c) Great Britain (d) Holland.
19. The largest producer of wood pulp is
    (a) Canada (b) U.S.A.
    (c) China (d) Chille.
20. Chicago, Colombo, Delhi comes under the strategic location
    (a) Portal (b) Nodal
    (c) Local (d) None of these.

21. Who is the author of the book "Anthopo G eography"?
    (a) Friedrich Ratzel (b) D. Morris
    (c) William Blake (d) Renner.

22. Which of the following regions of USA is not an industrial region?
    (a) Ohio
    (b) New Castle and its adjoining areas
    (c) New York
    (d) Detroit.

23. The iron and steel industries of -------- is by and large dependent on imported raw materials.
    (a) Japan (b) Great Britain
    (c) France (d) Germany.

24. Which of the following countries is the richest coal producing nation in Europe?
    (a) West Germany (b) France
    (c) Great Britain (d) Holland.

25. According to Cuvier, the Caucasoid race is
    (a) Black coloured (b) White coloured
    (c) Brown coloured (d) Pink coloured.

26. Whose classification of human races is based on skull measurements?
    (a) Ronald Raven (b) Ronald Divon
    (c) Victor Parez (d) Ronald James.

27. The belief in the existence of one God is termed as
    (a) Mohotholeism (b) Mohotheism
    (c) Binotheism (d) None of these.

28. There is only one language in Europe preserved from the period prior to the Indo-European invasion. The particular language is
    (a) Braque (b) Polish
    (c) Pasture (d) None of these.

29. Which of the following is the largest rubber manufacturing centre of the world?
    (a) Arkon (b) Sicily
    (c) Kolkatta (d) Ohio.

30. Natural polymers are the fibers developed from
    (a) Cellulose and proteins (b) Oil and natural gas
    (c) Coal (d) Iron ore.

31. The temperate grasslands of Asia and Europe are known as
    (a) Veldt (b) Steppes
    (c) Campos (d) Pampas.

32. Crude petroleum is carried from the wells to the refineries mainly through
    (a) Tankers (b) Pipelines
    (c) Airways (d) None of these.

33. Among which of the following Biotic resources are obatined?
    (a) Ionsphere (b) Biosphere
    (c) Stratosphere (d) Lithosphere.

34. Half of the World's Cocoa comes from
    (a) East•Africa (b) Cental Africa
    (c) West Africa (d) East Europe.

35. The European coal and steel community was formed after the
    (a) World War II (b) Year 1982
    (c) World War I (d) Americans put obstacles.

36. After smelting iron ore with coke in a blast furnace, the resultant molten iron is known as
    (a) Pig iron (b) Pure iron
    (c) Tough iron (d) Cast iron.

37. Reafforestation helps to conserve one of the richest natural resources
    (a) Mica (b) Timber
    (c) Coal (d) Spices.

38. A type of Jungle 'Selvas' is related to
    (a) Amazon basin
    (b) Gangetic basin
    (c) Nile basin
    (d) Congo basin.

39. The classic example of fragmented form is
    (a) Canada (b) India
    (c) Nepal (d) Japan.

40. The theory of industrial location on the basis of empirical data was propounded by
    (a) Alfred Weber (b) Max Weber
    (c) G. Taylor (d) E. Durkheim.

41. Though Amazon basin has tremendous potential for rubber production, but can not compete with the south-east Asian countries due to
    (a) Low availability of labour due to sparse population
    (b) Wild diseases is a great hindrance
    (c) Rubber trees are widely scattered in deep dense forest of the Amazon
    (d) All of the above.

42. Truck farming refers to
    (a) Vegetable crops for marketing
    (b) Cultivation of spices
    (c) Cultivation of cereals
    (d) All of the above.

43. A porous, sandy well aerated soil is essential for the cultivation of
    (a) Ground nuts (b) Mustard
    (c) Maize (d) Millets.

44. The moisture-retentive loamy or clayey soils are best suited for the cultivation of
    (a) Rice (b) Maize
    (c) Ground nuts (d) None.

45. Major products of horticulture includes
    - (a) Fruits and flowers
    - (b) Pulses
    - (c) Vegetables and spices
    - (d) All of the above.

46. Pelagic fishes are found in
    - (a) Open oceans
    - (b) Ponds
    - (c) Small rivers
    - (d) Small artificial lakes.

47. Japan is the leading fishing nation in
    - (a) North-West Pacific region
    - (b) North-West Atlantic region
    - (c) North-East Pacific region
    - (d) None of these.

48. Pigmy tribes are found in
    - (a) Central Africa
    - (b) Northern Burma
    - (c) India
    - (d) Eastern China.

49. Nomadic herding is a subsistence economic activity in
    - (a) The region extending from 5° south latitude to 5° north latitude
    - (b) Southern extent of the Tundra in Eurasia
    - (c) South-West Africa and Western part of Malaria
    - (d) All of the above.

50. ABO is a type of blood group that do not exist in
    - (a) Human race
    - (b) Animals
    - (c) Mammals
    - (d) Cold blooded animals.

ANSWERS

1.	(b)	2.	(d)	3.	(d)	4.	(d)
5.	(d)	6.	(c)	7.	(c)	8.	(b)
9.	(d)	10.	(d)	11.	(b)	12.	(c)
13.	(b)	14.	(a)	15.	(b)	16.	(b)
17.	(a)	18.	(b)	19.	(b)	20.	(c)

21.	(a)	22.	(b)	23.	(a)	24.	(a)
25.	(b)	26.	(b)	27.	(b)	28.	(a)
29.	(a)	30.	(a)	31.	(b)	32.	(b)
33.	(b)	34.	(c)	35.	(a)	36.	(a)
37.	(b)	38.	(a)	39.	(d)	40.	(a)
41.	(d)	42.	(a)	43.	(a)	44.	(a)
45.	(a)	46.	(a)	47.	(a)	48.	(a)
49.	(d)	50.	(a)				

SET 4
ASSESS YOURSELF

1. Lake Eyre is the lowest point of
   (a) Africa (b) Europe
   (c) North America (d) Oceania.

2. Which of the following rivers is older than Himalaya
   (a) Yamuna (b) Sutlej
   (c) Ganga (d) Kali.

3. Anchorage city is situated in
   (a) Iceland (b) Greenland
   (c) Siberia (d) Alaska.

4. Which of the following is not a commerical crop?
   (a) Spices (b) Sugarcane
   (c) Oilseeds (d) Cotton.

5. Largest ship canal of the world is
   (a) Gota (b) Panama
   (c) Suez (d) Kiel.

6. Which of the following is not a tributary of Indus
   (a) Ravi (b) Luni
   (c) Beas (d) Jhelum.

7. The length of the HBJ pipe line is
   (a) 1200 km (b) 1500 km
   (c) 1700 km (d) 1000 km.

8. Which of the following glacier is not in the Ladakh range
   (a) Hinarchi (b) Siachin
   (c) Punmesh (d) Baltora.

9. The Nicobar group containing several Islands extends between
   (a) 6° to 12° (b) 6° to 10°
   (c) 5° 30' to 9° 30' (d) 6.30° to 9.30°.

10. At each trophic levee, about how much energy is wasted
   (a) 60% (b) 70%
   (c) 90% (d) 80%.

11. Which state is leading producer of tobacco in India
   (a) Tamil Nadu (b) Gujarat
   (c) Andhra Pradesh (d) Karnataka.

12. Which of the following dam is not related to Chambal project
   (a) Konar Dam (b) Rana Pratap Sagar
   (c) Kota Barrage (d) Sagar Dam.

13. The houses made by the bushmen of Kalahari is known as
   (a) Igloo (b) Masai
   (c) Wurlies (d) Sherms.

14. The Karewa formation in Kashmir is of
   (a) Eucene age (b) Pleistocene age
   (c) Oligocene age (d) Miocene age.

15. Ice-caps are confined to
   (a) Siberia (b) Greenland
   (c) Northern Canada (d) Iceland.

16. National Tea Research Laboratory is in
   (a) Siliguri (b) Darjeeling
   (c) Jorhat (d) Kolkatta.

17. Central Power Research Institute is located in
   (a) Bangalore (b) Nagpur
   (c) Durgapur (d) Singrauli.

18. Which state in the country has highest road length?
   (a) M.P. (b) U.P.
   (c) Andhra Pradesh (d) Maharashtra.

19. Which is the second largest basin of all the Indian rivers?
   (a) Ganga (b) Godawari
   (c) Cauvery (d) Narmada.

20. Which is the second largest river of Africa
   (a) Zambezi (b) Zaire
   (c) Niger (d) Orange.

21. Azores is in the mid-oceanic ridge of
   (a) Arctic ocean (b) Pacific ocean
   (c) Indian ocean (d) Atlantic ocean.

22. Blue Ridge mountains are found in
   (a) Sweden (b) Finland
   (c) USA (d) Canada.

23. Atacama desert is situated in
   (a) South America (b) Australia
   (c) North America (d) Africa.

24. Which is the leading ship building state of Europe?
   (a) Germany (b) U.K.
   (c) France (d) Sweden.

25. Largest island of Japan is
   (a) Honshu (b) Hokkaido
   (c) Shikoku (d) Kyoshu.

26. The height of thunderstorms may vary from
   (a) 20-40 km (b) 10-50 m
   (c) 4-20 km (d) 100-500 m.

27. The origin of the simplest life is attributed to
   (a) Cambrian Era (b) Archaezoic Era
   (c) Proterzoic Era (d) Carboniferous Era.

28. Which of the following sea has greatest depth?
    (a) Caribbean Sea (b) Gulf of Mexico
    (c) Beriong Sea (d) Mediterranean Sea.

29. Which is the highest waterfall of the France?
    (a) Staubbach (b) Ribbon falls
    (c) Gavarnie (d) Mardola.

30. Which is the largest producer of sugarbeet?
    (a) China (b) USA
    (c) Turkey (d) Russia.

31. Soil contain
    (a) Nitrogen (b) Oxygen
    (c) Carbon di-oxide (d) All of the above.

32. The longest National Highway of India is
    (a) N.H. 2 (b) N.H.1
    (c) N.H. 7 (d) N.H. 6.

33. Which is the largest producer of Mica?
    (a) India (b) Russia
    (c) China (d) Turkey.

34. The intensity of the Insolation depends upon
    (a) longitude (b) winds
    (c) altitude (d) latitude.

35. India's urban population equals the total population of
    (a) Indonesia (b) Japan
    (c) Brazil (d) Australia.

36. Vera Cruz is a port city of
    (a) Colombia (b) Brazil
    (c) Mexico (d) Salvador.

37. Which of the following is weight losing industry?
    (a) Iron and steel (b) Sugar
    (c) Heavy machinery (d) Copper.

38. Which of the North-Eastern States has the lowest literacy rate?
    (a) Meghalaya (b) Tripura
    (c) Nagaland (d) Arunachal Pradesh.

39. Which North-Eastern States stands second only to Kerala in literacy rate?
    (a) Mizoram (b) Assam
    (c) Meghalaya (d) Manipur.

40. North-Eastern Council has its headquarter located at
    (a) Imphal (b) Aizwal
    (c) Shillong (d) Guwahati.

41. Cauvery rises in the
    (a) Cardamon hills (b) Brahmagiri hills
    (c) Satpuras (d) Mahadeo hills.

42. Black mountains are located in
    (a) Bhutan (b) Nepal
    (c) Germany (d) Sikkim.

43. Burzil pass is on a height of
    (a) 5425 m (b) 3900 m
    (c) 4386 m (d) 3750 m.

44. What is the estimated drought-prone area of India?
    (a) 190 m hectares (b) 220 m hectares
    (c) 260 m hectares (d) 300 m hectares.

45. Palicut lake is in the state of
    (a) Madhya Pradesh (b) Andhra Pradesh
    (c) Orissa (d) Gujarat.

46. New Moore Islands is situated in
    (a) Bay of Bengal (b) Arabian Sea
    (c) Gulf of Martaban (d) Gulf of Mannar.

47. Which state has the highest reserves of dolomite?
    (a) Bihar (b) Rajasthan
    (c) Orissa (d) Andhra Pradesh.

48. Indira Gandhi Canal, one of the most ambitious plans for irrigating Rajasthan extends up to the length of

(a) 468 kms (b) 428 kms
(c) 552 kms (d) 518 kms.

49. The mean density of earth is

(a) 3.8 gm/cm^3 (b) 4.4 g.m/cm^3
(c) 5.5 gm/cm^3 (d) 6.2 gm/cm^3.

50. Wicklow mountains of Ireland and Upland of Britany, France are an example of

(a) Batholith (b) Dyke
(c) Sill (d) Lapolith.

ANSWERS

1.	(d)	2.	(b)	3.	(d)	4.	(a)
5.	(a)	6.	(b)	7.	(c)	8.	(a)
9.	(d)	10.	(c)	11.	(c)	12.	(a)
13.	(d)	14.	(b)	15.	(b)	16.	(c)
17.	(d)	18.	(b)	19.	(c)	20.	(d)
21.	(c)	22.	(c)	23.	(a)	24.	(d)
25.	(b)	26.	(c)	27.	(b)	28.	(a)
29.	(c)	30.	(d)	31.	(d)	32.	(c)
33.	(a)	34.	(d)	35.	(a)	36.	(c)
37.	(b)	38.	(d)	39.	(a)	40.	(c)
41.	(b)	42.	(a)	43.	(d)	44.	(c)
45.	(b)	46.	(a)	47.	(d)	48.	(a)
49.	(c)	50.	(d)				

SET 5
ASSESS YOURSELF

1. A highway has been constructed by China to join Lhasa and
   (a) Beijing (b) Tsugtco
   (c) Cheugdu (d) Ghanzhar.

2. Which soil area is known as the 'bread basket of world" ?
   (a) Chernozel
   (b) Prairie soil
   (c) Chestnus and Brown soil
   (d) Meadow soil.

3. Which lake was formed due to the forces of diastrophism?
   (a) Victoria (b) Titicaca
   (c) Pepin (d) Reelfoot.

4. The diameter of the hurricane ranges from
   (a) 100 to 200 km (b) 500 to 600 km
   (c) 300 to 400 km (d) 400 to 500 km.

5. Which of the following is not a characteristic feature of rivers?
   (a) Delta (b) Outwash plain
   (c) Oxbour lakes (d) V-shaped valleys.

6. Lough Neagh is the largest lake of
   (a) Ireland (b) Scotland
   (c) England (d) Iceland.

7. Earth, has its speed
   (a) Remains the same (b) Greatest in Aphelion
   (c) Greatest in Perihelion (d) None of these.

8. The highest peak of Australian Alps is
   (a) Mt. Blanc (b) Kosciusko
   (c) Kilimanjaro (d) Mt. Vinson.

9. New Siberian Islands are situated in which of the following seas?
   (a) Laptev sea (b) Bering sea
   (c) Kara sea (d) Baltic sea.

10. Which is the 'index plant' of tropical monsoon climate?
   (a) Sal (b) Rubber
   (c) Cinchona (d) Teak.

11. Deccan Lava Region was a product of
   (a) Silurian period (b) Tertiary period
   (c) Eretaccous period (d) Ouiaternary period.

12. Which of the following is a cold current?
   (a) Kuroshio current (b) Okhotskl current
   (c) Gulf stream (d) Agulhas current.

13. Hill area development programme does not cover
   (a) Darjeeling hills (b) Nilgiris
   (c) Mikir hills (d) Mahadeo hills.

14. Hindan and Selani rivers are of
   (a) Middle Himalayas (b) Greater Himalayas
   (c) Siwaliks (d) None of these.

15. Which of the following glacier is of transverse type?
   (a) Punmesh (b) Biyafo
   (c) Siyachin (d) Bataro.

16. Which is the predominate rock of the Aravallis?
   (a) Eeldspar (b) Quartz
   (c) Marble (d) None of these.

17. Which is second largest lake of the world?
    (a) Tso Zilland (b) Mansarovar
    (c) Hemkund (d) Gourikund.

18. Which of the following Himalayas is most extensive?
    (a) Kumaun Himalayas
    (b) Punjab Himalayas
    (c) Nepal Himalayas
    (d) Assam Himalayas.

19. Which of the following country is known as "two nations in one state"?
    (a) Canada (b) India
    (c) Brazil (d) Germany.

20. Chhota Nagpur Plateau has
    (a) Laterite soils (b) Forest soils
    (c) Alluvial soils (d) Red soils.

21. Reh, Kallar, Usar belong the group of
    (a) Arid and Desert soil
    (b) Forest soil
    (c) Saline and Alkali soil
    (d) Black or Regur soil.

22. The largest producer of cement is
    (a) Former USSR (b) USA
    (c) Japan (d) China.

23. Mesabi, the most important iron-ore field of USA is situated near
    (a) Pacific Coast
    (b) In the vicinity of Great Lakes
    (c) Atlantic coast
    (d) None of these.

24. Baleric Islands are the part of :
    (a) Italy (b) Spain
    (c) Denmark (d) Portugal.

25. Canterbury plains from a part of
   (a) France (b) Hungary
   (c) Australia (d) New Zealand.

26. Which is the longest pipeline of the world?
   (a) Comecon (b) HBJ
   (c) Tapline (d) Big Iuch.

27. Trans-Siberian Railways has a length of about
   (a) 9100 km (b) 9300 km
   (c) 8500 km (d) 8800 km.

28. Southerly Burster is local wind which blows in
   (a) South-East America
   (b) E. China
   (c) Australia
   (d) South Africa.

29. Which of the following is known as "Mother of Pearls"?
   (a) Demersal (b) Cod
   (c) Oyter (d) Herring.

30. Guyana highlands have which of the following grasslands
   (a) Llanos (b) Pampas
   (c) Veldt (d) Campos.

31. Yucatan channel is in between
   (a) USA & Cuba (b) Cuba & Haiti
   (c) Mexico & Cuba (d) None of these.

32. Cape Farewell is in
   (a) Brazil (b) New Zealand
   (c) Australia (d) Argentina.

33. Which of the following is the primary source of "Pearl cultivation" ?
   (a) Demersal (b) Herring
   (c) Cod (d) Oyster.

34. Which of the rivers does not make a Estuaine delta?
(a) Hudson (b) Mackenzie
(c) Elbe (d) Mekong.

35. Rio Grande river drains into
(a) Atlantic (b) Pacific
(c) Gulf of Mexico (d) None of these.

36. Alaskan Highway links Anchorage with
(a) Edmonton (b) Regina
(c) Calgary (d) Victoria.

37. Trans continental railway of Africa would be between the cities of
(a) Capetown to Tunis (b) Cairo to Cape Town
(c) Tripoli to Pretoria (d) None of these.

38. Western Ghats Developement Programme cover the length of
(a) 1200 km (b) 1400 km
(c) 1600 km (d) 1800 km.

39. Which of the following is not a trans Himalayan river?
(a) Brahmaputra (b) Jhelum
(c) Sutlej (d) Indus

40. Zarga Hills is found in the state of
(a) Arunachal Pradesh (b) Rajasthan
(c) Himachal Pradesh (d) Uttar Pradesh.

41. Which port has the highest contribution to India's exports trade?
(a) Marmogao (b) Cochin
(c) Vishakhapatnam (d) Mumbai.

42. Which of the following river has most extensive deltaic plain?
(a) Godavari (b) Ganga
(c) Brahmaputra (d) Indus.

43. Which is known as the desert state of Australia?
(a) South Wales (b) Sothern Australia
(c) Western Australia (d) None of these.

44. Which of the following is known as"Juvenilo water"?
(a) Magmatic water (b) Rain
(c) Con nat water (d) None of these.

45. How much time is needed by the sun-rays to reach the surface of earth?
(a) 12 minutes (b) 18 minutes
(c) 6 minutes (d) 8 minutes.

46. Which of the following is not found in the saline soils?
(a) Sodium (b) Magnesium
(c) Sulphate (d) Carbonate.

47. Stalactites and stalagmites are features related to
(a) Desert land forms (b) Karst land forms
(c) Glacial land forms (d) Volcanic land forms.

48. Which is not a temperate grassland?
(a) Steppes (b) Prairies
(c) Selvas (d) Downs.

49. Angel falls, the highest in the world is situated on the tributary of
(a) Utshi (b) Carboni
(c) Magdalena (d) Rio Grande.

50. In the 16 km. depth of earth surface about what percentage rocks are igneous?
(a) 68 (b) 80
(c) 90 (d) 95.

ANSWERS

1.	(c)	2.	(a)	3.	(d)	4.	(b)
5.	(b)	6.	(a)	7.	(c)	8.	(b)
9.	(a)	10.	(d)	11.	(c)	12.	(b)

13.	(d)	14.	(c)	15.	(a)	16.	(b)
17.	(d)	18.	(c)	19.	(a)	20.	(d)
21.	(c)	22.	(a)	23.	(b)	24.	(b)
25.	(d)	26.	(a)	27.	(b)	28.	(c)
29.	(c)	30.	(a)	31.	(c)	32.	(b)
33.	(d)	34.	(d)	35.	(c)	36.	(a)
37.	(b)	38.	(c)	39.	(b)	40.	(b)
41.	(a)	42.	(d)	43.	(b)	44.	(a)
45.	(d)	46.	(b)	47.	(b)	48.	(a)
49.	(b)	50.	(d)				

SET 6
ASSESS YOURSELF

1. Generally people are attracted to democratic countries where individual decision can be made freely and independently is called
   (a) Political pull (b) Political hold
   (c) Political stability (d) Political push.

2. Agriculture is the most widespread form of human activity, more basic than any industry and one of the vital feature of agriculture is its
   (a) Yield (b) Fertility
   (c) Permanency (d) Stretch.

3. The lowlands are the most suited to a wide range of crops and rubber's latex yield . . . appreciably above the 2,500 foot contour.
   (a)- Diminishes (b) Increases
   (c) Remain unchanged (d) Increases by three times.

4. The areas having scanty rainfall and minimum irrigation facilities practise
   (a) Humid farming (b) Dry farming
   (c) Wet farming (d) All of the above.

5. Savanna is a
   (a) Flurio cycle
   (b) Temperate grasslands
   (c) Tropical grassland in Africa
   (d) Contour farming.

6. Halt-kel Agha-Jaria, Lali, Musjid-i-Suleman are the oil-fields of
   (a) Iran (b) Libya
   (c) Kuwait (d) Iraq.

7. Mica is
   (a) Used in electrical appliances
   (b) Tough, flexible and resilient
   (c) Non-conductor of heat and useful for electrical usage
   (d) All of the above.

8. Diego-Garcia island is a classic example of
   (a) Pelagic form
   (b) Deltaic form
   (c) Isthmus form
   (d) Tombolo form.

9. Which region of the world is with highest arithmetic density?
   (a) Central Asia (b) South Asia
   (c) North Africa (d) Eastern Europe.

10. Except ---------- others are the leading producers of Vanadium in the world.
    (a) Peru, South Africa (b) Japan and India
    (c) U.S.A. (d) Rhodesia.

11. Largest producer of Manganese in the world is
    (a) Pakistan (b) India
    (c) Former USSR (d) Cuba.

12. The only source from which aluminium is extracted is
    (a) Cryolite (b) Bauxite
    (c) Ferrum (d) None of these.

13. The pioneer of 'Migration zone theory of Race Evolution' is
    (a) Hooton (b) R. Dixon
    (c) G. Taylor (d) R. James.

14. The inhabitants of northern Finland, north Western Russia and northern Scandinavian are called the
    (a) Lapps (b) Igloos
    (c) Tonto (d) Eskimos.

15. The people of the world can be divided on the basis of the kind of substances their red cells contain into------ types.
    (a) 8 (b) 4
    (c) 16 (d) 20.

16. The synthetic fibre industry was first developed in
    (a) France
    (b) England
    (c) USA
    (d) Belgium.

17. Which among the following occupies the first place both in terms of area and production of sugarcane?
    (a) Canada (b) Cuba
    (c) China (d) India.

18. Which among the following regions 'Selva' is not associated?
    (a) Amazon basin of South America
    (b) Mediterranean region
    (c) Zaire and Congo basin
    (d) South-East Asian region.

19. Which among the following is the greatest gold producing?
    (a) South Africa (b) Spain
    (c) Brazil (d) Italy.

20. The famous industrial districts of the world are located along the
    (a) Coal fields
    (b) Hydro electric project
    (c) Nuclear energy project
    (d) None of these.

21. -------- is the greatest producer and consumer of rice and accounts for one third of world's rice, mainly in its three river basins.

(a) China (b) Japan
(c) India (d) Indonesia.

22. Which country is the world's largest producer of 'Fazenda-grown' coffee?

(a) China (b) Brazil
(c) Srilanka (d) India.

23. The main plantation crops of Philippines is

(a) Coconuts
(b) Rubber
(c) Coconuts, cane sugar, Manila hemp
(d) Coffee.

24. Which is the chief plantation crop of Malaysia and Indonesia?

(a) Tea (b) Rubber
(c) Jute (d) Coffee.

25. Which of the following is the largest producer of salt?

(a) U.S.A. (b) China
(c) Japan (d) India.

26. The first industry to benefit from Watt's steam engine was

(a) Iron (b) Textile
(c) Chemical industries (d) Coal mining.

27. In India -------- features are met with amongst the Andaman islands, Kadras of Kerala, Uralis of the Nilgiri.

(a) Cacasoid (b) Negritos
(c) Mongoloids (d) Dravidians.

28. Persons who have a definite combination of distinguishing physical traits which is passed on from parents of offsprings are known as

(a) Species (b) Race
(c) Gene (d) None of these.

29. Who divided the human groups as Vlotrichi, Leiotrichi and Cymotrichi on the basis of colour and texture of hair?
   (a) G.R. Mayor (b) Alfred Gayor
   (c) Tom Gayor (d) G.R. Gayor.

30. Subsistence fishing is practised in the
   (a) Open sea (b) Closed sea
   (c) Fresh water (d) None of these.

31. Which of the following countries is the world's largest exporter of beef?
   (a) Australia (b) Argentina
   (c) Ireland (d) Bangladesh.

32. Highly fuel efficient cars are maximum produced in
   (a) North Korea (b) France
   (c) Japan (d) Thailand.

33. The greatest automobile manufacturing industries are located in
   (a) China (b) Canada
   (c) England (d) U.S.A.

34. The Kinki, a very famous industrial centres is located in
   (a) Russia (b) Japan
   (c) China (d) North Korea.

35. Industries which produce raw materials for other industries are called
   (a) Basic industries
   (b) Small scale cottage industries
   (c) Small scale industries
   (d) Raw industries.

36. Major ship-building centres of USA are
   (a) New York
   (b) Kearney and Quitney
   (c) Boston and Detroit
   (d) Dallas.

37. Cuvier divided the human groups into three races according to the
    (a) Colour of skin (b) Size of tooth
    (c) Length of the head (d) All of the above.

38. Negroid stocks are divided into which of the following subdivisions?
    (a) The Negritos of Andaman islands, the Philippines
    (b) The Bushman of Kalahari desert
    (c) The Tongo of Sahara
    (d) Both (a) and(b).

39. According to whose classification, Vlotrichi race has frizzly hair
    (a) Deniker (b) G. Taylor
    (c) Haddon (d) Ghurye.

40. Which of the following countries comes under the North-West Pacific fishing grounds?
    (a) Newfoundland (b) South Korea
    (c) Japan (d) Malaysia.

41. ------- is the most densely populated continent in the world according to 1984 population statistics.
    (a) Asia (b) Australia
    (c) Japan (d) Africa.

42. Which country out of the following has reached the stage 4th of the demographic transition
    (a) Denmark (b) Japan
    (c) Norway (d) Netherlands.

43. The main occupations of people in mountainous regions are
    (a) Lumbering (b) Pastorlism
    (c) Counter farming (d) All of the above.

44. About 71% of the total area of the globe is covered with
    (a) Water (b) Desert
    (c) Land (d) None of these.

45. Who was the father of Human Geography?
    (a) Ratzel
    (b) Friedrich
    (c) E.C. Semple and Renner
    (d) None of these.

46. Ability to use more than one language is termed as
    (a) Lingua franca (b) Bi-franca
    (c) Bilingal (d) Dialect.

47. Which among the following is very sensitive to frost?
    (a) Cotton (b) Jute
    (c) Silk (d) Mulberry.

48. Slightly acidic, nitrate rich soil without calcium is suitable for
    (a) ground nut (b) Tea
    (c) Maize (d) Barley.

49. -------is the leading producer of coal.
    (a) India (b) Great Britain
    (c) U.S.A. (d) China.

50. Which of the following countries was the first to exploit coal-fields in the 19th century and was the then the leading producer of coal in the world?
    (a) France
    (b) Germany
    (c) Great Britain
    (d) West Germany.

ANSWERS

1.	(a)	2.	(c)	3.	(a)	4.	(b)
5.	(c)	6.	(a)	7.	(d)	8.	(a)
9.	(b)	10.	(b)	11.	(c)	12.	(b)
13.	(c)	14.	(a)	15.	(b)	16.	(a)
17.	(b)	18.	(b)	19.	(a)	20.	(a)

21.	(a)	22.	(a)	23.	(c)	24.	(b)
25.	(a)	26.	(a)	27.	(b)	28.	(b)
29.	(d)	30.	(c)	31.	(b)	32.	(c)
33.	(d)	34.	(b)	35.	(a)	36.	(d)
37.	(a)	38.	(d)	39.	(c)	40.	(c)
41.	(a)	42.	(a)	43.	(d)	44.	(a)
45.	(b)	46.	(c)	47.	(a)	48.	(b)
49.	(d)	50.	(c)				

SET 7
ASSESS YOURSELF

1. Which country has the highest percentage of cultivated land?
   (a) China (b) India
   (c) USSR (d) USA.
2. Which of following is a leguminous crop?
   (a) Gram (b) Millets
   (c) Tobacco (d) Tea.
3. Sultanpur Lake Bird sanctuary is in
   (a) Punjab (b) Gujarat
   (c) Rajasthan (d) Haryana.
4. Which is second coldest inhabited place in the world?
   (a) Greenland (b) Dras
   (c) Siberia (d) Alaska.
5. Which of the following Indian states has highest reserve of Gypsum?
   (a) Orissa (b) Gujarat
   (c) Rajasthan (d) Karnataka.
6. Chukha power project is in
   (a) Himachal Pradesh (b) Meghalaya
   (c) Bhutan (d) Nepal.
7. Rashtriya Chemicals and Fertilizers has its plant at
   (a) Durgapur (b) Barauni
   (c) Mumbai (d) Sindri.

8. The first superphosphate plant was set up at
   (a) Ranipet (b) Sindri
   (c) Ramagunden (d) Alwaye.

9. At which of the following place heavy machinery plant is situated?
   (a) Hospet (b) Bangalore
   (c) Faridabad (d) Hyderabad.

10. At which of the following places, the plant for heavy electricals is not located?
    (a) Bhopal (b) Hyderabad
    (c) Naini (d) Tiruchirapalli.

11. At which of the following places lead is manufactured ?
    (a) Alwaye (b) Alupuram
    (c) Manubhandar (d) Indoo.

12. Bokaro Steel Ltd. was formed in 1964 and the first blast furnace commenced production in -------.
    (a) 1968 (b) 1970
    (c) 1974 (d) 1972.

13. Sandalwood is a product of
    (a) Tropical rain forest
    (b) Tropical deciduous forest
    (c) Thorn forest
    (d) Tidal forest.

14. The 'chhos' of northern Haryana and Punjab have occurred due to
    (a) Sheet erosion (b) Gulley erosion
    (c) Rill eorsion (d) Wind erosion.

15. The black colour of black soils is attributed to the presence of
    (a) Titaniferous magnetite
    (b) Compounds of calcium and magnesiam
    (c) Nitrogen
    (d) Phosphoric acid.

16. Very fine and relatively new alluvium is found in the flood plains and the deltas. It is locally known as
    (a) Bhangar (b) Khadar
    (c) Bhalar (d) Kallar.

17. Permanent pastures constitute around -------- per cent of total land in India.
    (a) 4 (b) 6
    (c) 5 (d) 7.

18. Island Arcs have the characteristics
    (a) They are associated with the greatest deep trenches
    (b) They are site of volcanic and igneous activities
    (c) They are ports of circular arcs, concave towards the nearest continent
    (d) All of the above.

19. The mid-oceanic ridges are situated over the rising limbs of --------current in the Earth's surface.
    (a) Conduction
    (b) Convection
    (c) Continental
    (d) None of the above.

20. Isostasy is a condition of rest or balance. This theory says that the crust floats in equilibrium on a substratum in the mantle. Which of the following is not related to the theory of Isostasy?
    (a) Dutton (b) Jeffreys
    (c) Airy (d) Heiskasen.

21. Which of the following is not related to transportation function of river?
    (a) Dissolved load (b) Suspended load
    (c) Head load (d) Bed load.

22. Tsunamis are seismic ------ waves.
    (a) Land (b) Sea
    (c) Air (d) Shake.

23. Which of the following layer of earth is known as nife
(a) Mantle (b) Inner core
(c) Outer core (d) Crust.

24. Mt. Popa is an example of
(a) Active Volcano (b) Dormant Volcano
(c) Extinct Volcano (d) Fold Mountain.

25. San Andreas fault is an example of
(a) Transform fault margin
(b) Rift valley
(c) Groben
(d) None of these.

26. Which countries are separated by the Durand Line?
(a) India and Afghanistan
(b) India and China
(c) India and Pakistan
(d) India and Srilanka.

27. Which countries are separated by the MacMohan line?
(a) India and Pakistan (b) China and Tibet
(c) India and China (d) India and Bangladesh.

28. Which countries are separated by the 49th parallel·?
(a) U.S.A. and Mexico (b) USA and Canada
(c) USA and Panama (d) India and Pakistan.

29. For what is Philadelphia well-known
(a) Ship building (b) Silk Textiles
(c) Dairy Industry (d) Locomotives.

30. The boundary between North and South Korea is marked by the
(a) 38th parallel (b) 49th parallel
(c) Radcliffe line (d) 18th parallel.

31. Which countries lie on either side of the Radcliffe line?
(a) Sri Lanka and India (b) India and Pakistan
(c) India and Bangladesh (d) India and China.

32. The boundary between Germany and Poland is called the
    (a) Durand line (b) Maginot line
    (c) Hindenberg line (d) 17th Parallel.

33. Earthquakes are recorded and measured by
    (a) Seismographs (b) Banograph
    (c) Quakograph (d) Shock detector.

34. Trees shed their leaves in winter season to
    (a) escape being eaten by animals
    (b) take rest after the summer growth
    (c) conserve water
    (d) conserve heat.

35. Cotton fibre is obtained from the
    (a) Fruit (b) Leaf
    (c) Stem (d) Root.

36. On which of the rivers is the famous Kariba Dam located?
    (a) Zambezi (b) Niger
    (c) Nile (d) Amazon.

37. Earthquakes are recorded and measured by
    (a) Quakograph (b) Barograph
    (c) Seismograph (d) Shock detector.

38. In on oil well, what is the ascending order (from bottom) of oil, water and gas ?
    (a) Oil, gas, water (b) Water, gas, oil
    (c) Gas, water, oil (d) Water, oil, gas.

39. Echo-sounding is the technique applied to
    (a) measure the depth of the sea
    (b) record the density of air in the atmosphere
    (c) measure the amplitude of sound waves
    (d) measure the density of water.

40. Which of the folowing are the causes of earthquakes?
    (a) Volcanic causes (b) Surface causes
    (c) Tectonic causes (d) All of the above.

41. Which is the highest peak of Zasker Range?
   (a) Nanda Devi (b) Makalu
   (c) Kamet (d) Kanchenjunga.

42. Which of the following glaciers of all Karakoram Range is of longitudinal type?
   (a) Mohilyaj (b) Yajgil
   (c) Batoira (d) Khurdopin.

43. Parshwanath is the highest peak of
   (a) Malwa Plateau (b) Chota Nagpur
   (c) Deccan Plateau (d) Aravallis.

44. The rivers of the Deccan Plateau are mostly of ------ stream.
   (a) Conequent (b) Insequent
   (c) Obsequent (d) Inconequent.

45. The West Coast Plain convers the narrow strip of land along the western coast of India in a length of
   (a) 1200 kms (b) 1400 kms
   (c) 1500 kms (d) 1600 kms.

46. Konkan coastal plain extends from ------- to Goa and over a length of ------ kms.
   (a) Roha, 600 (b) Daman, 500
   (c) Daman, 650 (d) Mangalore, 500.

47. Brazil has the area 94 times the areas of the country which one colonised it which is that country?
   (a) Spain (b) Portugal
   (c) Demark (d) England.

48. Mountain building activity is known as
   (a) Epeirogenetic cycle (b) Oroganic cycle
   (c) Exogenetic cycle (d) None of these.

49. Crustal fracture of rocks take place due to
   (a) Cracks (b) Joints
   (c) Faults (d) All of the above.

50. The above fig shores which of the following faults ?
(a) Thrust fault (b) Strike ship fault
(c) Oblique fault (d) Overthrust fault.

ANSWERS

1.	(b)	2.	(a)	3.	(d)	4.	(b)
5.	(c)	6.	(c)	7.	(c)	8.	(a)
9.	(a)	10.	(c)	11.	(d)	12.	(d)
13.	(b)	14.	(b)	15.	(a)	16.	(b)
17.	(a)	18.	(d)	19.	(b)	20.	(b)
21.	(c)	22.	(b)	23.	(b)	24.	(c)
25.	(a)	26.	(a)	27.	(c)	28.	(b)
29.	(d)	30.	(a)	31.	(b)	32.	(c)
33.	(a)	34.	(c)	35.	(a)	36.	(a)
37.	(c)	38.	(d)	39.	(a)	40.	(d)
41.	(c)	42.	(c)	43.	(b)	44.	(a)
45.	(c)	46.	(b)	47.	(b)	48.	(b)
49.	(d)	50.	(b)				